MACMILLAN HISTORY OF LITERATURE

General Editor : A. NORMAN JEFFARES

MACMILLAN HISTORY OF LITERATURE
General editor: A. Norman Jeffares

Published

SIXTEENTH-CENTURY ENGLISH LITERATURE
Murray Roston

SEVENTEENTH-CENTURY ENGLISH LITERATURE
Bruce King

TWENTIETH-CENTURY ENGLISH LITERATURE
Harry Blamires

ANGLO-IRISH LITERATURE
A. Norman Jeffares

Forthcoming

OLD ENGLISH LITERATURE
Michael Alexander

ENGLISH GOTHIC LITERATURE
Derek Brewer

EIGHTEENTH-CENTURY ENGLISH LITERATURE
Maximillian Novak

NINETEENTH-CENTURY ENGLISH LITERATURE
Margaret Stonyk

THE LITERATURE OF SCOTLAND
Rory Watson

COMMONWEALTH LITERATURE
Alistair Niven

THE LITERATURE OF THE UNITED STATES
Marshall Walker

A HISTORY OF LITERATURE IN THE IRISH LANGUAGE
Declan Kiberd

MACMILLAN HISTORY OF LITERATURE

SIXTEENTH-CENTURY ENGLISH LITERATURE

Murray Roston

M

First published 1982 by
THE MACMILLAN PRESS LTD
Companies and representatives
throughout the world

ISBN 0 333 27143 2 (hc)
ISBN 0 333 27144 0 (pbk)

Typeset by
CAMBRIAN TYPESETTERS
Farnborough, Hants
Printed in Hong Kong

Contents

List of Plates

Acknowledgements

The author and publisher wish to acknowledge, with thanks, the following illustration sources:

By kind permission of his grace the Duke of Bedford, The Woburn Abbey Collection   12; The Bodleian Library   8, 9; The British Tourist Authority and by permission of the Marquis of Salisbury   10; The Folger Library, Washington/ John Cranford Adams   13, 14; The Frick Collection   5; The Mansell Collection   2, 7; The National Gallery   6; The Newberry Library   3; The Royal Library, Windsor — by gracious permission of H.M. The Queen   4; Master & Fellows of St John's College, Cambridge   1; The Victoria and Albert Museum   11.

Editor's Preface

THE study of literature requires knowledge of contexts as well as texts. What kind of person wrote the poem, the play, the novel, the essay? What forces acted upon them as they wrote? What was the historical, the political, the philosophical, the economic, the cultural background? Was the writer accepting or rejecting the literary conventions of the time, or developing them, or creating entirely new kinds of literary expression? Are there interactions between literature and the art, music or architecture of its period? Was the writer affected by contemporaries or isolated?

Such questions stress the need for students to go beyond the reading of set texts, to extend their knowledge by developing a sense of chronology, of action and reaction, and of the varying relationships between writers and society.

Histories of literature can encourage students to make comparisons, can aid in understanding the purposes of individual authors and in assessing the totality of their achievements. Their development can be better understood and appreciated with some knowledge of the background of their time. And histories of literature, apart from their valuable function as reference books, can demonstrate the great wealth of writing in English that is there to be enjoyed. They can guide the reader who wishes to explore it more fully and to gain in the process deeper insights into the rich diversity not only of literature but of human life itself.

A. NORMAN JEFFARES

1
The dual vision

IN the earlier part of the sixteenth century, English literature
certainly has its finer moments — the urbane prose of Sir
Thomas More, the sonnets of Wyatt and Surrey, and the
boisterous comedy of *Gammer Gurton's Needle*. Yet nothing
within that century can match the surge of creativity which
was so brilliantly to mark its final decades. In the brief space
of some ten to fifteen years, what had been until then an
essentially imitative literature looking towards the continent
for its models came suddenly into its own, and the poetry of
Sidney and Spenser, Marlowe and Shakespeare not only
projected England to the forefront of the European scene,
but set new standards against which the drama and poetry of
future generations would be judged.

Modern scholarship now views with some scepticism the
two traditional explanations for that phenomenon. The
theory that it arose from England's national self-confidence
as a growing economic and military power under the settled
monarchy of Queen Elizabeth is less securely based than
might at first appear. The country had indeed undergone.
profound changes during the century. The dissolution of the
monasteries as Henry VIII broke away from Rome had transferred no less than one sixth of all cultivable land from the
inefficient control of the monks to private hands, where it
began to be worked intensively. The cloth trade boomed,
coal mining was developed, and cannon foundries were
established to free the country from dependence on importation from abroad. By 1585 England had taken over the
European lead in finance from Antwerp and become the
centre for foreign investment. Elizabeth and her faithful
advisor William Cecil, with the aid of the astute financier Sir
Thomas Gresham, brought England from near bankruptcy in
the mid-century to economic prosperity within the course of

thirty years, till it rivalled the dominant power, Spain. War became inevitable, and the defeat of the Spanish Armada in 1588, when England's swift-sailing vessels outclassed the cumbersome and heavily manned Spanish vessels, changed naval strategy and left England with sufficient mastery of the seas to expand and develop its own independent trade routes.

'Economic prosperity', however, is an umbrella term that can cover a multitude of less attractive features. The rich had indeed become far richer, and the middle class was now established as a growing power in the land; but the poor, who still constituted the large majority in the country, had become miserably poorer. Food prices soared fivefold during the century with only a small rise in the average wage. The enclosure of land deprived many peasants of their livelihood, and rents were raised cruelly to cover the lavish expenses of the nobility. Accordingly, vagrancy and pillaging, the last resort of the desperate, became a major problem, which neither whipping nor repeated attempts at poor relief could stem. London teemed with beggars, whores, and cutpurses, the dross thrown up by waves of unemployment, and throughout Elizabeth's reign the tensions created by a discontented populace threatened to erupt into open rebellion. In brief, the economic boom of this period was often seen by the contemporaries who experienced it as a catastrophe rather than a blessing, in which, as Nashe put it, ' . . . the usurer eateth up the gentleman, and the gentleman the yeoman, and all three, being devoured one of another, do nothing but complain.'[1] Lastly, in considering such new national wealth as the possible source of the literary revival, it should be remembered that writers in that period generally benefited least from it, the overwhelming majority struggling desperately against financial privation.

Even apart from that deeper disturbance in the country, the question remains whether national self-confidence based upon growing economic and military prowess is itself a prescription for producing great literature. The very reverse has often been proved true. Russian society was decaying and the Czarist regime on the way to its demise when Tolstoy, Dostoevsky, and Chekov produced their finest work; and in the 1930s Nazi Germany possessed to a remarkable degree both those qualities of military might and abounding national

confidence and yet produced no literature of lasting significance. Even within the period we are now examining the
indications are against that theory. Shakespeare's maturer
plays, such as *King Lear*, *Othello*, and *Macbeth*, were written
not during Elizabeth's reign but in the gloomier period of
unrest at all levels of society under James I, and that fact
suggests that it was, if anything, the insecurity of his time
rather than the confidence which deepened his literary
sensitivity.

The second theory placed the sudden burgeoning of
English poetry and drama within the broader European
setting as England's response to the continental revival of
classical learning. The new interest in ancient authors which
Petrarch and Boccaccio had helped to foster in fourteenth-
century Italy received an added boost when a number of
Greek scholars found their way westward at the fall of
Constantinople to the Turks in 1453. With growing enthusiasm,
libraries were searched for forgotten manuscripts, and scribes
hired to copy them out for inclusion in private collections.
Plato became a model for philosophical speculation, Cicero
for prose 'eloquence', Ovid's *Metamorphoses* a source-book
for mythology; and academies were established for the study
of the ancient classics. This continental reverence for the past
began to reach England in the early sixteenth century when
Greek was included as a subject to be taught at the universities
under William Grocyn and John Colet, with the encouragement of the famed Erasmus who was visiting England at that
time. By mid-century the new grammar schools, such as
Merchant Taylors, which had now been either founded or re-
established to replace those previously conducted under
monastic supervision, furthered this interest, devoting the
main part of their curriculum to classical studies.

On the other hand it has been argued with justice that
within this golden period of sixteenth-century English
literature there is little intrinsic to its greatness which is
recognisably classical in timbre, form, or theme. Neither
Sidney's sonnets nor Spenser's *Faerie Queene* can legitimately
be regarded as modelling themselves on the verse of Greece or
Rome. In drama, if the dramatists had learned from Seneca's
unacted closet plays a taste for blood and violence, for scenes
of amputated limbs and declamatory rhetoric, those were not

the qualities which gave the Elizabethan stage its imaginative range and poetic splendour. On the contrary, it gained those only as it moved away from such classical tutelage into independence. As a result, C. S. Lewis, in one of the best-known studies of English literature in this period, begins his work by denying that the literary vigour achieved at this time can be attributed to the humanist revival of classical learning. It should be regarded, he argues, as simply an inexplicable phenomenon, the chance appearance at one time and in one country of a few individual writers of genius.[2]

The weakness of that argument is the very narrow conception of humanism on which it is based. The Renaissance was far more than a revival of classical learning or the imitation of an ancient style. It represented, rather, a complex shift in human thought of which the return to classical models was more a symptom than a cause. The early humanists, whether consciously or not, were really conducting a search for an alternative authority, also bearing the sanction of antiquity, which could serve as complement and at times as counter-weight to that which had dominated the Middle Ages. The search was less for styles of writing than for new styles of thought. It was eclectic, choosing to adopt only those elements in classical philosophy or art theory which suited the requirements of the searchers, and the sixteenth-century flowering of English literature needs to be seen not merely in terms of stylistic indebtedness but within the context of those larger changes.

Those changes are not easy to define, but it can, I think, be argued that the strength of the Renaissance in all its ramifications and complexity can be traced to its extra-ordinary duality, its incorporation of two markedly different concepts, sometimes clashing openly within it, sometimes fruitfully intermingling, but always ensuring on the part of the writer and thinker a widened range of perception. The appearance of the Italian *rinascimento* or cultural 'rebirth' may have seemed sudden to those experiencing it at the time as it reached its peak around 1500, but it was in fact the culmination of movements originating as early as the thirteenth century. In that earlier period, it had been universally assumed that Christian humility demanded from the scholar a reverential acceptance of respected sources. The mind of the medieval scholar, sharp as it might be in arguing points of theology, was not attuned to questioning received information. Thomas Aquinas, in his *Summa Contra Gentiles* (1259—64), mentions as if it were an indisputable fact the existence of a fish called a *remora* which, although only eighteen inches long, was supposed to possess the mysterious power of immobilising the largest of ships. Now, however, there appeared the first signs of a change. Roger Bacon, attacking such blind acceptance of untested tradition, began in the thirteenth century to insist that such facts be verified by a study of nature. Only by experiment, he argued, could the truth be known. A little later William of Ockham, resisting the prevailing faith in universals, posited a Nominalist philosophy in which he accorded validity only to the single, verifiable object, thereby opening a path, in an age which had always given primacy to theological truth, for the pursuit of scientific research.

The effects of the scientific revolution to which it eventually led were not to be fully felt until the seventeenth century, but that new interest in the isolated fact, the object as it really is, was enormously relevant for our period. It led in the arts to a new concern with the accurate rendering of material substances and objects. There is a careful painting of a rabbit in the corner of an *Annunciation* by Giovanni di Paolo, a lively interest in the details of clothing as a mark of social status in the manuscript illustrations of the Limbourg brothers, and, by their contemporary, Chaucer, an amused description of the small coral 'gauded all with green' on the arm of the Prioress, as well as her brooch of shining gold on which a flourishing *A* introduces the inappropriate motto *Amor vincit omnia*.

The significance of this empirical tendency is that it marked one extreme within a polarised view of the world. The opposite pole found its fullest expression in the teachings of Marsilio Ficino. In a villa near Florence presented to him in 1462 by Cosimo de' Medici, he founded an academy devoted to Plato's teachings. The group of devotees he gathered about him was more of a cult than a scholarly academy. A lamp was left permanently burning before a bust of Plato, celebrations were held in honour of his birthday, and hymns sung in his praise. But the votaries did also engage in serious scholarship, and under Ficino's guidance the dialogues of Plato were translated into Latin in order to ensure their wider dissemination, as were the works of Plotinus and others. Of greater consequence was the creation there of a revived form of Neoplatonism remarkably congenial to the needs of that age, a merger of Platonism and Christianity which was to serve as a bridge from the Middle Ages to the new world. According to that philosophy, although man belonged within the material world, his soul was held to participate in the divine. No longer seen as doomed from birth by original sin and utterly dependent upon God's grace, here the human soul held within its power the ability to ascend by reason and by love (its yearning for the celestial) until it finally reached the realm of the divine itself. By becoming part of the godly, it was endowed also with the ability to create, so that the merely skilful craftsman of the past now achieved an elevated status, as the 'divine' artist or poet of the new era. His task was to produce the universal harmonies of art. More generally, man, by clothing the particular in this world in its spiritual or allegorical meaning, could now soar into the universal, towards the ideal 'Beautiful-and-Good' identified with God himself.

Here, then, were two extrapolated views. On the one hand, a sober empirical insistence upon the provable fact or object, and on the other a movement away from physical reality towards a concept of man unbounded in his abilities and reaching up to the universal ideals in heaven itself. Sometimes the views drift far apart, and seem utterly alien. Pico della Mirandola, in his oration *Of the Dignity of Man* (1486), urged his contemporaries to devote themselves only to the celestial: 'Let us disdain earthly things, strive for heavenly things, and finally, esteeming less whatever belongs to this world, hasten to that court which is beyond the world and nearest to the Godhead.' Against his view is set the harsh pragmatism of Machiavelli's *The Prince* (1513), which cuts through the mists of moral idealism to see the actuality of power politics in the Italian states as he had witnessed them. The age might talk nobly of ethical responsibility in leadership, of Christian charity, of the need to love one's fellow man, but the facts spoke differently. The only way Machiavelli himself had seen princes like Cesar Borgia (the latter had assassinated his own brother and murdered all possible successors) gain power and hold on to it effectively was by ruthless cunning and cynical self-interest. Accordingly, the advice he offers any aspiring political leader is to follow where the historical and tangible facts point, irrespective of moral scruples.

So much for the dichotomy. But in art and literature of the time that duality of concept, the idealistic and the pragmatic, when enrichingly integrated, provided the artist with an amazing range, a vision of man reaching as high as the heavens, yet still rooted in this tactile earth. The Renaissance hero is seen as rivalling the gods themselves in splendour, yet tripping through some small factual error of human judgement, a moment's thoughtlessness, a minor spot or blemish which corrupts his virtues, be they as pure as grace. He may command the storms in his wrath, yet at the same time is seen realistically as no more than a poor, forked animal, vulnerable to rain and cold, and succumbing at the last to the cold touch of death. In a speech of wider significance than his own specific dilemma, Hamlet epitomises that vision in all its grandeur and in all its melancholy:

> What a piece of work is man, how noble in reason, how infinite in faculties, in form and moving how express and admirable, in action how like an angel, in apprehension how like a god: the beauty of the world, the paragon of animals; and yet to me what is this quintessence of dust?   [II, ii]

This is not the medieval view that in the midst of life we are in death, for ever reminding man that this world is as nothing, a shadowy anteroom before the Day of Judgement. On the contrary, it is an assertion of man's magnificent potential, his infinite faculties, his godlike apprehension; but offset by the sobering fact of his physical limitations. The only tangible evidence remaining after his noble achievements in this world is the putrefying flesh in the grave and the nauseating stench of a decaying skull. The astonishing poetic and dramatic spectrum offered by this twofold vision, the empirical and the spiritual, made possible for the era the breadth and range of its artistic productions.

The duality operates in the visual arts too and it may be helpful to glance there briefly before turning to literature. As painting deserts the medieval tradition, there emerges throughout Europe a new interest in physical reality, a concern with carefully recording the details of the natural world as they actually are. Van Eyck catches exactly the reflection of an orange in a convex mirror, Dürer painstakingly pictures every blade of grass, every thistle-spur and stalk growing within a tiny patch of ground, and Leonardo da Vinci, long before the appearance of Vesalius' anatomical charts, dissects over thirty corpses in order to determine the precise positioning of muscles, arteries and tissues for his depiction on canvas of the human form. After an age which had presented the world in terms of eternity and symbol, artists now constructed machines to allow them to plot perspective accurately, and provide on canvas the representation of a scene as the eye would actually perceive it. Yet, integrated with this determination for factual accuracy and correct architectural perspective, there develops in tandem an increasing tendency towards idealisation, taking its model from classical philosophy and practice.

In ancient Greece, Plato, relying upon Pythagoras' discovery that music was dependent on fixed mathematical ratios which produced harmonious chords, deduced the existence of universal laws prevailing throughout nature to ensure the preservation of perfect concord and culminating at the highest level in the music of the spheres. Now in the fifteenth century, the renowned humanist and architect, Leon Battista Alberti revealed that Roman architects had themselves carefully conformed to those Pythagorean proportions in designing their buildings so that the comparative size and relative positioning of the walls, doorways and columns should create a visually unified whole. In his *De re aedificatoria* (1452) he formulated the new principles for his age. The true work of art, he argued, must participate in this higher order. It must constitute a perfect, harmonious whole from which nothing can be subtracted, nothing altered without damaging its unity. Following his lead, artists now began sketching out circles, squares, and intersecting parabolas to serve as the substructures for their canvases and frescoes. Even the sketch of a face would have measured lines superimposed upon it in the early stages to ensure that the individual features should conform to the correct proportions and attain the ideal concept of beauty. Painting was thereby elevated in this era from mere visual representation into a participation in celestial harmony.

The striving for factual accuracy on the one hand and the trend towards an idealised harmony on the other, contrary as they may appear, joined forces to create that form of art specific to the High Renaissance. Where an earlier painting by Cimabue or Duccio would place the suffering Madonna against a background of gold in the stylised tradition of the ikon, da Vinci's *Madonna of the Rocks* adopts a different technique. The scene presented is dreamlike, a haunting glimpse of celestial beauty where, in accordance with Alberti's dictum, the figures are so perfectly placed in relation to each other that the slightest change would disturb the overall harmony. Yet the scene, despite its rarified sanctity remains realistically within this world. The rocks of the grotto are true geological formations, the plants and shrubs, the drape of the voluminous cloak, the fall of the curled hair utterly convincing, bringing the dream vision into conjunction with the tangible world as we know it.[3] In the same way, Michelangelo's sculptural group *Pietà* so idealises the Madonna that she appears there as a beautiful young girl, no older than the dead son lying before her. The artist here is aiming at a heightened concept of perfect beauty, if necessary at the expense of historical truth; and yet the beauty both of the mother and the son is an utterly human beauty, the beauty of astonishingly real flesh, with veins branching along the dead Christ's arm, a fold of cloth caught between two fingers, and the shape of the Madonna's rounded breasts visible through the loose and magnificently draped garment she wears. Instead of drifting away from the world into some impossibly heavenly perfection, the Renaissance artist integrates the two concepts, linking man with the elevated and celestial, while leaving him rooted in this earth.

Within our period, that ambivalence of a sharply actualised reality contrasting with, complementing, and merging with the nobly idealised vision is a primary source of achievement in all genres of literature. The following chapters will be examining these genres in detail, so that only a brief sketch of that interaction need be offered here. In romance, for example, the two worlds are sometimes partially separated, sometimes intimately joined, but they are never completely divorced. Shakespeare's *Merchant of Venice* provides us with two settings. Belmont, the home of Portia, is the golden palace of flowing wealth, of ideal generosity and wit, where dreams come true and magic caskets unite deserving lovers; against it is set the harshly realistic city of Venice, ruled by contracts and the vicissitudes of trade, where Shylock demands his pound of flesh and his legal claim must be enforced by the Duke to protect the commercial standing of the city. But the two polarised settings meet and blend as Portia comes from that dream world to bring the quality of mercy and true justice which must be made to prevail in the world of actuality, with the marriage of Bassanio to Portia symbolising the wedding of those two worlds. In poetry too, Spenser's *Faerie Queene* may suggest an imaginary world of medieval knights fighting impossibly evil monsters but the epic takes its force from our awareness throughout that those knights and monsters are in fact our own noble aspirations battling with sinful impulse and the vivid clarity of description intensifies its actuality. Moreover, to highlight its relevance to his own times, he projects into that allegorical world recognisable figures drawn from the Elizabethan court he knew at first hand, thus tying it into the real world. Sidney too, in the midst of a sonnet idealising his mistress in elevated Petrarchan terms will, unlike his mentor, unhesitatingly insert a few contemptuous thrusts at her real-life husband who stands between him and the consummation of his love. And Marlowe's Dr Faustus, revelling in the limitless power afforded him by magic, uses it 'to prove cosmography', to measure the coasts and kingdoms of this earth, and to grasp Helen of Troy in his own arms.

These are the qualities which lend such distinction to poetry and drama in the late sixteenth century. Other periods have offered elevated views of man's spiritual and imaginative yearnings, as did the Romantic poets in later years; but Wordsworth's response to the beauty of nature and its effect upon man's soul excludes completely, as if it were non-existent, the vicious realities of bird and beast tearing each other apart. The twentieth century, in contrast, sees that cruelty only too clearly in both man and beast, but it has on the other hand lost the vision of splendour; it no longer believes in man's ability to reach to the divine. The Renaissance writer at his best embraces both worlds. He possesses an acute awareness of the handling of a ship's tackle, the technicalities of falconry, the materialistic greed of man; but with it he has a sense too of the celestial harmonies to which man may attain, of human possibilities infinite in their range.

Some historians have attempted to separate the two elements, to speak as E.M.W. Tillyard did, of an Elizabethan world-picture consisting of hierarchy and moral order, in which Machiavelli's philosophy is merely an awkward anomaly. Hiram Haydn, in contrast, seeing that anomaly as more intrinsic to the age, isolated the group to which such sceptics as Montaigne belonged together with the Machiavels as being a 'Counter-Renaissance', militating against the major movement.[4] But to divorce the two elements is, I think, to deprive the era of its most splendid quality, the dynamic interplay between an ennobling sense of man's infinite possibilities in his ascent to the divine and a sharply pragmatic awareness of the realities within the human condition. Such duality produces the drama of Othello, dreaming of a love far excelling a world of purest chrysolite, set against a ruthless Iago, shrewdly putting money in his purse.

2

In search of a prose style

THE main tide of humanism did not reach England until the early sixteenth century, and even then it advanced slowly, one obstacle to its progress being the state of the English language. French had long been, with Latin, the language of international diplomacy, and Italian, with a tradition reaching back uninterruptedly to the period of ancient Rome, possessed the range and vocabulary requisite for the various genres of literature. But English remained in many ways unformed. The distinguished literature it had produced, including the poetry of Chaucer and, more recently, the prose of Sir Thomas Malory's *Morte Darthur* (1470), had relied for its effect on a simplicity and directness of style which English even in its less developed form was able to supply. Queen Guenever's parting from Launcelot is moving in its elemental purity of diction, employing mainly mono-syllabic words in a series of loosely joined and unsubordinated sentences:

> Therefore, Sir Launcelot, go to thy realm, and there take thee a wife, and live with her with joy and bliss, and I pray thee heartily pray for me to our Lord, that I may amend my mis-living. Now, sweet madam, said Sir Launcelot, would ye that I should return again unto my country, and there wed a lady? Nay, madam, wit you well that shall I never do; for I shall never be so false to you of that I have promised. [XXI, ix].

Such language, perfectly fitted to its narrative context here, was a tool as yet unsuited for hewing out sophisticated philosophical ideas or the rolling periods of great oratory; and the lack was sorely felt. Translation was hampered. Castiglione's widely read *The Courtier*, published in Italy in 1528, had already appeared in Spanish by 1534 and in French by 1538, yet it was to take thirty-three years before the first English translation by Sir Thomas Hoby became available in 1561. Though read in the Italian by educated Englishmen before then, it could not be absorbed into the life-blood of English literature nor contribute to its prose tradition until the latter part of the century when the serious work of translation into English began, and North, Holinshed, Golding and others at last made the major classical and continental works available to all.

Moreover, English had remained markedly regional as a language, with strong overtones of local dialect. At court, even in the latter part of the century the Queen's English was by no means universal. Sir Walter Ralegh 'spake broad Devonshire to his dying day', and how far local pronunciation deviated from what was eventually to become the norm is suggested by the spelling of the time which, as yet unsystematised, reflected the actual sound of the words. The Marchioness of Exeter concludes a letter to her son ' . . . by your loving mother Gertrude Exeter' but writes '. . . by your *lowfyng* mothar, Gartrude Exet*tar*' [author's italics].[5] The setting up of Caxton's printing press in Westminster in 1476, although it produced mainly late-medieval works and therefore contributed little to the dissemination of humanism, did help towards the standardisation of spelling, and hence pronunciation, in accordance with the prevailing London dialect, but progress was slow.

The need for a more sophisticated prose, both in range of vocabulary and in more complex sentence structure, is indicated by the changed curriculum introduced into the schools by leading scholars during the first half of the century. John Colet, in founding St Paul's school in 1509, encouraged the teaching of classical literature for the value of its form even though, as a churchman and dean of the cathedral, he recognised the danger of its pagan content. Accordingly the boys there, as in all grammar schools in the country, began concentrating the major part of their studies on the improvement of their style, translating from Latin into English and then back again into Latin, endeavouring to preserve in both versions the formal elegance of the Latin model. Numerous textbooks on rhetoric began to appear in the following decades, and Richard Sherry's *A Treatise of Schemes and Tropes* (1550) confirmed the general view that

Cicero's *De Oratore* was, together with Quintilian, the best model for prose because of its 'high' style of eloquence and its rich vocabulary. ' . . . for it hath an ample majesty, very garnished words . . . and grave sentences.' These were precisely the elements which were felt to be lacking in the English prose of the day.

This educational innovation, effective as it was in moulding the style of the next generation of writers, was in itself an expression of a trend already recognisable among the scholars who had introduced the change. A comparison of the two most substantial Latin—English dictionaries produced in the fifteenth century, *Promptorium Parvulorum* (1440) and *Catholicon Anglicum* (1499) reveals that in the years between them a shift was already taking place, with the latter volume offering a much wider range of weighty Latinate words in English, such as 'confabulation' and 'taciturnity', reflecting under early humanistic influence a growing desire for classical sophistication and expanded vocabulary within the English language.[6] By the middle of the sixteenth century the movement had grown to such proportions that protests began to be raised against the exaggerated importation of what Thomas Wilson's *Art of Rhetoric* (1553) called 'inkhorn' terms, that is, words introduced merely to display the writer's erudition. He offers in that work an amusing parody of the new vogue of writing which, he insists, he has heard many people praise extravagantly. The supposed epistle begins:

> Pondering, expending, and revoluting with myself your ingent affability and ingenious capacity for mundane affairs, I cannot but celebrate and extol your magnifical dexterity above all other. For how could you have adepted such illustrate prerogative and dominical superiority if the fecundity of your ingeny had not been so fertile and wonderful pregnant?

Understandably, Sir John Cheke, the Regius Professor of Greek at Cambridge, wrote in a letter to the translator Hoby: 'I am of opinion that our own tongue should be written clear and pure, unmixed and unmangled with borrowing from other tongues, wherein, if we take not heed by time, ever borrowing and never paying, she shall fain to keep her house bankrupt.'

However inappropriate the image of bankruptcy here (no country has to repay loan words), the sentiment is clear; the purity of the English language both in style and vocabulary must be protected against corruption. The danger was not only in the use of imported words, but also the often mindless imitation of Ciceronian triplets, substituting mere tautology for the powerfully incremental repetitions of the original. Berners, in the preface of his translation of Froissart (1523) argues, in a series of pointless synonyms, that historians ' . . . show, open, manifest, and declare to the reader, by example of old antiquity, what we should enquire, desire, and follow, and also what we should eschew, avoid, and utterly fly.'

However, to side with the purists in the controversy as if they were the noble defendants of the English heritage is to misunderstand the subtle changes taking place. The more perceptive critics, such as Wilson, while they justifiably scoffed at the indiscriminate use of Latinate words solely for a display of supposed scholarship, did at the same time welcome their importation as a much-needed enrichment of the language. For in the development of English prose in the sixteenth century, the new flexibility and variety of the language arose from a judicious blending of the simpler native forms with the more ornate 'eloquence' learned primarily from classical sources and to a lesser extent from French and Italian.

Style at its best is always organically related to content, and that blending of basic Anglo-Saxon forms with the more elaborate syntax of classical rhetoric was integral to the duality of Renaissance modes discussed in the previous chapter. By nature, the simpler, often monosyllabic vocabulary of earlier English was more suited to the accurate rendering of the factual and everyday, while the newly imported classical tradition, with its wealth of abstract nouns and more complex, rhythmic structures could express more effectively the loftier, sophisticated concepts. Time and again in the best prose of this period we find the more abstract or generalised philosophical discussion brought sharply to earth by a factual analogy or concrete illustration; and for the latter the language shifts back stylistically to the older more elemental forms:

Augmentation of honour and substance . . . not only impresseth
a reverence, whereof proceedeth due obedience among subjects but
also inflameth men naturally inclined to idleness or sensual appetite
to covet like fortune, and for that cause to dispose them to study or
occupation. Now to conclude my first assertion or argument, where
all thing is commune, there lacketh order; and where order lacketh,
there all thing is odious and uncomely. And that have we in daily
experience; for the pans and pots garnisheth well the kitchen, and
yet should they be to the chamber none ornament. Also the beds,
testers, and pillows beseemeth not the hall, no more than the carpets
and cushions becometh the stable.[7]

Basically, it was the same technique as Francis Bacon was to
use so tellingly at the end of the century, the contrast between
an arrestingly simple opening sentence — 'Men fear death as
children fear to go in the dark' — monosyllabic, factual, and
unelaborated — and the subsequent rising in tone and Latinate
resonance as the argument develops its broader philosophical
theme.

Sir Thomas More

The mingling of classical forms with native English diction is
exemplified in the writings of Sir Thomas More (1478—1535),
often called England's first true humanist. He indeed deserved
that title for the combining of his broad intellectual pursuits
with their translation into active and public terms as a learned
theologian, a secular jurist, a tolerant and perceptive observer
of contemporary affairs, who was eventually to take his place
as Lord Chancellor of England under Henry VIII. In a deeper
sense, however, he marks rather the transition between the
old world and the new, a man who, though stepping boldly
into the sixteenth century as an involved participant in
secular human activities, cherished, often secretively, an
abiding loyalty to the cloistered asceticism of the medieval
monastery. What endeared him to all who knew him was the
combination in his character of the best qualities of both
spheres — the ready wit, classical learning, and intellectual
curiosity of the humanist with the personal humility, incor-
ruptibility, and self-abnegation of the religious recluse.

Born to a London lawyer, More was sent as a boy to join
the household of John Morton, Archbishop of Canterbury,
where he distinguished himself by his ready humour and wit,

traits which were to accompany him throughout his life, even to the steps of the scaffold. From Morton's household he proceeded to Oxford, responding warmly to the new humanist trends, and thence to law studies in London. More's career now appeared assured, when unexpectedly he turned his back on the world. In 1499 he entered the Charterhouse in London, at that time a monastery belonging to the austere Carthusian order. There for a period of four years he lived in seclusion, though without as yet taking vows, and from a remark made towards the end of his life it would seem that part of him always yearned to return. At the end of that four-year period his confessor, Dean Colet, persuaded him that his task lay in the world outside, and he was urged by him to marry and set up a household.

The household he established was a model of its kind, with encouragement for every form of useful study and discussion. After one visit, his life-long friend Erasmus compared it enthusiastically to Plato's academy ' . . . yet more rightly to a school for Christian religion.' In women's liberation, More marked a considerable advance for his time, educating his daughters so well that they became famed for their learning. Yet, although he had moved out of the monastery into the secular world of marriage and career, the change did not go as deep as might appear; for beneath his doublet and gold chain of office, certainly during his years as Chancellor and possibly before then too, he wore unknown to all but his eldest daughter the rough hair-shirt of a monk.

In 1513, More composed, possibly for political reasons, a brief *History of Richard III* which, although only published years later in a mutilated form, was to serve as a primary source for Holinshed and, through him, for some of the most vivid scenes in Shakespeare's play of that name. Based upon a Latin version perhaps by Archbishop Morton (which would account for the eye-witness effect) yet emerging in the English form as a work in its own right, it marks, as did More's own life, a turning-point between the old and the new. The medieval idea of history as a collection of unsubstantiated legends is replaced here by a responsible search for accuracy. He distinguishes carefully between verified information and what may be mere hearsay, reported, as he says, by 'men of hatred' towards the king. The result, however, is not a drily factual account, but a powerful and lively portrait in which the language of the prose leaps forward from the older Malory-like forms still preserved here in the narrative sections ('for well they wist that the queen was too wise to go about any such folly') to a dramatic intensity and imaginative force at the climactic moments, boding well for the future of the English theatre. Richard III is described as racked by guilt after his murder of the two young princes in the Tower:

> Where he went abroad, his eyes whirled about, his body privily fenced, his hand ever on his dagger, his countenance and manner like one alway ready to strike again; he took ill rest at nights, lay long waking and musing, sore wearied with care and watch, rather slumbered than slept, troubled with fearful dreams, suddenly some-time start up, leap out of his bed, and run about the chamber, so was his restless heart continually tossed and tumbled with the tedious impression and stormy remembrance of his abominable deed.

More's most famous work *Utopia* (1516) lies technically outside the range of this present volume since it was written in Latin. It was, however, so widely read in England both in the original and in the English translation published in 1551 by Ralph Robinson that it cannot be ignored, particularly in view of the literary offspring it fathered, including Bacon's *New Atlantis*, Swift's *Gulliver's Travels*, and Samuel Butler's *Erewhon*. The work resulted from a six-month visit on an embassy to the Low Countries which serve as the locale for the discussions in the book, and in the tradition of the Platonic dialogue he mingles true with fictional characters. His use of Latin recalls once again the dilemma of the scholar at this time, needing to choose between the wider range of educated readers on the continent and the more parochial audience at home.

The first of the two books is a perceptive survey of England's moral and economic ills, often sounding remarkably modern in its suggestions for change. He attacks the cruelty of rack-renting and the enclosing of sheep-grazing land, the ostentatious extravagance of the wealthy, and the unjust penalty of death for stealing, in a society which had deprived the poor of their livelihood. All this More places very prudently in a period some twelve years before Henry VIII's accession to the throne, lest it should be interpreted as an attack on the King's command of the country.

The second part, with its account of the country of Utopia is the more famous. In More's day, the utopia of which men dreamed nostalgically was the mythological golden age of the past, the classical version of Eden before the Fall, when the conditions of man's life were ideal and the earth yielded its fruits in abundance. As a humanist, More turned from the idyllic conditions of such imaginary existence to this world, enquiring how man could create in it a viable society by relying on his own rational faculties. For its topical setting, therefore, he uses the voyages of discovery undertaken by explorers in his own day and the supposed visit of one such traveller to a country existing across the seas. If the country of Utopia ('No-place') is an acknowledged fiction, its description serves throughout as an ironic commentary on the shortcomings and irrationalities of contemporary European society, and it is that which is being explored rather than Utopia itself.

In that distant country, we learn, there is no indolent aristocracy living off the labour of the poor as in his own land, everyone being employed there in productive work. Ownership of property is equal, with houses reallocated by lot every ten years; and gold, while preserved as payment for foreign mercenaries should war be unavoidable, is kept in the form of chamber-pots and slave-rings so that wealth should be despised by the citizens. While marriage is encouraged, extra-marital intercourse is severely punished (with the rather sour justification that few would tolerate the trials of marriage were sexual activity permitted outside it), and both divorce and remarriage are permitted, the latter not for proven adulterers who have shown their inability to function correctly within the marital framework.

So brief a summary can only offer the bare bones of what is an extraordinarily witty and stimulating account, brimming over with novel ideas; and its very unconventionality has led to markedly different interpretations. For some critics More is seen as the forefather of modern socialism, distributing the country's wealth to ensure the greatest happiness of the greatest number. Others perceive in the work the very reverse, a return to medievalism, whereby Utopia becomes (with the exception of marriage) one large monastery with everyone forced to wear the same rough habit, to eat communally with meals preceded by instructive readings, to have their hours regulated, and property held in common. What, moreover, has troubled many readers is the contradiction between the principles advocated by the book and the religious convictions held by More himself. *Utopia* permits euthanasia under certain conditions, allows women to become priests, and approves of divorce and remarriage, all in direct contravention of basic tenets in the Catholic church; and this quite apart from milder suggestions upon which the church would undoubtedly frown, such as the requirement that prospective marriage partners should always examine each other naked before finally plighting their troth.

Part of the answer, but not all, lies in More's teasing tone which often undercuts his own seriousness and leaves the reader unsure where the author's real commitment rests. The narrator who admiringly describes the Utopia he has visited is named Hythloday ('A talker of nonsense'), the king is Ademus ('Without a people'), and More, who appears as a participant in the discussion, on occasion expresses his own disagreement with the arguments his own book presents. In real life More was known for his poker-faced jesting, once being charged: 'You use . . . to look so sadly when you mean merrily that many times men doubt whether you speak in sport when you mean good earnest'; and allowance must be made for that humorous vein within the account. On the other hand, as its impact on its era and on subsequent generations has shown, the book deals too seriously with matters of great moment for it to be dismissed as a mere joke.

Perhaps the true answer is to be found in the dichotomy within More's own personality, the rationalist committed to a religious faith with a hair-shirt concealed beneath his humanist garb. It may well be that in this book he is indulging his intellect, allowing the humanist side of his character to range freely, temporarily released from the restrictions of his faith, in order to speculate as a Renaissance thinker how in a country as yet untouched by Christianity man might use the resources of his reason to establish rules of social and moral behaviour without the aid of divine imperatives. Utopia would be for him, then, the 'green world' of Shakespeare's plays, a mythical country in which the imagination can roam at large, untroubled by personal commitments, before returning to this world with the moral insights it has gained.

In his later writings, the theologian in him took precedence, but even then he laced his prose with wit and humorous anecdote. He attacked Tyndale in his *Dialogue Concerning Heresies* (1529) and in resisting a move to have church property confiscated, in his *Supplication of Souls* published in the same year, instead of solemnly attacking the move he puckishly draws a picture of past donors gathering mournfully in purgatory to beg that they be not deprived of the prayers promised for the gifts they had bestowed. More had now become so eminent a figure on the European scene that his refusal to countenance Henry VIII's claim to the Supremacy of the Church could not be tolerated by the King. He resigned from the Chancellorship in 1532 and two years later was arrested and tried for treason on the grounds that he would not take the new oath of allegiance. His ability as a jurist and perhaps also as a humorist did not desert him even at such a time: he argued with tongue in cheek that since silence means consent, his refusal to take the oath should be regarded as perfectly satisfactory. But the decision had already gone against him before the trial began. While imprisoned in the Tower he composed his *Dialogue of Comfort Against Tribulation*, a devotional work whose prose style, generally more weighty and solemn than his earlier works, is enlivened repeatedly by homely images which contrast with the general tone by their simple forms of expression:

> . . . he that in tribulation turneth himself into worldly vanities to get help and comfort from them, fareth like a man that in peril of drowning catcheth whatsoever cometh next to hand, and that holdeth he fast be it never so simple a stick, but then that helpeth him not. For that stick he draweth under the water with him, and there lie they drowned both together.

Towards the end of his imprisonment he was deprived of writing materials, but from *The Life of More* written by his son-in-law William Roper in the 1550s we learn how, on being told that the King whom he had served so faithfully had ordered his execution, he replied to the courtier with gentle sarcasm:

> I have always been much bound to the King's Highness for the many benefits and honours that he hath still from time to time most

bountifully heaped upon me; especially that it hath pleased his
Majesty to put me here in this place where I have had convenient
time and leisure to remember my last end; and now most of all am
I bound unto his Grace, that I shall so shortly be rid out of the
miseries of this wretched life.

Educated governors

The eminent scholars surrounding More, such as William
Grocyn, John Colet, and Thomas Linacre, had by their
enthusiastic dedication to learning, succeeded in transplanting
to English soil the seeds of Florentine humanism; but they
were not themselves literary figures. It fell to the lot of a
younger member of that circle, Sir Thomas Elyot (c. 1490–
1546), to produce what was perhaps the first literary work in
English which both advocated and exemplified the New
Learning. His early career had only advanced him to the
office of Clerk of the King's Council, an unpaid post of
which he was deprived when his patron Wolsey fell from
power. Only partially consoled by the award of a knighthood
in lieu of more tangible renumeration, he withdrew to his
country manor where he turned his attention to writing. The
work he produced, *The Book Named the Governor* (1531),
which achieved immediate success and went into eight
editions before 1580, marked the introduction into England
of the so-called 'courtesy' book, the guide to a gentleman's
education.

The title derives from the specific meaning he bestows on
the term 'governor'. Unlike More, Elyot did not believe in the
possibility of a classless society. All nature, he maintained, is
constructed on hierarchical principles, and in human society
too an all-powerful monarch must of necessity stand at the
head of the state or 'weal' (hence the book's dedication to
Henry VIII, and the favour it found in royal eyes). Such a
ruler, however capable he may be, cannot govern unaided,
but requires immediately below him a stratum of magistrates
or lesser 'governors' to implement the laws of the realm. The
concern of his book is the nurturing of such a class.

The significance of education in the overall humanist
programme can scarcely be overestimated. Under the feudal
system of the Middle Ages, sons of the aristocracy were sent

(as More had been) to serve as pages in another household, where they acquired by daily experience rather than by any planned course of study the attributes of a courtier, their only formal lessons being in the arts of reading and writing. The humanism which More had met later, on attending the university, made heavier demands. It assumed as axiomatic, the perfectability, or at least the near-perfectability of man. Let a gentleman be thoroughly grounded from childhood in classical literature, let him study the actions of great men of history, learning from their achievements and their failings, let him develop a sensitivity to poetry, music, and art, and he would emerge as the all-round civilised man capable of ruling with 'magnanimity' in the broad Roman sense of that term. Today we are perhaps more sceptical of the effects of education, but in its day the system did produce such distinguished personalities as Federigo di Montefeltro in whose elegant court at Urbino the painter Raphael was reared, and in England under the tutelage of Roger Ascham a queen who amazed foreign visitors by her fluency in French, Italian, Spanish, and Latin, her comprehension of the responsibilities of high office, her intimidating command of administrative detail, and not least her ability to cultivate about her a court in which music, poetry, theatre, and dance could flourish in a manner rarely, if ever, equalled in other eras.

Elyot justifiably deplored the contempt for learning prevalent in his day among members of the upper class. Scholarship was still associated with the threadbare university 'clerk' as Chaucer had described him, so that, Elyot complained, 'to a great gentleman it is a notable reproach to.be well learned and to be called a great clerk.' It is largely to the credit of Elyot and his fellow humanists that the attitude changed so fundamentally during the century and learning became an indispensable part of the fashionable courtier's accoutrements. With that change came a rise in the status of the schoolmaster or private tutor. Elyot scorns noblemen who expend more care and money in choosing their cook than in selecting the educator of their offspring, and are satisfied with some poorly trained bachelor of arts who imparts a superficial knowledge 'which will be washed off with the first rain.' Instead he demands the highest qualifications, summarising, in effect, the ideal schoolmaster of the new era, and placing his emphasis too on classical training and stylistic analysis. He must be one:

> . . . that speaking Latin elegantly, can expound good authors, expressing the invention and disposition of the matter, their style or form of eloquence, explicating the figures as well of sentences as words, leaving no thing, person, or place named by the author undeclared or hidden from his scholars. Wherefore Quintilian saith, it is not enough for him to have read poets, but all kinds of writing must also be sought for: not for the histories only, but also for the propriety of words.

The requirement for propriety of words he extends from Latin composition to include English prose too, and his choice of English rather than Latin as the vehicle for his treatise was, as he remarked in later years, a conscious attempt 'to augment the English tongue.' His decision set a precedent, helping to wean subsequent writers away from Latin to their native English. The care he shows for propriety of words in his own writing reveals an awareness on his part that English vocabulary was in need of enrichment, and accordingly he generally prefers a longer Latinate word such as *commendation* or *decoction* where a simple word would do as well. The result is a prose often weightier than the content requires, although the firm sentence structure and controlled rhythms help to counteract this failing and to ensure an overall clarity of meaning. A typical passage runs:

> Although I have hitherto advanced the commendation of learning, specially in gentlemen, yet it is to be considered that continual study without some manner of exercise shortly exhausteth the spirits vital and hindereth natural decoction and digestion, whereby man's body is the sooner corrupted and brought into divers sicknesses, and finally the life is thereby made shorter; where contrariwise by exercise, which is a vehement motion . . . the health of man is preserved, and his strength increased.

He was a pioneer of the new prose rather than an accomplished stylist, but he did possess one quality rare in this period, a flexibility of style enabling him to adapt to the needs of his subject. In illustrating the virtue of amity, he retells with masterly skill the tale of Titus and Gisippus from Boccaccio, deserting the formal rhetoric of his treatise in

favour of a lighter diction and smoother-flowing sentence out
of which the later Elizabethan narratives were to develop:

> But at last the pain became so intolerable, that could he or no, he
> was enforced to keep his bed, being for lack of sleep and other
> sustenance brought in such feebleness that his legs might not sustain
> his body. Gisippus missing his dear friend Titus was much abashed,
> and hearing that he lay sick in his bed had forthwith his heart
> pierced with heaviness, and with all speed came to where he lay.

The programme he designs for the education of the young
nobleman is, in accordance with the new humanist trends,
strongly inclined towards the classics both in the historical
figures selected for emulation and in the writers who are to
serve as models. As a result, the ideal to which the programme
aspires approximates to the Roman *virtus* rather than the
traditional Christian virtues. There are brief nods in the
direction of the Bible and the Church Fathers, but it is clear
that Alexander the Great, Hannibal, and Mark Antony have
begun to replace as models for behaviour the lives of Francis
of Assisi and the patron saints.

In the same year as the book appeared, with its dedication
to Henry VIII, its author was rewarded by an appointment as
ambassador to the court of Emperor Charles V; but he
continued his literary activities, publishing numerous translations from the classics, a dialogue in Platonic style, and in
1538 the first major Latin–English dictionary incorporating
the New Learning, which in an enlarged form served scholars
throughout the Elizabethan era. His layman's guide to good
health based upon Galen and entitled *The Castle of Health*
proved even more popular than his educational treatise and
reached fifteen editions by the turn of the century. It has
little literary value but is a valuable source-book for sixteenth-
century views on hygiene, diet, the humours, and the peculiar
mingling of fact and fantasy which constituted medical practice in that period.

Elyot had defined the ideal schoolmaster from the
viewpoint of the 'governor' class, but Roger Ascham
(1516–68) did so as an experienced teacher himself, the past
tutor of one royal scholar who, as he proudly informed her
courtiers, went 'beyond you all in excellency of learning'
and, despite her busy schedule, spent more hours studying

each day than six of them together. An outstanding classicist
and a pupil of Sir John Cheke, Ascham was appointed to a
readership in Greek at Cambridge, but found the payment
too meagre for his needs (possibly because of an unscholarly
addiction to dicing and cockfighting which, according to a
contemporary, kept him poor throughout his life). Like so
many of the more ambitious young men of his day, he turned
his eye towards the court, to which Cheke himself had made
his way as a tutor to Prince Edward. In a successful attempt
to catch the King's attention, he published in 1545 a book on
archery, particularly the use of the long-bow, entitled
Toxophilus. As the long-bow was still regarded with patriotic
pride as the Englishman's truest weapon in battle, the treatise
found favour with Henry VIII, who awarded him an annual
pension worth double his salary at Cambridge, on which
presumably he could now indulge his sporting instincts more
liberally.

What might have been a dull instructional booklet is so
enlivened by the learned historical references, the mythological allusions, the writer's enthusiasm for his subject, and the
frequent excursions into fascinating bye-ways, that it arouses
the ardour of readers who have never taken a bow in hand.
Ascham graphically compares the archer resisting wind-drag
to a captain at the helm of his vessel. 'The master of a ship
first learneth to know the coming of a tempest, the nature of
it, and how to behave himself in it, either with changing his
course, or pulling down his tops and broad sails, being glad to
eschew as much of the weather as he can: even so a good
archer will first with diligent use and marking the weather,
learn to know the nature of the wind, and with wisdom, will
measure in his mind how much it will alter his shot, either in
length keeping or else in straight shooting . . . .'

The diction here is markedly simple, particularly when we
recall Ascham's excellent classical background; and the
simplicity was deliberate on his part. In the preface to the
book, he answers those who have introduced Latin, French,
and Italian words on the assumption that it will enrich the
language in the same way as wine, ale, and beer improve a
feast: 'Truly, quod I, they be all good, every one taken by
himself alone, but if you put malvoisie and sack, red wine
and white, ale and beer, and all in one pot, you shall make a

drink neither easy to be known, nor yet wholesome for the body.' Similarly, he was one of the first to attack legal jargon or what he called 'indenture' English. However, although he was a conscious purist in diction, a close reading of the quotation below on wind direction will reveal how the rhythms of Latin prose have entered his style, the repetitions for rhetorical effect, the subordinate participial clauses, and the echoing of a word or phrase which together create the more intricate and sophisticated tone of the sentence. Yet, on the other hand, the simplicity of his diction lends a sharp clarity to his writing, the crispness and exactitude of his description of the varying eddies and drifts created by the wind forming part of that empirical closeness of observation which was an essential part of the Renaissance outlook. Its combination here with the emotional responsiveness on the part of the spectator elevates it far above mere factual tabulation, creating a superb piece of prose.

> That morning the sun shone bright and clear, the wind was whistling aloft and sharp according to the time of the year. The snow in the highway lay loose and trodden with horses' feet: so as the wind blew, it took the loose snow with it, and made it so slide upon the snow in the field which was hard and crusted by reason of the frost overnight, that thereby I might see very well the whole nature of the wind as it blew that day. And I had a great delight and pleasure to mark it, which maketh me now far better to remember it. Sometimes the wind would not be past two yards broad, and so it would carry the snow as far as I could see. Another time the snow would blow over half the field at once. Sometimes the snow would tumble softly, by and by it would fly wonderfully fast. And thus I perceived also that the wind goeth by streams and not whole together.

Shortly after he completed this book, his pupil William Grindal who, under his guidance, had served as Princess Elizabeth's tutor, died suddenly, and in 1548 Ascham agreed to take over the task. That move marked his entry into the English court, where he was to become a respected and influential figure. In the course of time he was appointed Edward VI's Latin secretary (the composer of official letters to foreign governments), and despite his Protestantism, continued to serve under Catholic Mary and then again under Queen Elizabeth until his death in 1568. It was in the later period that he wrote *The Schoolmaster*, published posthumously in 1570, a book justly famed for the warm humanity and understanding it displayed in a period when education was still associated with the birch-rod. The wise advice it offers is often as relevant today as it was then. He observes, for example, that a slower pupil may not always be inferior to the quick-witted, nor always deserving of punishment. The teacher should consider future potential rather than present disposition. 'For this I know, not only by reading of books in my study, but also by experience of life abroad in the world, that those which be commonly the wisest, the best learned, and best men also when they be old, were never commonly the quickest of wit when they were young' and he analyses with great perception the reasons which may lie behind such slowness in youth.

His gentleness and tolerance as a teacher are strangely offset by irritable diatribes against the corruption prevalent in Italy (now no longer viewed as the source of humanism but as the hotbed of Catholicism), against Malory's *Morte Darthur* in which 'those be counted the noblest knights that do kill most men without any quarrel and commit foulest adulteries by subtlest shifts', and against the ostentatious apparel worn by courtiers in his day. If we may not always accept his moral or literary criteria, there can be only admiration for the force and dignity of his language, the rhetorical power to which prose had attained during the passing decades of the century:

> Take heed, therefore, you great ones in the Court, yea though ye be the greatest of all, take heed what you do, take heed how you live. For as you great ones use to do, so all mean men love to do. You be indeed makers or marrers of all men's manners within the realm. For though God hath placed you to be chief in making laws, to bear greatest authority, to command all others: yet God doth order that all your laws, all your authority, all your commandments do not half so much with mean men, as doth your manner of living.

The tone of the preacher rings out in that last passage, and we should recall that no study of English prose can afford to ignore the sermons of this era. In contrast to the great preachers of a later age, such as John Donne, Dean of St Paul's, or Bishop Launcelot Andrewes, who carefully wrote out their sermons before delivery, the preachers of this era generally extemporised. One of the greatest was Hugh Latimer (c. 1485–1555), Bishop of Worcester who, in the purges conducted under the Catholic Queen Mary, was to end his life at the stake in the Protestant cause with the stirring exhortation to his fellow martyr: 'Be of good comfort, Master Ridley, and play the man: we shall this day light such a candle by God's grace in England as, I trust, shall never be put out.'

The sermons we possess by him are in all probability based on notes taken by attentive auditors, but they convey even in that form his extraordinary ability to grip the attention of his listeners. There are no lengthy classical periods. The sentences are short and to the point, dramatic in their immediacy, the series of questions arousing curiosity, the images drawn from the world of everyday experience. In a sermon delivered in 1548, he chides the prelates of England for failing in their task of caring for the people, comparing them to idle plough-men absent when the soil needs them most — 'the plough standeth; there is no work done; the people starve.' Then he pauses:

> And now I would ask a strange question: who is the most diligent bishop and prelate in all England, that passeth all the rest in doing his office? I can tell, for I know him who it is; I know him well. But now I think I see you listing and harkening that I should name him. There is one that passeth all the others, and is the most diligent prelate and preacher in all England. And will ye know who it is? I will tell you: it is the Devil. He is the most diligent preacher of all others: he is never out of his diocese; he is never from his cure; ye shall never find him unoccupied; he is ever in his parish: he keepeth residence at all times; you shall never find him out of the way. Call for him when you will, he is ever at home.

This passage owes little to the classics, and a phrase such as 'I know him who it is' suggests the reason. For while the purists were protesting against the deliberate infusion of classical and continental 'inkhorn' terms into English, unobtrusively an additional force was at work, a further model contributing its own rhythms and idioms to English prose. At church services and in the daily readings customary in many family circles, the new English translations of the Bible were becoming familiar to the ear, their imagery, phraseology, and cadences being gradually absorbed into the language.

Bible translation

After the early attempts at such translation under Wycliffe in the fourteenth century a long interval had elapsed, but the Reformation movement gave it renewed impetus and, through the advent of printing, vastly improved powers of dissemination.

In England the work began inauspiciously. William Tyndale's version of the New Testament (1526), produced on the continent, aroused the ire of More and the English bishops by its tendentious use of *congregation* instead of *church*, *senior* instead of *priest* with their overtly Protestant implications (the Protestants were bitterly opposed to the priesthood), and all copies of the book upon which the authorities could lay their hands were publicly burned at St Paul's Cross. Tyndale's earlier withdrawal across the Channel did not save him, and in 1536 he was betrayed and executed near Brussels as a heretic. Ironically, by the time of his execution the climate in England had changed radically. The break with Rome had been implemented to suit Henry VIII's marital needs, his antagonist More had himself been put to death for his religious views, and Henry VIII, although moving hesitantly towards changes in dogma or ritual, had agreed to act as patron for the complete Miles Coverdale Bible of 1535, which incorporated much of Tyndale's own work. Three years later, a royal decree required every church to possess its own large copy of an English Bible for the use of parishioners and, with only a temporary set-back under the Catholic rule of Queen Mary (1553–8) when the translators wisely moved to the stronghold of Calvinism in Geneva, the process of translation proceeded in England undisturbed.

The acknowledged beauty of these translations, beginning with Tyndale and culminating in the Authorised Version of 1611, has often been attributed to their coinciding with the maturing of the English language, to the existence at that time of a prose sufficiently rich and flexible to serve their needs. The facts, however, point in a very different direction suggesting that it was the literal translation of the Bible which helped change the form of English prose. For a contemporary, the fidelity to the original which the sanctity of the scriptures required made those new versions of the Bible foreign-sounding in English ears, the imposition of an

ancient idiom and unfamiliar cadences on the native forms of
English rather than a translation into an indigenous tongue.
Since the Reformation in many ways formed part of the
Renaissance, the ferment of activity in Bible translation had
been prompted very largely by a humanist urge for accuracy,
for the empirical testing-out of knowledge. No longer prepared
to accept the scriptures in the form in which they had been
filtered through Catholic exegesis, the Reformers were
determined to inspect the sources at first hand, to go beyond
the venerated Latin Vulgate to the original Hebrew of the
Old Testament and the Greek of the New. Fidelity to the
original was at a premium, and as a result, however natural
the rhythmic patterns and biblical phrases may appear today
after they have already been absorbed into the language, at
the time John Selden complained bitterly at their strangely
un-English form:

> There is no book so translated as the Bible. For the purpose, if I
> translate a French book into English, I turn it into English phrase
> and not into French English. *Il fait froid* I say 'it is cold', not 'it
> makes cold'; but the Bible is translated into English words rather
> than into English phrase. The Hebraisms are kept and the phrase of
> that language is kept, as for example 'he uncovered her shame',
> which is well enough so long as scholars have to do with it, but when
> it comes among the common people, Lord what gear do they make
> of it!

As knowledge of Greek and Hebrew improved during the
century, so the progressive versions of the Bible moved
against the stream of developing English prose, away from
the native English rhythms and Ciceronian rhetoric towards
more literal renderings which preserved the cadences of the
ancient original. Ciceronian prose, now fully entering the
English language, achieved its rhetorical effects by the repetition of clauses or phrases within a larger sentence, the
repetition often being threefold. Thus Ascham trusts that the
King will perceive his treatise ' . . . to be a thing honest for
me to write, pleasant for some to read, and profitable for
many to follow.' In contrast, the biblical pattern was an
oscillatory parallelism of complete sentences or ideas, an ebb
and flow in which the second half of the verse, approximately
equal in length, doubled back on the meaning of the first,

amplifying, emphasising, or particularising the earlier thought.
Coverdale, relying on the Latin and German translations,
although he does catch something of that rhythm, often
blurs the effect, but the later Authorised Version, adhering
scrupulously to a word-for-word rendering of the Hebrew,
transfers the original parallelist form directly to the English
tongue:

> *Coverdale*: From that time forth shall not one people lift up
> weapon against another, neither shall they learn to fight from
> thenceforth.   [Isaiah ii, 4]
> *Authorised Version*: Nation shall not lift up sword against nation,
> neither shall they learn war any more.

These rhythms, together with the phraseology of the Bible,
became part of English prose, from the time that Coverdale's
translation gave the first hints of them and with increasing
effect as the versions became more literal. They are particularly recognisable at those moments when a writer temporarily
dons the mantle of the prophet to speak with the authority
of the scriptures. John Foxe's *The Book of Martyrs* (1563)
won its wide popularity in part by its unpretentious narrative
style in which were described as if by eye-witness account the
dreadful sufferings of the Christian, and especially the
Protestant, martyrs throughout history. As he pauses to
comment on the implications of their passage from this world
to the next, the prose suddenly takes fire with the fervour of
the believer. The words are his own, but the parallelist
cadences and idiom draw unmistakably on the scriptural
source:

> The more hard the passage be, the more glorious shall they appear in
> the latter resurrection. Not that the afflictions of this life are worthy
> of such glory, but that it is God's heavenly pleasure to reward them.
> Never are the judgements and ways of men like unto the judgements
> and ways of God, but contrary evermore unless they be taught of
> him.

Similarly, Hugh Latimer, preaching against London, writes:

> The butterfly gloryeth not in her own deeds, nor prefereth the
> traditions of men before God's word; it committeth not idolatry nor
> worshippeth false gods. But London cannot abide to be rebuked,

such is the nature of man. If they be pricked, they will kick. If they be rubbed on the gale, they will wince. But yet they will not amend their faults, they will not be ill spoken of.

Now that England had turned away from the Roman Church, a Latin breviary or missal would no longer serve, and Cranmer's *Book of Common Prayer* (1549) was completed to take its place, henceforth accompanying English men and women to baptisms, weddings, and funerals, to divine services and private meditation, and thereby injecting into their consciousness the measured dignity of Cranmer's own versions of the prayers, interspersed with passages quoted from the Coverdale Bible. Classical influence still remained predominant in English prose at this time, but it blended with the scriptural rhythms and idioms as well as with the older simpler forms of fifteenth-century English. By the latter half of the sixteenth century, therefore, English prose could already offer a much wider range of vocabulary and rhetorical syntax as a result of the revived interest in classical, continental, and biblical sources, while preserving through the insistence of such purists as Cheke, Wilson, and Ascham (who had themselves contributed so greatly to the deepening of classical studies), the native diction and structural simplicity of earlier times.

3
The music of poetry

THE state of English poetry before the new styles were imported from Italy is vividly exemplified by the verse of that lively, caustic, and often bawdy cleric John Skelton (*c*. 1460–1529). Highly regarded in his day as poet and scholar, and a laureate of both Oxford and Cambridge universities, he was singled out for praise by Caxton and Erasmus as a leading luminary of the English literary scene. Yet within a few decades his reputation went into eclipse. His rugged verse held little appeal for the more polished age of the sonneteers, and with the appearance of an anonymous jestbook which used his name to advertise its wares, the *Merry Tales Made by Master Skelton* (1567), he began to be remembered more as a buffoon and mad-wag than as a serious poet. Only in our own century, with its rebellion against the smooth-flowing verse of the Victorians and its search for unconventional and often dissonant forms, did his 'Skeltonics' come back into favour, admired afresh for their native vigour and satirical pungency.

For a reader unacquainted with Skelton's life, the coarse ribaldry in much of his verse can be misleading. His boisterous description of a female tavern-keeper, with its earthy language and jogging rhythms, might appear to be the work of some peasant tippler with a lively imagination and a flair for rhyme:

> Droopy and drowsy,
> Scurvy and lousy,
> Her face all bowsy,*   *bloated
> Comely crinkled,
> Wondrously wrinkled,
> Like a roast pig's ear,
> Bristled with hair.
> Her lewd lips twain
> They slaver, men sain . . .

He was, in fact, a distinguished classicist, renowned for his elegant translation of many Latin works, including Cicero's letters, into an 'aureate' English prose; and the discovery in 1956 of his only surviving translation, a version of Diodorus Siculus, confirms the justice of his reputation. However, if Skelton was a classicist he was by no means a humanist. In an era marked by the revival of Greek studies, his own knowledge of that language remained negligible. He was deeply suspicious of the Reformist tendencies within the church, and actively opposed the changes being introduced into the school curriculum. His Latin scholarship was, in fact, of the old style, rooted in the late medieval tradition, and in his poetry too he harked back to the Chaucerian world in which he felt more at home. 'The Tunning of Elinor Rumming' (1517), from which the above quotation comes, has an obvious kinship with the description of the Wife of Bath, not merely as an unflattering and amusing vignette of a woman, but more fundamentally in its use of telling detail as a means of creating character. He focuses upon the bare threads in Elinor's 'huke' or cloak which she fondly imagines is as splendid as when she bought it forty years before:

> Her huke of Lincoln green,
> It had been hers, I ween,
> More than forty year,
> And so it doth appear;
> And the green bare threads
> Look like sere weeds,
> Withered like hay,
> The wool worn away.
> And yet I dare say
> She thinketh herself gay
> When she doth her array . . .

The interest in meticulous description is here, but not as yet any striving for aesthetic elevation of the scene such as was to motivate the following generation of writers and artists. There is rather a confrontation with an unadorned truth, the realism being allowed to speak for itself.

In the development of his verse-forms, Skelton moved in the opposite direction from the norm. He began with an ornate sophistication in his poetry, but in his search for more vigorous modes he gradually rejected the ornate in favour of a rough plainness, often crude in its diction as well as its rhythms. His earlier, more elaborate verse is typified by 'The Bowge of Court' ('Court Rations') of 1498. The poem is in the tradition of the allegorical dream-sequence, applied here to the falsity of court life. The court is represented as a goodly ship, richly outfitted, upon which Deceit, Dissimulation, and Disdain sail together with sundry other Vices, a technique which leans heavily upon the morality play, and the verse employed is the established seven-line stanza of rime royal, used in Chaucer's 'Troilus and Criseyde'. At the end of the poem, the speaker, appalled by what he has seen, determines to leap overboard, fleeing from such corruption. In doing so, he awakes; but lest the moral be missed, he concludes with the warning to the reader that 'ofttimes such dreams be found true'.

Skelton was in a position to speak knowledgeably of the court, having been appointed in 1489 as court poet and later as tutor of the future Henry VIII. In 1498, the year this poem was published, he took holy orders at the comparatively advanced age of thirty-eight and was soon afterwards appointed rector to the parish of Diss in Norfolk. Neither his entrance into the priesthood nor his position as rector to a Christian community seems to have restrained his penchant for ribald verse. One of his best-known poems, the lament for 'Philip Sparrow' (1508) moves towards 'Elinor Rumming' in its adoption of colloquial speech patterns. It is an elegy supposedly recited by a young girl at the loss of her favourite pet, a sparrow eaten by a cat, and the lament is cunningly intertwined with passages from the Latin Office for the Dead. It provides remarkable psychological insight into the personality of the girl, her fondness for nature, her fears of Hell's terrors, and, not least, her own erotic experiences with the bird allowed to play beneath the blanket, to which description is added her plaintive comment 'God wot, we thought no sin!' Interestingly, Skelton places in her mouth his own reasons for rejecting the new-fangled words being introduced by the humanists, and his preference for the cruder but more natural language he has adopted in his poetry. The English language, he maintains, is too weather-beaten to be renewed ('ennewed') by such importations:

Our natural tongue is rude,
And hard to be ennewed
With polished terms lusty:
Our language is so rusty,
So cankered and so full
Of frowards and so dull,
That if I were to apply
To write ordinately,
I wot not where to find
Terms to serve my mind.

and he concludes by choosing the pleasant, easy, and plain language of Chaucer.

By now his pupil Henry VIII had ascended the throne, and Skelton became embroiled in a controversy with Cardinal Wolsey. In the 1520s he composed three poetic invectives against contemporary abuses in the Church, 'Colin Clout', 'Speak Parrot' and 'Why Come Ye Not to Court' which at first indirectly but with increasing outspokenness reproved Wolsey for his humanist policies and his driving ambition. One main object of attack there is the system of non-residence prevalent in the Church at that time, and for many years to come, whereby a clergyman would accept livings and omit to carry out the duties of the incumbent, living in London far from the parishioners he was supposed to serve. It was the same abuse as Latimer had castigated in his sermon on the absent ploughmen, and a vice of which Wolsey was particularly guilty, amassing from such sinecures the enormous income for those days of £50,000 per year (at a time when even an archbishop earned only £3,000) with which he was able to build Hampton Court. The irony is that Skelton, while composing this vituperative attack was himself permanently resident in Westminster, one hundred miles distant from his Norfolk parish (and the story that he was taking sanctuary there from Wolsey's wrath has long been disproved). At all events, his mordant satires may have been partly responsible for the fact that on Wolsey's fall from power in 1530, Parliament passed legislation against pluralism in livings, though the legislation was largely ineffective.

His adoption of the role of Colin Clout for his attack on the Church was an attempt to resist the more cultivated styles beginning to enter literature. By that device he was able to speak in the guise of a rustic figure, bewildered by the

ecclesiastical corruption around him and flagellating it in the
language and imagery of an untutored peasant. Skelton could
thereby use more naturally the rough unpolished verse to
which he had gravitated in his later years, a vigorously native
English untouched by the perfumed diction wafting across
from Italy and France:

> For though my rhyme be ragged,
> Tattered and jagged,
> Rudely rain-beaten,
> Rusty and moth-eaten,
> If ye take well therewith,
> It hath in it some pith . . .

But there was to be no halting of that continental influence
and his rearguard action failed to stem its advance. Such
country verse, with its deliberately jerky rhythms and jogging
rhymes was to disappear before the refinement of the new
poetry. The following stanza by Wyatt was probably written
during the very same year as 'Colin Clout', yet stylistically
the two are worlds apart:

> When first mine eyes did view and mark
> Thy fair beauty to behold;
> And when my ears listened to hark
> The pleasant words that thou me told,
> I would as then I had been free
> From ears to hear and eyes to see.

The sound is smooth and mellow, the controlled pauses
heighten the rhythmic pattern, and the rhyme scheme is
more subtly interwoven to create a melodiousness new to
English poetry. That melodiousness needs to be seen within a
larger context. The love of music had been long established in
England. Its composers had been acknowledged as the leaders
of Europe until John Dunstable's death in 1453, and even
after that, joy in music had continued unabated. Erasmus, as
a foreigner visiting the country, had been particularly
impressed by the ploughman singing at his furrow and the
workman at his bench. Local parish churches were being built
from the profits of the booming wool trade (an inscription
by one donor, John Barton, reads: 'I thank God and ever
shall. / It's the sheep hath paid for all'), and as part of the
prosperity organs were now being installed in them to bring
church music from the great cathedrals to the smaller

communities. But a change in direction occurred during the early decades of the century in response to the new fashions affecting Europe at large.

In music, as opposed to literature, the humanist return to classical sources was by necessity theoretical, for there were no musical scores to be imitated from the ancient period; and even theory, surviving in various philosophical treatises, was very generalised. As a result, music could develop with greater freedom. The Pythagorean concept of universal harmony, with the music of the heavenly spheres intimately related to the harmony in men's souls gave, in its revived form in this century, an enhanced dignity to the arts of song, dance, and musical instrumentation. No longer were they simply pleasant relaxations but were now regarded as a valued conduit for achieving inner concord of spirit, moral integrity, and social acceptability. Castiglione reminded the prospective courtier that '. . . the universe is composed of harmony, the heavens produce music, the human soul is formed on the same principles, and therefore it revives and, as it were, awakens its virtues through music.' An ability to play an instrument and sing from musical notation became prerequisites for the courtier, accomplishments without which he could not participate effectively in social activities, with all their importance for personal advancement. Where paintings and triptychs of an earlier era had depicted the angels playing musical instruments in heaven, now, as in the canvas by Lorenzo Costa (*Plate 6*), interest has turned to human players, achieving a harmony of souls through their unison in part-song. The girl's hand is placed sociably on the lutanist's shoulder, and the positioning of the participants' facial muscles indicates that each singer is producing a different note, blending in musical accord.

England welcomed the vogue from abroad, again as part of a larger educational and moral concept. Henry VIII, who read music at sight and composed his own songs, had by the time of his death assembled one of the finest collections of musical instruments in all Europe, numbering over 380 valuable items; and his own love of dancing he bequeathed to his daughter Elizabeth, whose favourites often included those who were the most accomplished dancers.

The most notable transformation in European music at

this time was a shift away from polyphony (the interweaving of numerous voices, each singing its own specific text, so that the words were generally indistinguishable) to the harmony of one or more voices singing a single text together. In line with Alberti's dictum that an artistic work must consist of the integration of all its parts, the words of the song attained a new prominence. Music was now to correspond closely to the actual words of the text, reflecting each changing mood. Thomas Morley's *A Plain and Easy Introduction to Practical Music* (1597) summarised the principle which had entered English music much earlier in the century, that ' . . . you must in your music be wavering like the wind, sometime wanton, sometime drooping, sometime grave . . . .' The variety now desired by the musician made fresh demands on the poet, and consequently a new expressiveness entered contemporary verse. The lyric particularly and to a lesser extent the sonnet, strove for a generally mellifluous effect but was also modulated internally by the lover's protestations, his sinking into grief, rising into hope, quavering in despair; yet all avoiding dissonance. It may well be that the very division of the sonnet into octet and sestet in this period, with a change of mood at the transition, arose from that tendency towards contrasted emotion within an overall harmony.

Interest in the new modes spread far beyond the court, and the growing demand for songs to be rendered in unison by small groups at all levels of society ensured that the connection between music and poetry was maintained. The most popular poetic miscellany produced during this century, quaintly named *The Paradise of Dainty Devices* (1576), claimed that its poems were '. . . aptly made to be set to any song in five parts, or sung to instrument', and throughout this period even when a poet was not consciously composing for a musical setting, the close inter-relationship of verse and music left its mark upon his writings, contributing to the qualitative difference between Skelton's rougher forms and the harmonious effect of Wyatt's verse.

The Petrarchan sonneteers

Sir Thomas Wyatt (1503—42) was a man of many parts even beyond his distinction as a poet. He was the all-round achiever, excelling in the manifold arts appropriate for the Renaissance courtier. A skilled athlete and swordsman, handsome in appearance, an accomplished linguist and scholar, a knowledgeable astronomer and musician, he was also held in high regard as a diplomat, both by his own King and by Emperor Charles V. His life had all the makings of splendid success; yet both domestically and politically he had cause for the sadness and sense of missed opportunities which tinge most of his verse. His marriage resulted in an early separation on the discovery of his wife's infidelity. There is strong evidence that he was later Anne Boleyn's lover, compelled to relinquish her with as good a grace as he could muster when it transpired that the rival for her affections was no less than Henry VIII himself. And if his condition was no worse than others in the highly dangerous game of court politics, he was twice imprisoned in the Tower, and on both occasions fortunate to escape with his life. Saved from the executioner's block in 1541, in part by his brilliant defence speech prepared for the trial in which he wittily turned his accuser Bonner into a laughing-stock, he was returned to royal favour. However, in the following year he fell victim to a fever caught while travelling on the King's affairs and died at the early age of thirty-nine.

The melancholy tone pervading his poems may owe something to his personal disappointments, but it derives also in no small part from the love tradition which he introduced into English poetry on his return from a diplomatic mission to Italy in 1527. There the Petrarchan love-poem, fostered and developed for over a century after Petrarch's death, had reached the height of popularity, the tradition in which the despairing lover mourns with icy chills and burning passion the mistress who has denied him her love:

> I find no peace, and all my war is done,
> I fear and hope, I burn and freeze like ice;
> I fly above the wind, yet can I not arise . . .

Such verse sounded a new note in England. Its introspective focus upon the emotional state of the speaker, and even its validation of love as an absorbing theme for poetry had little precedence in the English poetic tradition. Earlier poets preferred ballads on the themes of death and ancient battles, or chose narrative, satire, and country scenes for their subject-matter. When they did treat of love, they did so either allegorically or with a lusty forthrightness far removed from the sensitivity of the Petrarchan, as in this anonymous poem of the sixteenth century:

> Western wind, when wilt thou blow,
> The small rain down can blow?
> Christ, if my love were in my arms,
> And I in my bed again!

Now, however, the lover adopts a refined suppliant and mournful tone, pleading for mercy from his cruel mistress, warning the world of the pain inherent in love's bondage and, for all his complaints, obviously revelling in his role as the suffering victim of Cupid's darts. Whether written for a musical setting or not, the following stanza, like most of Wyatt's poems, possesses all the qualities of a text for lute accompaniment. There is the slow plangency of the opening line, the pauses after 'pain' and 'cry' to allow for a more protracted note, soon to be echoed by the rhyming 'I', as the subjective climax of the passage:

> Lament my loss, my labour, and my pain,
> All ye that hear my woeful plaint and cry;
> If ever man might once your heart constrain
> To pity words of right, it should be I,
> That since the time that youth in me did reign
> My pleasant years to bondage did apply,
> Which as it was I purpose to declare,
> Whereby my friends hereafter may beware.

Wyatt wrote a number of poems in this style which for all their intrinsic merit as individual poems and their real contribution to the development of English poetry, when read together lose much of their attractiveness by the repetition of theme and the recurrence of stock images imported with that tradition from abroad. Fortunately, they do not represent his best or his most typical work. Indeed, his modification of the Petrarchan pose, which constituted his finest writing, did much to damage his reputation during the period when that other tradition was in vogue, and even in later years when it

was assumed that his main purpose had been only to imitate
his fourteenth-century Italian master. He was accused of
failing to capture the inward significance of Petrarch's poetry,
as if that had been his aim. But Wyatt, we should recall, was
writing nearly two hundred years after Petrarch, for a
different age and with a different intent, using that tradition
for his own ends. In Petrarch's *Canzoniere* the tender longing
for an idealised Laura had functioned as a symbol of unful-
filled desire, a yearning for the impossible, representing for
the poet an image of life itself, the joy and anguish of man's
earthly longing for the divine. There was, for example, no
radical change in his poetry after Laura's death from plague
in 1348, and her angelic figure is only transposed a little
further heavenward.

While Wyatt does adopt the Petrarchan elevation of love as
an all-consuming power inspiring man to lifelong dedication or
reducing him to abject despair, he combines with that ennoble-
ment the Renaissance penchant for clear, objective perception
of fact. At the very moment that he bewails his lot and
participates emotionally in the sublime-love tradition, part of
him sees with cool cynicism the fickleness of the woman who
has caused his agony; and in manly refusal to be imposed
upon, he rejects the role assigned to him by the tradition.
The Petrarchan mode is thus authenticated and the lover's
pain felt by the reader through the speaker's overt rejection
of it. But by being viewed here with a certain detachment
and even mild humour, the clichés of the tradition are avoided,
and the poem achieves a vitality and freshness of its own:

> Divers doth use as I have heard and know,
>> When that to change their ladies do begin,
>> To mourn and wail, and never for to lin,*   *cease
>> Hoping thereby to appease their painful woe.
> And some there be, that when it chanceth so
>> That women change and hate where love hath been,
>> They call them false, and think with words to win
>> The hearts of them which otherwhere doth grow.
> But as for me, though that by chance indeed
>> Change hath outworn the favour that I had,
>> I will not wail, lament, nor yet be sad;
> Nor call her false, that falsely did me feed;
>> But let it pass and think it is of kind,
>> That often change doth please a woman's mind.

The more virile independence of the lover in such poems may also owe its source to a basic English dislike of 'unmanly' tears. With all their readiness to adopt the imported fashion for the greater sophistication it afforded in the articulation of emotional experience, temperamentally the English were uncomfortable with the role of disconsolate weeper bewailing his lot and in fact responded more readily in this century to the Stoic philosophy, with its demand for equanimity in the face of misfortune. As a result, in the poems they did produce within the sonneteering mode, they were usually at their best when they resisted a collapse into self-pity, displaying instead a slightly mocking tone, an awareness, as it were, of the absurd condition of inferiority in which they unexpectedly found themselves as lovers and a desire at the very least to restore their dignity by a witty rejoinder to their disdainful mistresses.

The sonnet form of this poem, appearing with Wyatt for the first time in England, suggests, together with the great popularity it was to achieve during the century, the need felt by poets for a firmer metrical discipline. The intricate rhyme scheme, the fixed pattern of fourteen iambic pentameters with a separation into octet and sestet, and such further refinements as the final epigrammatic couplet (an innovation of Wyatt's inspired by Serafino and adopted into the Shakespearean form of the sonnet) made sterner demands on the poet than the looser stanzaic modes of the earlier tradition; and the challenge it posed created in poetry a sophistication paralleling the effect which Ciceronian rhetoric had produced in Tudor prose.

In poetry, neither Greek nor Latin verse could serve as metrical models (although they did for subject-matter and genre), since they depended upon a quantitative, non-accentual metre unsuited to English as a non-inflected language. Even the incorporation of continental verse-forms into English required considerable ingenuity on the part of the poet, particularly as the language was still fluid. Spelling (modernised throughout this volume for the convenience of the reader) was, as has been noted, very different at that period, and to a large extent dependent on the passing whim of the writer. Wyatt, like Shakespeare, had various ways of spelling even his own name (Wyat, Wiat) and chose whichever happened to suit his fancy at the time. Such flexibility in spelling has implications both for rhyme and accent. In their original form, the opening lines of the above sonnet read:

> Dyvers dothe vse as I have hard and kno,
>   When that to chaunge ther ladies do beginne,
>   To morne and waile, and neuer for to lynne,
> Hoping therbye to pease ther painefull woo.

The rhyming of 'know' and 'woe' is seen to have been more dubious at the time the poem was written, particularly as the regional dialects prevailing at the time make it difficult to determine today how the words were actually pronounced. 'Painefull' seems here to contain only two syllables, but there are other times when 'kindely' or 'frendes' (friends) may well have sounded the now silent *e*, adding an extra syllable to the line. Are we always to read such words in the manner that produces the most regular metrical form, or are we to assume that sometimes Wyatt is deliberately varying the metre? When his poems were published in 1557, some thirty years after they were first circulated in manuscript and when Wyatt was no longer alive to supervise the printing, the publisher introduced a number of emendations, either to make words conform to a usage already becoming uniform by then or to regularise the line metrically; but the changes, it can now be seen, generally damage the subtler rhythms of the original, and insofar as it is possible to reconstruct the pronunciation at the time of their composition, they show Wyatt to have been a more sensitive metrist than his publisher had recognised.

The introduction of a final couplet in the sonnet to summarise the theme or sharpen its concluding point indicates the more logical structure of Wyatt's poems, the injection of a more formal reasoning to modify the yearning other-worldliness of the Petrarchan mode. It forms part of a sharper awareness of reality, and there is often in his poems a lively sense of astonishment, almost of rebellion, when he observes, as though standing outside himself, the change wrought in him by love:

> What meaneth this? When I lie alone
> I toss, I turn, I sigh, I groan;
> My bed me seems as hard as stone.
>   What meaneth this?

> I sigh, I 'plain continually;
> The clothes that on my bed do lie
> Always methinks they lie awry:
> What meaneth this?

Despite the sharp queries, the melodiousness of the poem is maintained by each stanza's being rounded off with a refrain, again evocative of lute accompaniment. In fact, sonnets constituted only a small percentage of Wyatt's poetry, and he was a keen experimenter in a variety of stanzaic forms. Like the above lyric, they continue, though with a marked refinement in technique and theme, the 'ballet' or 'ballade' tradition of a song to accompany dances which was popular in the previous century. In the following instance, the more complex metrical form of the stanza is used subtly to underscore the theme. As the lines progressively expand in length, the final line is cut short, the sudden ending of each phase marking the unpredictability of the mistress's moods:

> Is it possible
> That so high debate,
> So sharp, so sore, and of such rate,
> Should end so soon and was begun so late?
> Is it possible?
>
> Is it possible
> So cruel intent,
> So hasty heat and so soon spent,
> From love to hate, and thence for to relent?
> Is it possible?

The speaker's incipient rebellion against the role of the suffering lover breaks out at times into open revolt, and the joy of throwing off the yoke and laughing it to scorn comes as a refreshing release from the oppressive self-pity of the older tradition:

> Tangled I was in love's snare
> Oppressed with pain, torment with care,
> Of grief right sure, of joy full bare,
> Clean in despair by cruelty;
> But, ha, ha, ha, full well is me,
> For I am now at liberty . . .

A particularly endearing feature of Wyatt's poems is his habit
of addressing a poem not only to his mistress but also to his
pen, his heart, his mistress's fair hand in which his own heart
is held, and his lute. In each instance, the message of the
poem is still aimed at the mistress herself who is assumed to
be listening, but the device of addressing her indirectly frees
the speaker, as it were, from embarrassment, and creates a
greater sense of frankness and intimacy. One of the loveliest
of his lyrics is an extension of this device, in which his lute
having become the object of her wrath, is defended by him
on the grounds that it can only play the songs emanating
from its master's heart. If she wishes to change them, then
she must, he suggests, change her feelings towards their
author:

> Blame not my lute, for he must sound
>   Of this or that as liketh me;
> For lack of wit the lute is bound
>   To give such tunes as pleaseth me.
> Though my songs be somewhat strange,
> And speak such words as touch thy change,
>   Blame not my lute . . .

Within the history of English poetry, Wyatt is a seminal
figure. Anthologies have generally restricted him to only one
or two poems, such as his deservedly famed 'They flee from
me . . . ', with its extraordinarily vivid depiction of a memory
from earlier and happier days:

> Thanked be fortune it hath been otherwise
>   Twenty times better; but once in special
> In thin array, after a pleasant guise,
>   When her loose gown from her shoulder did fall,
>   And she caught me in her arms long and small;*   *slim
> Therewithal sweetly did me kiss,
> And softly said, 'Dear heart, how like you this?'

Yet the qualities which distinguish this poem, the mingling of
sharply etched actuality with dream-like meditation, of
idealised love with scorn for the changeability of women, of
melodious tone broken by direct colloquialism, hold true for
a large body of his poems which deserve to be classed among
the finest of his era. In addition to their own merit, they

were also the first to introduce into the language a new style
of verse in subject-matter, imagery, and metrical form. They
left their mark on English poetry for the following century,
including John Donne among the many heirs, not least in the
latter's use of a fully realised dramatic situation to question
the very Petrarchan convention which acts as its frame.
Nobody previous to Wyatt could have written such lines as:

> A face that should content me wondrous well
> Should not be fair but lovely to behold . . .

but there would be many afterwards who would try to imitate
them.

Poetic miscellanies

By the reign of Henry VIII enterprising printers had begun to
search for new markets, and as a result the poetic anthology
(or 'miscellany' as it was then called) came into being, moulding the tastes of readers during the century, and serving in
later generations as a valuable source for poems which might
otherwise have been lost in manuscript. Although it has only
survived in tattered form (some discarded pages were
discovered within the binding of a later sixteenth-century
volume), the earliest known miscellany is *The Court of Venus*,
probably printed in the 1530s, and containing together with
other poems by various hands some of Wyatt's early lyrics.
The fanciful name chosen for this collection of love poems
was mild compared with the riot of imaginative titles under
which subsequent miscellanies were offered for sale. There
was *The Paradise of Dainty Devices* (1576) which went into
ten editions, *A Gorgeous Gallery of Gallant Inventions* (1578)
orginally named *A Handful of Hidden Secrets* or *Delicate
Dainties, A Handful of Pleasant Delights* (1584), *The Bower
of Delights* (1591), and *The Arbor of Amorous Devices* (1597).
The most influential of them, however, had a more sober
name, *Songs and Sonnets Written by the Right Honorable
Lord Henry Howard Late Earl of Surrey and Others*, and
perhaps because of the solemnity of its formal title it became
commonly known as Tottel's *Miscellany* in tribute to its
publisher Richard Tottel, although the original name was not

forgotten. In Shakespeare's *Merry Wives of Windsor*, the diffident lover Slender, incapable of composing his own love songs, declares 'I had rather than forty shillings I had my Book of Songs and Sonnets here.'

Published in 1557, a year before Elizabeth's accession to the throne, it went into nine editions within the brief space of thirty years, an extraordinary sale by the standards of the time. Unlike most modern anthologies which offer selections from already established poets, this provided the first appearance in print not only for Surrey's poems, but also for the main body of Wyatt's verse, as well as for many individual poems by less famous poets of the generation. Moreover, it offered a dazzling variety of metrical forms, some of them quite new to the English tongue. There was a generous sprinkling of sonnets, ottava rima, terza rima, heroic couplets, blank verse, and rime royal, quite apart from a wide selection of stanzaic patterns for the lyric. In an age when poetry-writing was becoming a fashion at court, it offered a broadened range of models, and confirmed that the continental Renaissance had entered the poetry of England. Tottel at times tampered with the poems he printed, attempting to remove irregularities of metre or harshness of sound usually to the detriment of the original, but such liberties were amply recompensed by the impetus this collection gave to the poets of the Elizabethan era, and the change in reading tastes which it helped to inaugurate.

Although Tottel's *Miscellany* contained ninety poems by Wyatt and only forty by Surrey, the title gave pride of place only to Surrey, probably for reasons of political prudence. Only three years before publication, Wyatt's son had been beheaded for leading a rebellion against Queen Mary, who was still on the throne when the book appeared, and Wyatt's family name had sensitive associations. Surrey (1517–47), it is true, had also been executed for treason, but the circumstances were different. He had been arrested with his father, the Duke of Norfolk, on a transparently absurd charge trumped up by their bitter rivals the Seymours in the jockeying for power as Henry VIII lay dying. Even at that time, the death at the age of thirty-one of this attractive young man who had been a champion at court jousts and had distinguished himself on the battlefield aroused the ire of the populace.

Noble birth in the Tudor era was known to be a dubious
blessing, offering a glittering pathway strewn with honours
yet leading only too often to the scaffold for no better
reason than that the person's very existence as heir or relative
to a potential rival marked him out for destruction, and
Surrey's memory remained unsullied in men's minds. The
prominence accorded to him in the *Miscellany* was largely
responsible for his being regarded for many years as Wyatt's
superior, but the situation has been rectified in our own era.
It can now be seen that, although he did much to smooth
out the metrical wrinkles of Tudor poetry and to formalise
certain aspects of the sonnet, his own poetry lacks the
vitality and lyricism of his older friend and poetic mentor.

Surrey was, by all accounts, happy in his marriage (he
wrote a touching lament on his enforced separation from his
wife during his military duties) and perhaps for that reason
his poems, composed in the guise of the Petrarchan lover
scorned by a cold unfeeling mistress, emerge as artificial
pieces, as conscious literary exercises, offering an excuse for
introducing imagery but without the grief or passion which
should generate it:

> Give place, ye lovers here before
> That spent your boasts and brags in vain,
> My lady's beauty passeth more
> The best of yours, I dare well sayn,
> Than doth the sun the candlelight,
> Or brightest day the darkest night . . .

On the other hand, if the lover's suffering is only an excuse
for composing poetry, Surrey often leads that poetry in a
new direction, towards a deeper responsiveness to the beauty
of the English countryside. A love of the changing forms of
nature had long existed in English poetry, as in the sparkling
opening to *The Canterbury Tales*, but here it merges with
the introspective melancholy of the lover to create an
emotional bond between speaker and natural scene which has
no precedence in English poetry, and was to prove fruitful
for its future development. The mythologising of nature
familiar from Petrarch's verse is deserted here in favour of the
actual world of nature, the nightingale displaying its new
feathers in the spring, the adder casting off its winter garb,

the swallow swooping after small flies. In his finest sonnet, the mood is more solemn, the conventional anguish of the lover being contrasted with the peacefulness of nature; and the harmony of the verse here is a tribute to the improved control of sound and rhythm which Surrey has achieved:

> Alas, so all things now do hold their peace,
> Heaven and earth disturbed in nothing;
> The beasts, the air, the birds their song do cease;
> The night's chair the stars about doth bring.
> Calm is the sea, the waves work less and less;
> So am not I, whom love alas doth wring,
> Bringing before my face the great increase
> Of my desires, whereat I weep and sing
> In joy and woe, as in a doubtful ease.
> For my sweet thoughts sometime do pleasure bring,
> But by and by the cause of my disease
> Gives me a pang that inwardly doth sting,
>   When that I think what grief it is again
>   To live and lack the thing should rid my pain.

If only he had composed more often in this strain, his place in poetry would be secure; but rarely does he achieve such distinction and most of his poems fall below Wyatt's in quality. As this poem shows, incidentally, the so-called Shakespearean sonnet was already gaining ground, and Surrey did much to popularise what had been only occasional in Wyatt's writings. Here the form is still less disciplined than it was later to become. Although the rhyme scheme follows the pattern of three quatrains followed by a concluding couplet, the sense movement spills over those divisions and remains fluid, so that it would be easy for a reader to miss the fact that it is a sonnet.

Surrey's further contribution was to be far-reaching in its effect. For his translation of two books from Virgil's *Aeneid*, he experimented with a new metrical form, attempting to domesticate into English the non-rhyming metre of the classical epic. The unrhymed iambic pentameters or 'blank verse' he introduced proved so attractive in their combination of regular rhythm with freedom from the restrictiveness of rhyme that they became the accepted vehicle for Elizabethan drama. In Surrey's version, the line is often stiff and awkward, particularly in the narrative sections; but in the speeches set

within the epic it leaps into life, displaying the rhetorical
sweep and power which it was to offer the dramatist:

> He answered nought, nor in my vain demands
> Abode, but from the bottom of his breast
> Sighing he said: 'Flee, flee, O goddess's son,
> And save thee from the fury of the flame.
> Our enemies now are masters of the walls,
> And Troy town now falleth from the top . . .'

Much, then, stands to Surrey's credit as a metrist; but one
other verse-form he popularised was to spread like a canker
through the minor verse of the age. Jestingly called 'poulter's
measure' from the poulterer's habit at that time of adding
two extra eggs to the dozen for good measure, it consisted of
twelve syllables alternating with fourteen, that is, a six-foot
iambic followed by a seven-foot. A clumsy form, it created
long, unwieldy lines which pull the reader off balance:

> My soul is fraughted full with grief of follies past;
> My restless body doth consume and death approacheth fast.
> Like them whose fatal thread thy hand hath cut in twain,
> Of whom there is no further bruit, which in their graves remain.

The wonder is that it proved so attractive, becoming in the
1570s the most commonly used metre of all. The resulting
verse, abounding in the various Elizabethan anthologies, has
by now mercifully sunk into a deserved obscurity.

Surrey employed that metre for his metrical version of
certain biblical psalms. There had been a long tradition of
such psalm versification, not least because the psalter was so
obviously poetic in style, imagery, and content, and yet was
not set out as poetry even in the Hebrew original. Only in the
eighteenth century was Robert Lowth to discover that
Hebrew poetry in fact relied on parallelism, a rhythmic echoing of ideas, free from metrical restriction. Until then,
however, poets felt drawn to the task of versifying what
seemed such excellent poetic material, with the added
attraction that its sacred source might vicariously inspire the
poetiser too.

The renewed surge of interest in such activity at this time

was prompted by a further reason. Throughout the Middle
Ages, the singing of church masses and hymns had been the
prerogative of a clergy trained in polyphonic chant at the
various abbeys and monasteries. Now with the advent of the
Reformation, the Protestant insisted on a more direct com-
munion between the individual worshipper and his God, and
he was encouraged to participate actively in the hymn-singing,
preferably within a chapel or smaller church. A need was felt,
therefore, for simpler hymns which even the untrained voice
could sing, hymns making little demand on musical skill,
avoiding complicated polyphony and, if possible, consisting
of an easily learnt tune repeated verse after verse. For such
purposes, the stanzas needed to be brief, readily understand-
able even for the illiterate, and simple to remember. Various
attempts in this direction were made on the continent by
Luther, and later under Calvin. In England, after the dissolution of the abbeys and monasteries around 1539, the need
became urgent, and one version appeared which swept the
field. It held its position of prominence for centuries, however
undeserved that prominence may have been on literary
grounds. In 1549, a collection of versified psalms produced
by Thomas Sternhold and John Hopkins was published which
by the mid-nineteenth century had appeared in no less than
six hundred editions. Occasionally the authors used poulter's
measure, but more commonly they employed a variant of
ballad metre (a four-line stanza with alternating four-foot and
three-foot iambics, really the 'fourteener' broken into two
lines) with the difference from ballad metre that all four lines
were rhymed *abab* to aid memorising.

Sternhold and Hopkins unfortunately assumed that the
divine origin of the psalms was all the poetic inspiration that
their versions required. Accordingly, they merely chopped
the ideas of the psalm into metrical form, inserting a meaningless 'I say' or 'then' to fill out a short line or to create an easy
rhyme, a sure mark of the lazy poetiser. The result is a
succession of stanzas such as:

> O happy is that man, I say,
> Whom Jacob's God doth aid,
> And he whose hope doth not decay,
> But on the Lord is stay'd.

However poor their own attempts which are really doggerel and not poetry, their choice of metre did eventually prove itself and become the accepted mould in which later and more distinguished writers, including Isaac Watts and William Cowper, cast such hymns as 'O God our help in ages past' and 'God moves in a mysterious way/His wonders to perform'. In that respect at least, the sixteenth-century versions apparently found the right answer to the needs of the new Church.

In connection with this theme of pious verse, an oddity deserves to be mentioned which never became part of the mainstream of poetry but was to recur in various forms throughout the centuries, the attempt to counter the popularity of the secular love-song by adapting its success to religious ends much in the style of the rock-hymn sessions, held in churches in our own day. In 1565, John Hall, alarmed at the vogue of amatory verse and hoping to turn it to advantage, issued a volume entitled *The Court of Virtue* in obvious contrast to the secular anthology *The Court of Venus* which had appeared in a new edition three years earlier. In place of Wyatt's well-known lament for unrequited love, which appeared there, beginning 'My lute awake! Perform the last/Labour that thou and I shall waste', Hall offers a poem (to be sung to a popular tune), which opens:

> My lute, awake and praise the Lord,
> My heart and hands thereto accord,
> Agreeing as we have begun
> To sing out of God's Holy Word,
> And so proceed till we have done.

His volume, not surprisingly, did little to stem the tide of the secular love-song, but it does at least indicate how the hymns and religious poetry of this time did, as in subsequent periods, keep a wary eye on contemporary fashions in secular verse and song, lest the younger generation be led astray by its literary or musical attractions.

The change from the cruder notes of Skelton's verse in the earlier part of the century to the polished and sensitive lyrics of Wyatt and Surrey suggest that English poetry was breaking out of its medieval chrysalis to warm its wings in the sunlight of a new era. It was not alone. Drama was undergoing a similar metamorphosis and to that we shall now turn.

4

The growth of secular drama

BY the early sixteenth century, the great cycles of mystery plays spanning Christian history from Creation to Doomsday had begun to die a natural death. After their medieval beginnings, emerging before the high altar of the very church which had forbidden all drama, they had in England reached the height of their dramatic power in the revised Wakefield cycle of the fourteenth century. Such plays continued to be performed well into the sixteenth century and occasionally even beyond, but they had ceased to hold a position of centrality in drama or to attract the best creative writers of the age.

The message disseminated by the Church had itself begun to change. Alarmed at the growing attractiveness of the material world with its expanding economy and widening horizons, it had grown more strident in its reminders to man of the Day of Judgement awaiting him beyond the grave, and his need here in this earthly existence to prepare for the eternity of his soul. Below the fifteenth-century fresco of *The Holy Trinity* by Masaccio, with its startlingly realistic perspective, appears a skeleton laid out upon a coffin with the chilling caption addressed to the spectator: 'What you are, I once was; what I am, you will become!' Its positioning beneath the sacred scene indicated the direction the spectator was to look for eternal life.

In drama, the celebration of the Corpus Christi pageants climaxing in the Crucifixion and Resurrection of Jesus begins to be replaced by such morality plays as *Everyman* (*c.* 1485), where the focus has been transferred from the holy characters of scripture to man himself, to the *psychomachia* or struggle for his soul, with its message that worldly wealth and power would be of no avail to him in postponing either death or the Day of Judgement:

DEATH: Everyman, it may not be, by no way.
I set nought by gold, silver, nor riches,
Nor by pope, emperor, king, duke, nor princes.

As the decades moved on, dramatists were to gaze with increasing fascination at that very power of kings and princes which is so casually dismissed here; and if the theme of Death the Equaliser remains prominent in the later plays, the dramatist's growing sense of astonishment at the fall of such princes from their impressive heights creates in large part the sense of tragic waste.

The demise of the mystery cycles (their name probably arose from a corruption of the Latin *ministerium*) was hastened in England by the break with Rome. Once Henry VIII had claimed for himself the supremacy of the English Church, we find the town clerk of Chester in 1572 altering the document issued each year to announce the performance of the plays by scoring through the warning there that any disturbers of the performance would be cursed by the Pope. The plays, therefore, were now no longer under the jurisdiction or patronage of the Church as such, but of the monarch (a significant change for the development as well as the censorship of drama in England). In those dangerous times, men were understandably wary of risking their heads by performing plays so obviously Catholic in origin, and there is a noticeable drop in the frequency of performance of the cycles after the formal separation from Rome. In 1538, John Bale composed a new Protestant mystery cycle entitled *God's Promises* to replace the Catholic plays, as well as to rival the growing secular drama. It consisted of seven scenes or playlets in which biblical figures obtained from God a renewal of the Covenant, so central to Protestant belief. Noah, like the other characters appearing there, has a self-reliance and dignity in his plea for mercy to man which breathes the spirit of humanism, and the language too is that of the new era:

NOAH: Lose him not yet, Lord, though he hath deeply swerved.
I know thy mercy is far above his rudeness,
Being infinite, as all other things are in thee.
His folly, therefore, now pardon of thy goodness,
And measure it not beyond thy godly pity.

The structure of the drama is, however, outmoded, still clinging to the medieval pattern of the cycle which was to continue only spasmodically through the century before disappearing altogether. Bale had been pouring new wine into a cracked flask.

Some historians have attributed the end of the mystery cycles in England to their suppression by the Protestants,[8] but there is evidence that they would have disappeared in any case. As part of the growing naturalism of the stage, the mystery cycles had in their later period become less formal and stylised. The main characters remained grave preachers of theological doctrine, but among them appeared some with warmer human qualities, anger, humour, and satiric impishness. The change, however, was not uniform. It seeped into the plays only from below. The characters becoming humanised were, it transpires, only those at the lower end of the holy hierarchy. They were either the villains (and hence fair game for ridicule) or figures non-biblical in origin (hence not really holy). The liveliest figures in the more developed cycles included, therefore, Noah's shrewish wife, who does not appear as a recognised figure in the Bible, the shepherds of the Nativity before their conversion to Christianity and, among the villains, Cain with his cheeky servant Garcio and Herod raging among the Innocents. In the course of time the growth of realism spread up the ladder of sanctity until it began to endanger the solemnity of the holier figures. For painters the humanisation of the donors and spectators in the sacred scenes was no threat, since the artist remained in sole control; but an audience roaring with laughter at the antics of minor figures not always obeying the dramatist's instructions was liable to get out of hand. Juan Luiz Vives, a Spanish humanist resident in England, described the cat-calls and ribaldry which he had witnessed at a performance of a Passion play in the Low Countries in the early sixteenth century:

> And by and by this great fighter comes and for fear of a girl denies his Master, all the people laughing at her question and hissing at his denial; and in all these revels and ridiculous stirs, Christ only is serious and severe: to the great guilt, shame, and sin both of the priests that present this and the people that behold it.[9]

As a result the realism advancing up the rungs of sanctity from below caused inversely the gradual disappearance of the sacred characters at the top end of the ladder, in descending order of importance. In biblical plays written during the sixteenth century, the first to disappear from the cast is God himself, who could not co-exist with realistic scenes on the stage. Then Christ ceases to be seen in such plays. By mid-century the entire New Testament loses its eligibility for stage presentation, not through censorship but because the dramatists themselves came to realise its inappropriateness for an increasingly naturalistic stage. Dramatists still interested in biblical themes now moved to the less sacred Old Testament and its Apocrypha, which provided the themes for Thomas Garter's *Godly Susannah* (1568) based on the story of Susannah and the Elders, and George Peele's *The Love of King David and Fair Bethsabe (Bathsheba)* at the end of the century in 1594. The last subject with a biblical flavour available for dramatisation at the turn of the century is drawn from the histories of Flavius Josephus in Lady Elizabeth Carew's *Mariam, the Fair Queen of Jewry* (1613), after which even semi-biblical subjects disappear completely from the English stage for three hundred years, moving instead into the unacted closet drama of Milton's *Samson Agonistes* never intended for stage production, and Byron's *Cain*. From this growing sensitivity to the inappropriateness of dramatising the scriptures on an increasingly naturalistic stage, it may be deduced that the mystery cycles and playlets, though still performed in outlying areas, were in any case doomed to extinction.

Such religious plays did not simply disappear, leaving a vacuum behind. The evolution was more gradual, with the new secular drama preserving many of the more popular elements of the earlier plays out of which it had grown. To an Elizabethan audience, Shylock and his servant Launcelot Gobbo would have been immediately recognisable as sixteenth-century versions of the Devil and his comic Vice, particularly as Shylock in that era always wore the red wig and beard familiar from his prototype Judas in the mystery plays. Shakespeare's comic presentation of Vice in Gobbo and Falstaff was itself an outgrowth of those earlier plays. The minor devils of the mystery cycles, running among the

members of the audience amidst shrieks of laughter and
pretended terror as they laid about them with inflated
bladders, had formed an integral part of the festive spirit of
those plays, mingling solemnity with comedy; and the
moralities had continued that tradition with their humorously
leering Envy and supercilious Pride.

The mystery plays had become deeply rooted in the folklore of the people, and as late as 1575 the Mayor of Chester,
when called before the Privy Council for having permitted
the plays to be acted in his city against the regulations,
defended himself by insisting, no doubt truthfully, that the
people had demanded them. In creating the figure of Shylock,
therefore, Shakespeare was relying on a devil tradition still
very much alive in people's minds. Moreover, those early
plays left their mark on subsequent drama in many other
ways, prominent among them being the lavish spectacle
which audiences had come to associate with the stage. The
theory that pageants were presented from primitive waggons
has been considerably modified by recent research. Where
they did still move from station to station, it is now believed
that, after stopping, the waggons were unloaded and settings
used to employ a larger acting area. In later years, the plays
were often presented in a fixed setting, and then the investment in time and money was considerable. Indeed, the trade
guilds which, as semi-religious institutions, had taken over
from the Church the responsibility for the presentation of
the plays, were now no longer able to bear the financial
burden for individual pageants as in the past, but began to
amalgamate in order to share the heavy costs. We know from
records that dressmakers and carpenters were hired sometimes
four months in advance to prepare the show. In consequence,
when the professional stage took over, it was playing to
audiences who had come to expect gorgeous robes and
colourful processions, and the entertainments and masques in
the houses of noblemen had a high standard of spectacle to
equal.[10]

The actor's status

The growth of the secular drama in this era was inhibited by
the peculiar status of the actor, who was at that time neither

a recognised craftsman nor a professional. He had no guild to regulate his activities nor, even more necessary, to offer him the protection he required. The economic difficulties of the country had created problems of wide unemployment and poverty. The most obvious course for a destitute peasant was to wander through the countryside raiding hen-coops and orchards as he went. To contain this danger, which was a threat to all settled husbandry, Poor Laws were passed and strictly enforced, restricting such unemployed vagrants to their town of residence, where the authorities were made responsible for providing them with work or alms. Vagabonds who continued to wander were clapped in irons, 'grievously whipped and burnt through the gristle of the right ear with a hot iron of the compass of an inch about.' The simplest loophole was for such a vagrant to slip a jester's cap into his pocket and, if challenged, to claim that he was an itinerant actor. The loophole was closed in 1572. From that time, only groups of players possessing a document testifying to the personal protection of a nobleman were permitted to tour. Hence the nomenclature for the various actors' companies in this era, such as the Earl of Leicester's Players, or the Admiral's Men. The need for such protection also testifies to the low social status of the professional actor who was at that time rated close to the vagrant, and only towards the end of the century began to rise in public estimation. Hamlet's admonition to Polonius to see the players well bestowed because they are 'the abstract and brief chronicles of the time' was Shakespeare's own hint to the courtiers watching the performance that the actors enjoyed an enhanced social position in his day, and that therefore greater respect should be accorded to them.

In the earlier part of the century, the distinction between amateur and professional actor was less clearly defined. While the mystery plays were still performed mainly by amateurs, plays offered in noblemen's houses began to include in their casts players employed on the staff for that purpose. Moreover, having performed in the house, they would often be permitted to take the play out to the local public, acting at an inn, village green, or hall, so that there were times when an actor himself would be hard-put to define whether his own standing was that of an amateur or a professional.

Interludes

The dramatic form which contributed to the transition from religious to secular themes as well as from amateur to professional status was the Interlude. The origin of the Latin term *inter-ludum* may be a 'play between' the courses at a banquet, or more simply a 'play between' two or more actors; but whatever the source of the term, it generally did take place in the banquet hall during or after a meal. A particularly valuable contribution of the interlude was its break with the fixed festival days of the Christian calendar, upon which the earlier plays had always received their public performance. Presented within a nobleman's house, the interlude could now form part of any celebration, such as the visit of distinguished guests or a family wedding. Such occasions were still festive, and often coincided with the seasonal rites of Christmas, Twelfth Night, or Easter, so that much of the anthropological sense of rebirth or release from winter's stress, which modern critics have seen as a deeper motive force in comedy and tragedy, remained present. Yet the possibility of performance outside the prescribed dates, and their overspill into the public domain after presentation at the manor-house, opened the way for the professional stage which could eventually offer regular week-day performances unconnected with official public holidays.

Even more significant was the opportunity the interlude offered for a widening of scope. It could still supply morality themes, but since it no longer needed to justify itself in the eyes of the Church, the interlude could also present broad farce with no moral lesson to convey, scenes from English history, and even political topics of immediate contemporary relevance. At first sight these various categories may appear unrelated, but they were bound by an underlying unity. The medieval mind loved debate. Peter Abelard's twelfth-century *Sic et Non* ('For and Against') had offered contrasting views on theological matters; the universities had used public disputation as a basic tool of instruction; and a genre of poetry had arisen in that period called *débat*, in which two persons argued their case in verse before a third figure who adjudicated the prize. The morality play itself was a form of debate arising from that tradition. Man must judge between the conflicting advice of the good and bad angels, or between the persuasive claims of the personified Virtues and Vices, each eager to win the prize consisting of the adjudicator's eternal soul. With the advent of humanism, debate continued, but its nature had changed. In morality debates, the dice had been heavily loaded in favour of the virtues whose very names predetermined audience response. Wisdom versus Folly, Charity versus Avarice were black-and-white distinctions, oversimplifications which left little room for subtler discrimination or rational discussion. Hence, while the fate of Everyman may have been in doubt, the choice he ought to make was never in question.

In cultivated courts of the late fifteenth and sixteenth centuries such as Urbino a favourite pastime, as we know from Castiglione's colourful description, was a debate ranging over a wide spectrum of subjects, in which ladies and gentlemen alike would participate with wit and learning under the benign patronage of the Duchess or her deputy, whose only 'cruelty' was to threaten forfeits to anyone reluctant to speak when called upon. They would choose a theme such as the nature of love, the advantage of painting over sculpture, or the attributes desirable in the ideal courtier, and participants would be judged by the company both on their learned reasoning and on the humour with which they presented their arguments. The home of John Morton, in which Thomas More served as page, became at the turn of the century an English counterpart to Urbino, a civilised household presided over by a benevolent and scholarly head, involved at the highest level in the religious and political life of his country of which he was to become Archbishop of Canterbury and Lord Chancellor. More's *Utopia*, with its teasing yet serious discussion of ethical, political and religious topics, reflects the debates in that household much as Castiglione's *Courtier* does for Urbino. And it is not fortuitous that the new interlude emerged from Morton's household and the social and family circle of More who had been educated in it. For the interlude was in many ways a translation into dramatic form of the discussions taking place at the banqueting table, and often spiced by witty jest or humorous anecdote to enliven the argument.

Henry Medwall was a chaplain in Morton's house, who had

been known only for a minor morality interlude entitled
Nature until the discovery in 1919 of his *Fulgens and Lucrece*.
The latter won him recognition not only as the author of the
first known secular play in English, but also as an original and
lively dramatist. The interlude appears to have been performed
about Christmas time in 1497 at a banquet honouring the
ambassadors of Flanders and Spain during a period of sensitive
international negotiation when it was important to create a
warm social atmosphere. The play contains all the ingredients
of the interlude summarised above. The central plot is a
dramatised morality debate on the theme of Idleness versus
Studiousness, but removed from so simplistic and allegorised
a contrast into the area of humanist discussion, more in the
tradition of Cicero's *De Senectute*. Cornelius, a wealthy
young nobleman whose aristocratic forebears have served the
state well in the past competes for the hand of the fair
Lucrece again Gaius, a plebeian of studious, modest, and wise
nature. In addition to his aristocratic blood, Cornelius offers
her riches, a life of ease and comfort, beautiful clothes,
minstrels to dance by when the mood takes her, and hawks
for hunting. Gaius, in defence of his low birth, argues that
suitors should be judged by their own deeds, not those of
their ancestors, and that in place of idleness, he can offer her
a life of moderate riches but greater usefulness and satisfaction.
Her choice clearly will fall upon Gaius, but the choice is less
easy than the straightforward preference of good over evil and,
what is more, is transferred from the abstract world of
allegory to the actual world of contemporary social modes,
even though the setting is supposedly ancient Rome.

A further merit of the interlude lies in the clever interweaving of a comic sub-plot which, like so many such scenes
in later Elizabethan drama, humorously echoes or parodies
the main theme by being transposed to the knock-about
setting of the lower classes. Two servants, named simply A
and B, are also in competition for the hand of a 'fair' creature,
Lucrece's maid, and are commanded by her to undergo the
trial of singing, wrestling, and jousting with each other to
determine which is more worthy of her choice. After all their
efforts, their only reward at the end is a clout on the head for
each, as she laughingly informs them that she is already
promised to another.

Here too, as so often in the Renaissance, the lofty debate on the ideals by which humanity is to live becomes anchored by the sub-plot in the everyday setting of serving-men and their wenches, who also form part of that humanity. While the mystery plays had gradually permitted slapstick and humour to creep in from below, it never became an integral part of the overall plan. Noah's fisticuffs with his recalcitrant wife or Garcio's cheeky replies to his master Cain are marginal and later additions, rather like the so-called 'babooneries', those lively drawings of monkeys, a rabbit funeral, or a hunting scene which appear with no connection to the text in the margin of a sacred medieval manuscript, such as a collection of Psalms.[11] With parchment too expensive for an artist to purchase, there was nowhere else for him to draw such scenes except as a decoration to the manuscript he was transcribing. Similarly, with no stage existing in the Middle Ages other than the ecclesiastical, the only place for comedy to grow was in the 'margin' of the religious plays. Now, however, the concept changes. There is an intrinsic relationship between the two plot levels, with the farcical version not detracting from the main debate but enriching it, by broadening its relevance and reminding us that man, for all his noble aspirations, does not live in the clouds but on this solid earth.

The staging of this interlude in a banqueting hall during a festive meal is incorporated into the text as a device for creating rapport with the audience. At the opening of the play, A scolds the diners for sitting at table so solemnly, and asks if they are expecting some pretty girl to dance for them:

> A: For God's will,
>   What mean you, sirs, to stand so still?
>   Have you eaten, and your fill
>   And paid nothing therefore?

Half-way through the performance, as the climactic disputation between the main suitors is about to be presented, an interval is announced:

> A: We may not with our long play
>   Let* them from their dinner all day.   *keep
>   They have not fully dined.

The guests, he declares, jocularly, look half-starved, and in the name of the master of the feast, he calls for the next course to be served together with good wine, the play to be resumed when they have finished eating.

The crossing of the barrier between stage and audience — a dramatic device which the modern stage has repeatedly attempted to reintroduce after centuries of formal division at the curtain line — arises from the more convivial atmosphere of an indoor drama in a household where both actors and audience know each other well. When B knocks at one of the hall doors, a member of the audience is requested to open it for him. We know, in fact, that audience participation went much further. At one point during the interlude, the two servants are spectators watching the main action. B decides he must offer some advice to Cornelius. 'Peace, let be./By God, thou wilt destroy all the play!' cries A, but to no avail, and B enters the play, dragging his friend with him. In that setting, it is easier to appreciate the story told of More that, during the time he served in the household, to the amusement of all including the elderly Archbishop himself, he used to 'suddenly sometimes step in among the players, and never studying for the matter, make a part of his own there presently among them.'

More's interest in play-acting was shared by the men who married into his family. John Rastell (c. 1470–1536), who wedded More's sister Elizabeth, was a man of quite remarkable energy and versatility. Coroner of Coventry, active in artillery transportation, a shareholder in an overseas venture, member of parliament, and religious reformer, he was led by the latter zeal into conflict with the King and to eventual death in prison. Fortunately for the historians of drama, among his many enthusiasms was a love of interludes. In the 1520s he worked as a designer of royal and civic pageants, and was himself the author of at least one interlude, entitled *The Nature of the Four Elements*. He built a permanent wooden stage within his own gardens in Finsbury Fields, furnishing it with a wardrobe of players' costumes and settings. His most valuable contribution, however, was the blending of two of his interests — drama and the comparatively new art of printing.

The press owned by himself and his son was the very first

to publish plays in England. He printed *Fulgens and Lucrece*, and together with his son was responsible for printing two-thirds of all English plays published before 1534, many of which would not have survived were it not for his foresight. He holds the title also of being the first to print music in England, the score for a song included in his *Four Elements*. That interlude itself is interesting more for its allegorical concern with the embryonic sciences than for its intrinsic merit as a play. The morality theme of earlier allegories is secularised as Studious Desire instructs Humanity to apply its rational faculties to a study of astronomy, geography, and the world of natural phenomena.

It was John Heywood (*c.* 1497—1580), married to Rastell's daughter, who contributed most to the development of the interlude as such, leading it away from the sombre lessons of the morality tradition into sheer farce, in line with the *fabliaux* popular in France at that time. His playlet *The Four Ps* presents four men whose profession begins with the letter *P*, meeting by chance in an English country lane — a Palmer who claims to have visited Jerusalem and therefore can request alms, a Pardonner selling supposed saints' relics, a 'Pothecary or quack-doctor, and a Peddlar who beguiles women into spending their hard-earned savings on his trinkets. They vie with each other in defending their professions, but eventually admit cheerfully that they are all cheats, at which point the Peddlar suggests a competition (a variation on the adjudicated debate):

> PEDDLAR: And now I have found one mastery
> That ye can do indifferently,
> And is neither selling nor buying,
> But even only very lying!

He offers to act as judge in deciding which of them can tell the most impressive lie to prove his professional competence. The 'Pothecary tells a vastly exaggerated and bawdy tale of one of his miraculous cures, and the Pardonner relates how he once released a shrew from Hell to the great relief of the devils, who were only too glad to be rid of her. It is now the Palmer's turn. Instead of telling a story, he solemnly expresses his puzzlement at the latter tale on the grounds that he has never known any woman lose her temper. His remark is greeted with acclamation as the most monstrous lie of all, and the victory is his by common consent.

Apart from the good-natured scepticism towards relics and cure-alls, there is no real moral lesson conveyed, and the play exists solely for its entertainment value. The same holds true for his other interludes, such as *The Play of the Weather* (1533), in which Jupiter, in response to frequent complaints, holds court to decide what improvements should be made in it. One man demands constant strong winds to turn the sails of his windmill, another requires heavy rains to swell the streams for his water-mill, a laundress needs perpetual hot sun to dry her loads of washing, a lady requests an all-year temperate climate for her complexion, and a small boy insists on plenty of frost to permit snowballing. The decision, Merry Report informs us, is that the weather shall remain exactly as it was, to give everyone his fair share.

There is nothing great in these farcical interludes; merely light amusement in dialogue form with the introduction of occasional knock-about, as in *John John* (c. 1521) also probably by Heywood. There a foolish husband is cheated out of his supper by his wife and her paramour, whom he finally chases out of his house. This is all slapstick rather than comedy, but it has at least moved outside the religious framework, opening the way for secular comedy to develop independently. Yet it should not be forgotten that even in its later, more cultivated form, one great advantage of the English stage was that it avoided becoming an élitist drama — it never lost touch with the earthy humour of the folkloristic tradition out of which it had grown. Dogberry and the men of the watch, Bottom and his crew, the gravediggers in *Hamlet*, are drawn from the same rough world of labourers and artisans as populate these early farces. If later the humour becomes more subtly integrated into the overall themes of the plays, the endearing simplicity, jocularity, and ribaldry of England's native stock gave to drama an elemental quality which widened its appeal to include all levels of society.

Among the topics being debated at the banquet table and elsewhere at this time was the urgent question of the Reformation. There was little room there for the broad-minded tolerance and enlightened discussion associated with questions of general art and culture. Men and women were being burned at the stake for their views, and as the clash between Lutheranism and the Catholic Church took political overtones and countries aligned themselves formally with one or the other, the dangers grew in proportion. There was no opting out, and each individual was compelled to make his or her choice. The preachers on each side began to discover that the interlude could serve not only as dramatic framework for more genial debates on the pleasures of hunting versus the rigours of study, but also as a valuable propaganda weapon for glorifying their cause and publicly ridiculing their enemies.

There had been a precedent for such religious satire in John Skelton's playlet *Magnificence* (1515). Although ostensibly a traditional morality, it would have been understood at the time as directed against the author's usual target, Cardinal Wolsey. In this interlude, 'a prince of great might' named Magnificence dismisses his wise counsellor Measure in favour of such unsavoury characters as Counterfeit Countenance and Cloaked Collusion, who lead the prince towards ruin; fortunately, Good Hope and Perseverance return him to the right path and restore him to his former greatness. In isolation, it is a standard allegory, not particularly worthy of Skelton's talents, but as a thinly veiled attack on the King's chief advisor who, although the leading cleric of the English Church, was in Skelton's view squandering huge sums of his own and the King's wealth merely to enhance his own dignity, it takes on the quality of a mordant, topical satire.

Probably the most virulent of such dramatic polemicists was John Bale (1495–1563). Educated at a Carmelite convent in Norwich where he received a strict Catholic upbringing, he proceeded to Jesus College, one of the most monastic of Cambridge houses in that era. There he took holy orders, but becoming exposed to the new Reformist ideas before long changed sides, joining the Protestant cause. He created a public scandal by renouncing his vows of chastity and taking a wife. Like many converts, he proved to be more zealous in reviling his former faith than were the Protestants he had joined, and his splenetic attacks won him the unflattering nickname of 'bilious' Bale.

His composition of a Protestant mystery cycle to replace the Catholic was mentioned earlier, but he has earned a place in drama for a further innovation. In his *King John* (1538) he placed within a morality setting not simply 'a prince of great might' but the actual King John who fought a long battle against the Pope. It may seem a small change, but it marked the first use in drama of themes from English history, pointing forward to Marlowe's *Edward II* and Shakespeare's great monarchal cycle on the Wars of the Roses. The historical element in Bale's play was not confined to the central character despite the allegorical, morality setting, for the three main Vices are all identified as persons. Usurped Power, we find, is the Pope, Sedition is Archbishop Stephen Langton, the King's arch enemy who was responsible for his papal excommunication, and Private Wealth is Cardinal Pandolph. The parallel between King John's struggle against the papacy and Henry VIII's own break with Rome would have been clear for all to see when the play was performed in 1539 during the period when the King was asserting his own authority over the English Church. Quite apart from the virulence of the text, we can gain some idea of the ridicule conveyed by the acting and costuming from another play of Bale's, his *Three Laws*, where the stage directions instruct Sodomy to be dressed like a monk, Ambition like a bishop, and Hypocrisy like a Greyfriar. Here in our play, Bale's scorn for his former belief finds expression as Sedition offers for sale a series of relics including:

SEDITION: A louse of Saint Francis in this same crimson silk,
A scab of Saint Job, a nail of Adam too,
A maggot of Moses with a fart of Saint Fandigo . . .
In nomine Domini Pape, amen.

Such invective began to cause discomfort even to a Protestant monarch. From the moment that responsibility for the stage was transferred from the Church to the King, careful control became necessary. Plays when publicly performed drew crowds, and crowds are notoriously difficult to handle. This danger was particularly prevalent in the days when audiences were less disciplined, and would accompany a play with cat-calls, cheers, and ribald comments. It only required one hiss from a member of the audience whose religious scruples had been offended for him to be set upon by those around him, roused by the inflammatory rhetoric of the play, and then a general scrimmage would ensue often with serious consequences. In 1543, an Act was passed forbidding the performance of plays offering interpretations of scripture '... contrary to the doctrine set forth' by the King's Majesty, and that doctrine became so narrow as to make religious plays almost impossible to perform. Bale found himself compelled, on the fall of his patron Cromwell, to flee to the continent, and from there wrote bitterly of the new law, which he saw as muzzling the true preachers of God's word:

> So long as they played lies and sang bawdy songs, blasphemed God, and corrupted men's consciences, ye never blamed them, but were very well contented. But since they persuaded the people to worship their Lord God aright according to his holy law and not yours and to acknowledge Jesus Christ for their only redeemer and saviour without your lousy legerdemains, ye never were pleased with them. [12]

Bale's efforts to use drama in order to spread the good word before he left England throws interesting light on the actors' gradual transition from amateur to professional status in this sparsely-documented period. Apparently he formed his own group of travelling players, and lobbied for political and financial backing from the new Protestant leaders in much the same way as later companies turned to aristocratic patrons for protection. A note from Archbishop Cranmer to the Lord Chancellor Thomas Cromwell records that an inter-lude, enacted in his own house during the Christmas festivities at about eight or nine o'clock at night, demonstrated that 'King John was as noble a prince as ever was in England.' In Cromwell's account book appears an entry shortly after that date listing a payment of thirty shillings to 'Bale and his fellows' for a performance. By receiving payment for their labours they were, at least in that respect, moving towards professionalism.

School and university plays

There was one area of drama in this period which remained amateur and yet helped considerably to mould the future development of the English stage — the plays performed at schools and universities. Written by men of learning, they provided an early training for the dramatists of the next generation, by introducing them in their youth to the pleasures and challenges of full stage performances. The plays themselves were often taken over immediately by the professionals to become part of their repertoire. The role of education in bringing England into line with the continent has already been stressed. A century earlier only about one third of the population could read or write, but now the growth of trade had made it essential for a much larger percentage to be able to record transactions in writing. The more efficient administration of the country demanded a trained civil service, and made a knowledge of Latin, in addition to English, requisite for town clerks and bailiffs as well as those of higher office. While the monasteries existed, most schools in outlying areas had been supported and administered by them, with the clergy serving as teachers, and the disbanding of that system in the 1530s had left such areas without adequate facilities. As compensation, the grammar schools in the larger towns received an added boost after the mid-century, with poorer pupils from the local and surrounding areas being admitted by scholarship.

The school day was long, usually stretching from six in the morning to seven at night with two breaks for meals, and at that time sport had not yet become part of the programme. Some livening of the curriculum was needed to prevent boredom but there were in that era enlightened teachers such as Ascham and Mulcaster eager to arouse their pupils' interest in study rather than merely to cram them with information. One technique which had proved successful on the continent was imported to England. In addition to the passages of prose and poetry translated back and forth from Latin to English, full-length comedies by Plautus and Terence now began to be used, with the pupils acting out the plays in both languages. Thomas Ashton, the headmaster of Shrewsbury school, became famed for the plays he wrote and produced in the Quarry. In the course of the century that dramatic training raised the standard of boy-acting to such a level that it became a threat to the professional stage. One such professional, Ben Jonson, wrote a touching elegy in memory of a thirteen-year-old boy, Salathiel Pavy, who had acted old men so convincingly that, Jonson comments wrily, the Fates must have thought him to be one, and hence erroneously consigned him to his early grave.

From the 1530s onwards there was dramatic activity in the schools. The elusive Ralph Radcliffe, all of whose plays have vanished, took over, we know, an abandoned Carmelite monastery at Hitchin and opened a school there, converting the lower portion of the building into a spacious theatre for school productions to which he used to invite the local population. At a time when there was no regular professional stage, such performances had a wider appeal than they have today, and even royalty would invite schools to present plays before them. The boys of St Paul's school acted out Terence's *Phormio* before Henry VIII, and Queen Mary, because of her religious sensitivity, encouraged such school groups in preference to the professionals because she knew that the content of their plays would be either harmless or obediently catering to her own susceptibilities. Not only the ancient comedies but even the original interludes written especially for the boys by their masters were generally free of polemic and intended only to amuse and instruct, offering a relaxed humour and an unpretentious pleasure in entertaining situations such as was still lacking on the professional stage.

John Redford's *Wit and Science* may serve as one illustration for the many interludes of this kind written during this period. It was almost certainly composed between 1531 and 1547 when its author was Master of the Choristers of St Paul's Cathedral and responsible for their education. In form it is a morality play, but with one significant difference. The message it conveys is no longer religious but secular, aimed at instilling in the pupils a humanist love of learning. The main Vice, therefore, is no longer Pride which leads to Damnation but Sloth which leads to Ignorance and the play's main charm is the blending of the old allegorical tradition with the new romance mode. A young man, Wit, has determined to marry the fair lady Science (used here in its original meaning of 'Knowledge'), but in requesting her hand is informed by her father Reason that he must first slay the giant Tediousness. Eagerly he sets out on his way, accompanied by his faithful companions Instruction, Study, and Diligence, but the uncouth, Goliath-like Tediousness severely beats him, leaving him for dead. Discouraged, Wit lays his head in the lap of

Idleness, who in what may well have been a parody of one of the boys' own teachers castigating a backward student, takes her pupil Ignorance through his lessons with ludicrous results. As might be anticipated, Shame eventually drives Wit into challenging Tediousness once again. This time he is victorious and wins the hand of Science, promising never to forsake her; at which point the trained choristers conclude appropriately enough with a musical rendition of 'Remember Me!'. The purpose of such school interludes may have been primarily to sugar a didactic pill, but the sheer joy of acting which so obviously permeates the work, the strutting and ranting of the giant, the severity of Lady Science when her lover fails her, the absurdity of dull-witted and clownish Ignorance, show that drama was also being relished for its own sake, no longer functioning within a prescribed framework, but free to experiment and move out into the secular world.

One such new area was comedy, and the distinction of having written the first known English comedy belongs to Nicholas Udall (c. 1505–1556). He served as headmaster of Eton from 1534, but left under a cloud when he was called before the Privy Council in 1541 on a charge of sexual misdemeanour, and sentenced to imprisonment. After his release a few months later, he seems to have redeemed himself in the eyes of his accusers. For, despite his Lutheran leanings at a time when the reigning monarch was Catholic and his past misbehaviour, he was appointed Master of the Chapel under Queen Mary (who refers to him as 'our well-beloved Nicholas Udall') and later as headmaster of Westminster school. In all these appointments, he was active in organising dramatic performances, and won a wide reputation as a playwright, although only one play has been definitely identified as his and that only because of a passing reference to it by a contemporary.

The play known to be his is *Ralph Roister Doister*, which was in all likelihood written and performed during his period at Eton. In overall pattern it draws obviously enough on the Plautine-Terentian tradition in which a sharp-witted slave or parasite plays on other people's self-delusions to gull them into lining his own pockets with silver. This specific play employs as the gull figure the *Miles Gloriosus* or braggart soldier from Plautus' play of that name, the type who always boasts of his prowess but flees at the first sign of danger. Yet for all its indebtedness, including the importation of the classical or pseudo-classical names such as Philander ('Lover of Men') which had become customary in this period, here we meet Margery Mumblecrust, Tom Truepenny, and Tibet Talkapace. But the domestication of comedy goes much further. In the original plays by Plautus intended for adults and catering to a Roman society of looser moral standards, there was plentiful play with whorehouses, lechers and financial tricksters. Here, dissociating himself even from the milder indecencies of Heywood's interludes, Udall announces in the prologue:

> . . . all scurrility we utterly refuse,
> Avoiding such mirth wherein is abuse.

As a result, although Matthew Merrygreek, the main motivator of the action, has residual traces of the parasite about him (at one point he asks Ralph for a new coat in return for his assistance), his real purpose in manipulating the plot and planning the various misunderstandings is the sheer English love of mirth for its own sake.

The story involves Merrygreek's urging Ralph, who foolishly imagines he is a lady-killer, to press his suit on Dame Christian Custance, a widow already affianced to another. The scorn she pours upon this new suitor fails to penetrate the armour of his self-esteem and he is repeatedly beaten and berated before the lesson finally comes home. The plot is well constructed, moving smoothly from action to action, but the strength of the play lies less in the structure than in the main comic scenes, such as the battle between Ralph's band and Dame Custance's household, fought in order to force her into submission. When Ralph realises that he has forgotten his helmet, Merrygreek (who has in fact planned the fight in advance with the connivance of the 'enemy') decks him out with a kitchen cauldron which falls over his ears; and as they charge into the fray together with their absurdly-clad leader, Merrygreek's blows, (as pre-arranged) keep missing the enemy and falling instead on the unenviable Ralph. This is pure knock-about, far more effective on the stage than in any description here but the text of the play is often more subtle in its effect, using comic devices which were to reappear in Shakespearean comedy.

Ralph, for example, has paid a scrivener to compose a letter of proposal for him to Dame Custance. In reading the letter aloud to her on his behalf, Merrygreek deliberately misplaces the punctuation in a way which transforms the compliments into insults:

MERRYGREEK: 'Sweet mistress, whereas I love you nothing at all,
              Regarding your substance and riches chief of all,
              For your personage, beauty, demeanour, and wit
              I commend me unto you never a whit.
              Sorry to hear report of your good welfare . . . .'

The letter continues in this vein for over thirty lines. For the schoolboys it was an entertaining and salutary lesson on the need to mind their commas and colons, but it functioned for a wider audience too, as the prologue in the Pyramus and Thisbe scene of Shakespeare's *Midsummer Night's Dream* was to prove, with its untrained rustic actor repeatedly pausing in the wrong places, and thereby changing the meaning of the text. It was, incidentally, a quotation from Ralph's letter by Udall's past pupil Thomas Wilson which established this play's authorship for historians. In discussing 'ambiguities' in a treatise he wrote in 1553, he uses it as 'an example of such doubtful writing, which by reason of pointing may have double sense and contrary meaning, taken out of an interlude made by Nicholas Udall.'

In such scenes, the allegory of the morality interludes is discarded in favour of a refreshing realism, sorely needed on the English stage. In place of the religious didacticism which had predominated on the earlier stage, there is a new openness to the actual world of sixteenth-century England, and in fact the play even contains a lively parody of a church requiem. The latter is a late echo of the Boy Bishop ritual which on festive occasions had, as a release from the severities of normal discipline, allowed mock services to be held, sometimes with a braying *Hee-haw* from the worshippers to replace the usual *Amen*. Here Ralph wallowing in self-pity, moans that the pangs of unrequited love are breaking his heart. Merrygreek takes him at his word and holds a slightly premature funeral service with a makeshift tolling of church bells, interrupted at times by groans from the corpse:

MERRYGREEK:	Goodnight, Roger, old knave! farewell, Roger, old knave!
	Goodnight, Roger, old knave! knave, knap!
	Nequando. Audivi vocem. Requiem aeternam.
	Pray for the late master Roister Doister's soul!
	And come forth, parish clerk, let the passing bell toll.
	Pray for your master, sirs, and for him ring a peal.
	He was your right good master while he was in heal.
FIRST BELL:	When died he? When died he?
SECOND BELL:	We have him! We have him!
THIRD BELL:	Roister Doister! Roister Doister!
FOURTH BELL:	He cometh! He cometh!
GREAT BELL:	Our own! Our own!
ROISTER DOISTER:	Heigh-ho!

Dramatic activity was not confined to the schools, but continued into the universities. Oxford and Cambridge were very different then from their present form. They were smaller institutions both in the number of their colleges and in the size of their student body. Students were accepted there from as early as thirteen years of age, and generally studied for seven years before obtaining their degrees. Their training in drama at the schools was therefore still fresh in their minds. Between the universities and the royal court there was then a stronger connection, and that too affected the drama of the time. The reigning monarchs were eager to develop the centres of learning, partly in order to raise England's prestige among the cultured nations of the world, but partly also because of the power the universities held in influencing the religious direction of the country at a time (both preceding Luther and immediately after) when changes in that direction were liable to endanger the security of the throne. It was in the monarch's interest to know what ideas were being promulgated there. Henry VII's mother, Lady Margaret Beaufort, established a professorship of divinity at Cambridge, refounded Christ's College and supervised the opening of the new college of St John's (see *Plate I*); and both Thomas Cromwell as Henry VIII's chief advisor, and Lord Burghley as Queen Elizabeth's, served as university chancellors in the midst of their manifold other activities in order to keep an eye on their development.

In contrast to the schools, drama at the universities did not form part of the curriculum, but was an outgrowth there of the holiday celebrations. From the late fifteenth century, the statute books of the colleges had included regulations for the appointment of a Lord of Misrule during the Christmas period. One of the doctors of the college would be chosen and, for the period of his reign, was required to sit in mock judgement, administering ridiculous punishments for misdemeanours with heavy fines for anyone failing to comply in a true festive spirit.[13] From about 1540 a humanist leavening made itself felt, and a requirement was introduced for the performance of from two to five plays annually as part of the festivities. These were usually classical plays but also included plays written especially for the occasion in Latin, more rarely in Greek, and with increasing frequency in English.

In the earlier period, they were intended for the residents of the college only. However, in 1564 and 1566, Queen Elizabeth paid official visits to the two universities in order to strengthen her influence there, and in both instances dramatic performances by the students formed the main entertainment. Contemporary accounts record the great excitement that preceded the visits, the heavy financial outlay on staging and costumes, and the impressive spectacle that resulted. At Cambridge, a large stage was erected for a presentation of Plautus' *Aulularia* on the Sunday night, somewhat surprisingly within the nave of the majestic King's College Chapel; and in the hall of Christ Church, Oxford, a performance of Richard Edwards' *Palamon and Arcite* took place two years later. The latter attracted such large crowds through the rumour which had spread of its magnificent settings that a wall protecting the entrance steps collapsed, killing three persons. The play, the Queen decided, must go on, and it was performed as planned in two lengthy parts, one each evening. Particular admiration was evoked by a hunting scene in which boys standing at the windows of the hall responded to the cry of hounds coming up from the quadrangle below, a technique which extended the stage to include the entire college.[14]

The best-known university play from the mid-century and deservedly so, is *Gammer Gurton's Needle*. On the title-page of the 1575 edition, it is described as 'A right pithy, pleasant and merry comedy . . . played on the stage not long ago in Christ's College in Cambridge', and written by the mysterious 'Mr S., Master of Arts.' Many years of detective work by scholars have failed to establish with any certainty the identity of the author (most probably William Stevenson) and even the date of its first performance remains in doubt. From the fact that in the text an arrest is to be made 'in the king's name', and that from 1553 only queens reigned in England, it would appear to have been performed before that date under Edward VI, though the lapse of over twenty years between then and the 1575 title page scarcely accords with the statement that it was played 'not long ago'.

Whatever the authorship and exact date, the play remains one of the most endearing comedies produced at this time. Like Udall's, it adopts the classical five-act structure, but in content it is even more ruggedly English, providing a colourful picture of a contemporary farm in one of the poorer country areas of England. The thick rural dialect of the peasants, the deep mire clogging the paths, the tippling priest grumbling at being called away from his ale, the bickering and scuffling of the gossips, and above all the sheer poverty of a world in which a sewing needle is a treasured possession form the setting of the play. And yet for all the misery of that setting, the dominant mood is one of high spirits and good humour among people for whom such squalor constitutes the natural tenor of their lives. Hodge, the farmhand, may complain of the filthy clay clinging to his clothes as he digs a ditch and of the new split that has appeared in his breeches, but only as part of the normal way of things (in the following passage *cham* and *ich* represent rustic dialect for *am* and *I*):

HODGE: See! So cham arrayed with dabbling in the dirt!
           She that set me to ditching, ich would she had the squirt!
           Was never poor soul that such a life had.
           Gog's bones! This vilthy glay has drest me too bad!
           God's soul! See how this stuff tears!
           Ich were better to be a bear-ward and set to keep bears!
           By the Mass, here is a gash, a shameful hole indeed!
           An one stitch tear further, a man may thrust in his head!

Surprise has often been expressed that such realistic scenes of peasant life, capturing the intonations and thought-patterns of the lower class, should have come from the pen of an academic, a Cambridge master of arts, rather than from some rural playwright. Yet that is less of an anomaly when viewed in the social context of its time. Prior to this era, the gap between the classes had been much smaller. The furnishings in the house of a wealthy citizen of the later medieval period were incredibly meagre, and the physical comforts negligible. A few simple stools and a folding table provided for the main needs.[15] The surge forward in the late fifteenth and early sixteenth centuries as trade expanded resulted in the cultivation of polished manners among the upper strata of society and the building of elaborate homes. The aristocracy and burghers became the new patrons of art in place of the Church and the gap between the classes now widened considerably, making the peasant in his isolated village a curiosity for the townsman, to be examined as a creature almost from another world. There is evidence of this in the painting of the era. Peter Brueghel the Elder is often known as 'the Peasant Brueghel' because of his canvases depicting the daily life, pastimes and festivities of that class, but he was actually a highly cultivated man, and a friend of humanists intrigued by the unaltered traditions of the rustic community. His *Village Wedding* (1565), and *Peasant Dance* (1566), painted about the time of this play, convey in their depiction of the uncouth but harmless merriment of the dancers or the self-satisfied smirk of the bride seated for one day in her life in the position of prominence, the same amused and condescending sympathy for the country bumpkins as animates this English comedy.

The play itself has a simple, entertaining plot. Hodge has torn his breeches yet again, after they had only just been repaired by his employer Gammer (Grandma) Gurton. Embarrassed in such an exposed condition to meet the milkmaid who smiled at him last Sunday, he needs an urgent repair, but the vital needle is missing. Diccon, a light-hearted (and light-fingered) vagabond has appeared on the scene, full of mischievous schemes both to fill his stomach and to keep himself amused by stirring up the action. He swears that he saw the gossip next door pick up the needle, and sends the drunken curate to creep into her house to retrieve it. She,

warned by Diccon that robbers are about to break in, admini-
sters a sound drubbing to him unaware of the curate's identity.
Diccon, performing rather like Merrygreek the part of the
Plautine servant, now terrifies Hodge by pretending to call up
the Devil to help discover the whereabouts of the needle, the
academic author here ridiculing the foolish superstitions of
the peasants. After a number of similar escapades, Diccon's
subterfuges are revealed, and he is arraigned before the village
magistrate. Master Bailey, like the Lord of Misrule at the
college festivities, listens patiently to the unravelling of the
various stratagems and good-humouredly condemns Diccon
to a series of meaningless punishments, among them that he
is never to pay for the curate's drink if the curate should ever
offer to pay first. The high-spirited Diccon seals the bond by
giving Hodge a jovial thwack on the behind, which produces
a sharper squeal than had been expected. The missing needle
is discovered — left in his breeches from the previous repair!
Peace is restored and Gammer Gurton invites everyone to the
alehouse to celebrate the restoration of her missing darner.

The verse, as in most plays of this era, is often irregular, as
in the passage quoted earlier; but for the most part it employs
a rollicking fourteen-syllable line whose rhymed couplets
enliven the movement while the rhyme also probably aided
the amateur players in remembering their lines:

> She stooped me down, and up she took a needle or a pin.
> I durst be sworn it was even yours, by all my mother's kin.

Occasionally it is varied, for example to convey the simplicity
of the dim-witted Hodge in a speech with wonderful possibilities for a gifted comic actor:

> HODGE: My Gammer Gurton here, see now,
>   sat her down at this door, see now;
> And as she began to stir her, see now,
>   her needle fell to the floor, see now;
> And while her staff she took, see now,
>   at Gib her cat to fling, see now,
> Her needle was lost in the floor, see now.
> Is not this a wondrous thing, see now?

In form the comedy still shows marks of immaturity. The
Prologue, delivered before the play begins, reveals at that

early stage the comic conclusion which should provide the surprise ending by explaining that Hodge will eventually find the needle sticking in his buttocks. Such an opening belongs to the older tradition in which a play was the acting out of a story already familiar to the audience (a convention preserved, to Hamlet's annoyance, in the player's dumb-show preceding the performance of *The Mousetrap* — 'The players cannot keep counsel; they'll tell all'). As drama broke away from such traditions, it was to rely increasingly on unexpected twists or sudden revelations in plot to create tension or comic reversal; but the older patterns lingered on through much of the century.

Ralph Roister Doister and *Gammer Gurton's Needle* together mark a stride forward in English drama, a bold assertion of native strength basing itself on the revived classical models rather than the medievally-derived cycles and moralities which had dominated the earlier part of the century. On the other hand, while these comedies provided convincing evidence of the untapped potential of the English stage, they were not as yet drawing level in quality with the continental drama. Machiavelli's brilliant comedy *La Mandragola* (*c.* 1518), written much earlier than these two plays, has an agility of dramatic movement, a wit and satirical power which could only have emerged from a sophisticated and urbane society such as England could not yet provide. The pressures, however, were on, and if England was still hampered by its slow start, there was still time for the astonishing spurt which was to draw her ahead of her rivals.

5
Into the playhouse

IN religious drama of the Middle Ages, the celestial and the
mundane might appear together upon the stage but they
remained divorced from each other. The York Crucifixion
play, for example, depicts the instruments of torture with
chilling realism and the nauseating professionalism of the
soldiers driving in the nails. The central figure in that scene,
however, as he hung above them on the cross, spoke not in
the agony of his bodily suffering but with the quiet serenity
of a martyr already received into heavenly bliss. The spiritual
reading of the scene, his heavenly glory, was superimposed
upon the actual in order to encourage the spectator to despise
this earthly life and strive only for the eternal beyond the
grave.

In contrast, the new hero of the sixteenth century
embodies in his achievements that fusion of the celestial and
the mundane which typifies the Renaissance mode. He is a
creature of flesh and blood who has lived, fought, and
laboured in this world and yet his military, political or artistic
achievement have awesomely expanded the limits of human
potential beyond the earthly. The traditional view that the
revival of classical studies was responsible for the change is
here too as misleading as the cock's belief that his own crow-
ing brought the dawn. The desire for such heroes was an
integral part of the emergence from medievalism, a need
requiring to be satisfied, and men looked not only to the
classics, to the *Lives* of Plutarch or the heroes of Senecan
drama for their exemplars but also to their own age and to
their own national history for such models. Giorgio Vasari, in
writing *The Lives of the Most Eminent Italian Architects,
Painters and Sculptors* (1550), marvelled at the genius of his
own contemporaries who seemed to have set new standards
for mankind, soaring above the human to achieve some sort

of 'divinity'. Of Leonardo da Vinci he wrote in astonishment that the heavens ' . . . sometimes with lavish abundance bestow upon a single individual beauty, grace, and ability, so that whatever he does, every action is so divine that he outdistances all other men'.

In the same way as such creativity came to be admired by others, so the writer or artist himself began to look upon his own talents in more exalted terms. No longer prepared to make his anonymous contribution to the mystery cycle for the greater glory of God, he now sought for personal fame in this world, for public recognition of his own abilities, for an earthly eternity in the minds of men. As the proud inscription behind the portraits of Arnolfini and his wife 'Jan Van Eyck was here' assured the painter his recognition, so the poet saw his sonnet as perpetuating for mankind his own personal joys, aspirations, and sorrows, as well as conferring eternity on the loved one to whom it was addressed:

> So long as men can breathe, or eyes can see,
> So long lives this, and this gives life to thee.

When writers did turn to the classics for their models, their purpose was to use ancient authority to bolster their beliefs as they broke gradually away from the dominance of medieval thought. However, those sources were not easily accessible. The improvement in classical training in the schools and universities had left its mark, but many of the new generation of writers, although capable of construing a Latin passage if given the task, were not able to read the classical authors fluently and with pleasure. Now a change occurred. Where, previously, translation had been regarded with some contempt (rather like the 'cribs' schoolboys still use to avoid doing their Latin homework), in the mid-sixteenth century its status began to rise as being an art in itself and the use of such translations was legitimised — a change no doubt influenced in part by the Protestant insistence on translation of the Bible. Sir Thomas Hoby, in offering his influential English version of *The Courtier* in 1561, resisted the earlier view, arguing that ' . . . to be skilful and exercised in authors translated is no less to be called learning than is the very same in the Latin and Greek tongues.'

Senecan drama

In translation, the plays of Seneca were to exert a powerful influence on English drama in this period and on the heroes and villains stalking its stage.[16] As closet plays not originally intended for stage performance, they consisted for the most part of lengthy rhetorical speeches filled with noble maxims and relieved by little action. The dramatic moments occurred off-stage, the scenes of violence and horror being reported by eye-witnesses after the event. In the sixteenth-century revival of Seneca in England, the closet tradition was ignored or forgotten and these plays at sporadic intervals received stage presentation in Latin, usually for an academic audience. In 1559, however, Jasper Heywood, an Oxford scholar, translated Seneca's *Troas* into English, his version awakening immediate interest and going into three editions in as many years. During the following decade, further plays were translated by him and by other hands, and in 1581 they were collected and published together as *Seneca His Ten Tragedies*, establishing the Latin author as a major source for the contemporary stage.

The metre generally employed in the translations was the popular 'fourteener' or seven-foot iambic, which to modern ears is both heavy and tedious. However, for an age as yet unfamiliar with the flexibility of dramatic blank verse (at least as Shakespeare was to use it), with its range extending from magniloquence to light repartee, the fourteener served its turn; for there was no witty banter in Seneca's plays. His task, as he had seen it, was to transpose the lofty themes of Greek tragedy to a Roman setting. In the Greek theatre these tragic tales had been enacted within a religious frame-work, as part of a liturgical ritual; but that requirement did not hold true for the Senecan versions. Under the insane cruelty of Nero, the emperor whom Seneca himself served so faithfully, belief in a just heaven had collapsed. Hundreds of innocent citizens were being senselessly butchered at the whim of a madman, the best of them, like Seneca himself, dying after the noble Roman fashion by Stoic suicide when they saw their turn for imperial displeasure had come. Fate appeared blind and arbitrary, and man a mere pawn in its hands. The most admirable of men seemed to be those who had the courage to take their fate into their own hands, to avenge themselves on their enemies, and hence to assure that some semblance of justice had been achieved in this world. The dramatic equilibrium of Greek tragedy, in which a soothing chorus counters the tragic hero's protests against the gods by assuring us that all will yet be well, is missing here;[17] and Seneca's message amid the welter of blood and horror is that despite the arbitrariness of fate there is yet room for individual moral responsibility in human affairs.

For the Elizabethan age with its insistence on the significance of the individual this belief in personal responsibility proved a powerful attraction. The rhetorical over-statement of theme in these closet dramas enlarged man to superhuman proportions, with heroes and villains alike driven by consuming passions to the fulfilment of their ambitions or lusts. The reported scenes of murder or hacked limbs all served to heighten the dramatic effect and, where the Senecan play failed to rise to the occasion, Heywood and his fellow translators were prepared to lend a helping hand. In the original *Troas* Achilles' ghost is merely reported to have appeared, but Heywood now introduces it in person into his own translation, bursting through the ground and shrieking for vengeance. While it shrieks,

> The poles with stroke of thunderclap ring out,
> The doubtful stars amid their course do stand,
> And fearful Phoebus hides his blazing brand.

Whatever the defect of such plays, they did encourage at a crucial moment in English drama a movement away from the unpretentious entertainment of the interlude towards an ambitious striving for overwhelming theatrical effects, with the struggle between the individual and an inexorable fate as the theme. By their very exaggeration the English Senecan plays set new standards for the stage. They were often spoilt by ranting and bombast, but they were at least extending the range of English drama attempting to scale new heights and to experiment with larger themes. In their failures they warned later dramatists of the morasses to be avoided, and in their limited successes pointed towards the direction in which drama could be effectively developed.

That a search for exemplars of human conduct existed in England even before the importation of Seneca is evidenced by *A Mirror for Magistrates*, one of the major publishing successes of the century and itself a source-book for dramatists throughout the reign of Elizabeth and beyond. It was a work of multiple authorship. A printer interested in publishing a new edition of Lydgate's *Fall of Princes* approached William Baldwin with the suggestion that he provide a sequel devoted to the chief princes of the land who '. . . since the time of King Richard the Second have been unfortunate in the realm of England,' that is, who had achieved great power or distinction before fate or error cast them down. It focused therefore not upon classical precedent but upon England's own history at a time when national pride was awakening. Moreover, such an undertaking particularly suited an age regarding human history as a source of ethical guidance and concerned, as was Elyot in his *Governor*, with the task of instructing future rulers in the responsibilities of their office. Baldwin, feeling the project beyond his own powers, approached various other writers, commissioning a total of seven poems (of which he wrote three) in each of which the ghost of a past ruler laments the sad reversal of his fortunes and warns the reader to learn from his fate.

The first edition of 1555 was suppressed by the Lord Chancellor, presumably as an unwelcome questioning of the security of kingship during the precarious reign of Queen Mary, but in 1559, once Elizabeth had ascended the throne, it appeared in an enlarged form, now containing nineteen instead of seven such tales. The third edition of 1563 was expanded even further, including the famous tale of Jane Shore by Thomas Churchyard, and the 'Complaint of Henry, Duke of Buckingham' by Thomas Sackville, Earl of Dorset, who prefaced it with a remarkably fine 'Induction'. There, echoing Virgil and Dante, the author describes how a spirit led him down into Hell, where he met the ghosts of the kings and noblemen whose tales appear in the work and he is instructed to convey the message of their ruin to the sovereigns of his own day:

> 'Lo here,' quoth Sorrow, 'princes of renown,
> That whilom sat on top of Fortune's wheel,
> Now laid full low, like wretches whirled down,
> Even with one frown, that stayed but with a smile;
> And now behold the thing that thou, erewhile,
> Saw only in thought, and what thou now shalt hear,
> Recount the same to caesar, king and peer.'

> Then first came Henry, Duke of Buckingham,
> His cloak of black all pill'd and quite forworn,
> Wringing his hands, and Fortune oft doth blame,
> Which of a duke hath made him now her scorn;
> With ghastly looks, as one in manner lorn,
> Oft spreads his arms, stretch'd hands he joins as fast
> With rueful cheer and vapored eyes upcast.

These were poems not dramas, but they fostered the chronicle plays of the Elizabethan stage which were to present to audiences the rise and fall of the kings of England, their moral crimes, their thwarted ambition, their missed opportunities and, with all that, the splendour of their regal might before their fall. The plays revealed on the one hand a more universal concern with man's fate, with Fortune which raises and dashes to the ground. Yet they constituted also a form of political and ethical instruction for a country about to join the great powers of Europe. They sought to convey both to the Queen who loved watching the plays and to her subjects who formed the audience that stable government could only be attained in a kingdom ruled in justice and wisdom, and blessed with a people loyal to its rightful sovereign.

The prose historics of England which began to appear in this period in response to the growing pride in the country's heritage contained the germs of this concern with monarchal responsibility. Edward Hall's *The Union of the Two Noble and Illustrate Families of York and Lancaster* (1548) was aimed at glorifying the Tudor dynasty, and *The Chronicles of England, Scotland and Ireland* (1577), of which Raphael Holinshed contributed the English section, described in stirring phrases, often echoed in Shakespeare's dramatic versions, the dignity of England's past kings. He relates how Henry V, on the eve of the battle of Agincourt, overhears a soldier's wish that they had more English troops with them:

> The king answered: 'I would not wish a man more here than I have; we are indeed in comparison to the enemies but a few, but if God of his clemency do favour us and our just cause (as I trust he will) we shall speed well enough. But let no man ascribe victory to our own strength and might, but only to God's assistance; to whom I have no doubt we shall worthily have cause to give thanks therefore. And if so be that for our offences' sake we shall be delivered into the hands of our enemies, the less number we be, the less damage shall the realm of England sustain.

Two years later in 1579 Thomas North translated Plutarch's *The Lives of the Noble Grecians and Romans* into English, maintaining to his readers that a study of the work would be profitable since '. . . it is better to see learning in noble men's lives than to read it in philosophers' writings.' His work was a translation of a translation, as he used the French version by Jacques Amyot published some twenty years earlier; yet in the same way as that French version had been hailed as a masterpiece of French prose, so North's translation introduced into the English language a stylistic euphony coupled with a manly vigour which was to serve as a model for many subsequent writers. In the following description of Cleopatra the sentences flow with a smoothness and harmony such as we have met so far in the poetry of Wyatt and Surrey but rarely in prose. Cleopatra, we are told, was not unmatched in physical beauty:

> . . . but so sweet was her company and conversation that a man could not possibly but be taken. And, besides her beauty, the good grace she had to talk and discourse, her courteous nature that tempered her words and deeds, was a spur that pricked to the quick. Furthermore, besides all these, her voice and words were marvellous pleasant; for her tongue was an instrument of music to divers sport and pastimes, the which she easily turned to any language that pleased her.

Apart from its contribution to English prose, North's version of the *Lives* offered the English dramatist a further selection of fallen heroes, this time drawn from the classical period. In the plays based upon them, the setting may have been ancient times, but the kinship between the Roman Empire at the height of its power and England's own expanding might, between the sacrosanctity of past emperors and that of contemporary sovereigns was not missed. As an Elizabethan audience watched unfold before them the heavenly vengeance meted out to Julius Caesar's assassins in Shakespeare's play, they were aware that the lesson it taught applied to their own era no less.

The first English tragedy recognisably indebted to Seneca was *Gorboduc*, known also as *The Tragedy of Ferrex and Porrex*. Written jointly by two young 'gentlemen of the Temple', Thomas Norton and Thomas Sackville (the latter had in all probability already made his contribution to *A*

Mirror for Magistrates at this time), it was performed initially as part of the Christmas festivities in the Inner Temple in 1560. Two years later it was acted again before the Queen at Whitehall, and was published in 1565. The style is uniform, with no visible seams to distinguish the work of the two authors, but it is generally believed that Norton composed the first three acts and Sackville the last two.

With its gruesome series of revenge murders, the theme of the play was ideally suited to the Senecan mode which Jasper Heywood had just inaugurated. Based upon ancient legends of English history, such as those recorded by Geoffrey of Monmouth, it relates a tale not unlike that of *King Lear* (which had appeared in the same collection of legends). The aged King Gorboduc, resigning his throne to ease his last years, instead of passing on his kingdom in its entirety to the rightful heir, divides it equally between his two sons. Porrex at once invades the adjoining kingdom and slays his elder brother. Their mother, the queen, appalled at the deed, murders her surviving son in revenge, the people in their turn assassinate the royal couple, and the play ends with the bloody suppression of the insurgents:

> . . . slain in the field
> Or with the strangling cord hanged on the tree
> Where yet their carrion carcasses do preach
> The fruits that rebels reap.

However limited its merits as drama, *Gorboduc* does mark two significant advances on the English stage. The first is that the story it chose to relate at last shakes off the allegorical tradition of the morality plays to offer a genuinely humanistic drama, the account of a king's fatal error in judgement and the grim sequence of calamities which the responsibilities of kingship set in motion. The range of tragedy had begun to broaden, now examining the fate of an entire kingdom, an ancient heritage threatened with destruction, and with frequent appeals to 'the mighty gods' or Jove to intervene by restoring justice under a rightful ruler. Even the appeal to 'Jove' is symptomatic of a new universality, a Renaissance blending of pagan with Christian traditions by the use of the secondary name for Jupiter which associates him with the Jehovah of the Bible.

The humanistic direction of the play is interestingly revealed by one residue of the morality tradition applied here in a new way. In *Everyman* and the morality interludes, the central character had regularly been furnished with a pair of advisors — a good and a bad angel, or a Virtue and Vice — each urging him to accept the proffered counsel which was to lead to personal salvation or damnation. Those speeches constituted the dramatised debate on sin and righteousness which formed the primary theme of the piece. In *Gorboduc* the tradition of the advisors remains, but the subject is no longer spiritual salvation. It is now political expediency. The focus has shifted from the next world to this, from redemption in the kingdom of heaven to the security of a kingdom on earth. King Gorboduc's first words in the drama are to turn for counsel to:

> My lords, whose grave advice and faithful aid
> Have long upheld my honour and my realm . . ..

Of his advisors, Eubulus ('Good Counsel') strongly urges him to reject his plan for the division of the kingdom, stressing in Senecan axiom that:

> Within one land one single rule is best.
> Divided reigns do make divided hearts.

Gorboduc ignores the warning, and once they are installed on their separate thrones, both Ferrex and Porrex turn to their own pairs of advisors for further debates on the policies which each should pursue.

In addition to the broader theme of good government, there was a more pointedly topical message to be conveyed and the very topicality underscores the relevance to contemporary kingship which had entered drama. At the time of the play's first performance, Queen Elizabeth had already rejected Philip II's offer of marriage. Her subsequent half-hearted toying with other proposals was beginning to arouse grave suspicions that she might never marry and, by having no children, leave the succession in jeopardy. The choice of *Gorboduc* as the play to be performed before her in 1562 presumably was Burghley's device for applying a little indirect pressure. She would not have missed the main message of the play, the fear that calamities in the kingdom:

> . . . grow, when lo unto the prince
> Whom death or sudden hap of life bereaves,
> No certain heir remains.

The second innovation of the play was its introduction of blank verse to the English stage, a metre employed by Surrey for his translation of Virgil but never as yet applied to the drama, where it was to find so congenial a home. What is missing here for the reader familiar with the usage from Marlowe onwards is the variegated and wide-ranging imagery which was imaginatively to elevate and enrich such drama. *Gorboduc*, as Sidney acknowledged, is 'full of stately speeches and well-sounding phrases', but it remains generally prosaic. The habit inherited from Seneca of reporting all off-stage action coupled with the morality tradition of debate encouraged tediously long speeches unrelieved by movement or even verbal exchanges and its paucity of imagery increases the monotony. Yet, compared with the plays which had preceded it, the new style was endowed at times with a rhetorical force impressive in its majesty:

> GORBODUC: Oh cruel wight, should any cause prevail
> To make thee stain thy hand with brother's blood?.
> But what of thee we will resolve to do
> Shall yet remain unknown. Thou in the mean
> Shalt from our royal presence banished be
> Until our princely pleasure further shall
> To thee be shewed. Depart therefore our sight
> Accursed child!

The advance which *Gorboduc* marks is perhaps best illustrated by comparing it with a far poorer play written about the same time. Thomas Preston's *Cambises*, published in 1569, clumsily attempted to appeal to all tastes, creating a weird pot-pourri of a chronicle-type tragedy, the didacticism of a morality play replete with allegorical Vices and, for good measure, an admixture of farcical slapstick. The incongruous title *A Lamentable Tragedy Mixed Full of Pleasant Mirth, Containing the Life of Cambises King of Persia* was justly held up to ridicule in Shakespeare's *A Midsummer Night's*

Dream where the ham actors offer *The Most Lamentable Comedy and Most Cruel Death of Pyramus and Thisbe* as an example of 'tragical mirth' — and Falstaff elsewhere parodied too the bombast of 'King Cambises' vein'. The ridicule does at least indicate that the play succeeded in its purpose, holding its place on the popular stage until Shakespeare's day. The play, moreover, gives some indication of the realism with which scenes of violence were presented whenever Seneca's 'off-stage' convention was deserted. Cambises slays his own brother, his newly-wed wife, a brave lord and, with a little more reason, a corrupt judge he has appointed. The stage instructions call in one instance for a bladder filled with red vinegar to be burst at the words 'Behold now his blood springs out on the ground!', and even more gruesomely in another instance the victim is skinned on the stage after execution, the direction reading *'Flay him with a false skin'.* For an audience used to witnessing in real life men being hanged, drawn, and quartered, such realism was apparently necessary and explains the concluding scene in Shakespeare's *Macbeth* in which the king's head dripping with gore is triumphantly brought on to the stage by the victorious Macduff for all to see.

Ovid's *Metamorphoses*

The translations of Seneca and Plutarch helped foster monarchal plays on the tragic fall of princes, but the translation of Ovid's *Metamorphoses* in 1565–7 opened a further range of possibilities for poetry and stage alike. The Latin *Metamorphoses*, relating in verse a wealth of mythological stories, had been widely known in its day, not least for its erotic interest — tales of the rape of young maidens, or the myth of Actaeon peeping at the unwitting Diana as she bathes naked in the stream — all related with the amused urbanity of a poet whose *Ars Amatoria* had become a handbook for the profligate Roman society of his day. The preface to Arthur Golding's translation, in which he assures the reader that these stories are really moral lessons in allegorical form, might appear transparent hypocrisy were it not for our knowledge first that he was a Puritan of impeccably strict morality and secondly that the same allegorical interpretation held true for other areas of Renaissance art. Golding solemnly explains that in each of the myths are concealed ethical teachings:

> As for example in the tale of Daphne turned to Bay
> A mirror of virginity appear unto us may.

It is difficult for our own generation to appreciate that numerous seduction scenes in sixteenth-century painting, such as Titian's *Rape of Danaë* or Veronese's *Rape of Europa*, were recognised at the time within the new universal view linking pagan with biblical themes, as representing icono-logically the ravishing of the Christian soul by the divine spirit. The maiden's serene expression as she is 'raped' and the little angels or *putti* blessing the scene from above do, however, underscore those implications. On the other hand the allegorical reading (in which the nakedness of the female represented the soul freed from the 'clothing' of the flesh) did open the way for eroticism in the art and literature of the time. Soon after the appearance of Golding's version, Thomas Garter composed *The Most Virtuous and Godly Susannah* (*c*.1568) a play paralleling the scene of Diana's bathing from a biblical source, the surprising of Susannah in her bath by two lecherous elders. Garter's naming of one elder as Voluptas ('Lust') is intended as a moral warning, but the description of the heroine which he places in his mouth scarcely accords with the ostensibly didactic purpose of the play:

VOLUPTAS: Her breasts that are so round and fair, her arms that are so
   long,
   Her fingers straight with veins beset, of blue and white
   among.
   Her middle small, her body long, her buttocks broad and
   round,
   Her legs so straight, her foot so small, the like treads not on
   ground.

The didactic concern with 'fallen' rulers and with the lessons they offered for kings and magistrates helped blur the distinc-tion between heroes and villains. Self-will, passion, and inordinate ambition might be condemned as failings leading to the destruction of the monarch but those were qualities which, under the aegis of the English chronicles and the revival of Seneca, Plutarch, and Ovid, fired the imagination of Elizabethan audiences and broadened the scope of tragedy. Yet, vital as these qualitative changes were for drama, they did not themselves necessitate the new physical setting for the stage, which came into being at that time. The establishment of the Elizabethan playhouse as a permanent home for dramatic companies was dictated primarily by political and economic considerations rather than the content of the plays presented there.

The interludes and plays examined until now had been performed for the most part by amateurs or semi-amateurs, either within the Tudor banqueting hall or within the academic environment of schools, colleges, and the lawyers' Inns of Court. Professional groups did exist, but peripherally, often picking up interludes and plays for their repertoire from those more educated circles and adapting them to the needs of the common people. Such groups travelled through the country-side, setting up temporary 'booth stages' on top of barrels, with a curtained rear section to serve as a changing room or 'tiring house'. From the mid-century the reputation of the professional groups grew until by the last decades they had achieved a commanding position in the theatre.

A permanent stage

In the 1550s, at least two inns in London, the Saracen's Head at Islington and the Boar's Head in Aldgate, began to be used for regular theatrical performances by professional groups. The great advantage of inns over performances in open fields was that, in the open, audiences tended to melt away the moment a hat was passed round for contributions. The inns, in contrast, were constructed around an open courtyard entered by a single doorway, through which an audience had to pass, dropping its money into a box fixed firmly in the ground to prevent theft, (the origin of the term 'box-office' still used in theatres today). In 1574, the Corporation of London, angered at the unruliness prevailing at these temporary theatres and the immoral practices with which they had become associated, instituted stringent regulations for their licensing and control. The wording of the Act offers a colourful picture of these popular performances as viewed through the disapproving eyes of the more sober citizens who saw the theatre, no doubt with some justification, as a meeting-place for prostitutes, cutpurses and rabble-rousers. The Act maintains that:

> . . . sundry great disorders and inconveniences have been found to ensue to this City by the inordinate haunting of great multitudes of people, specially youth, to plays, interludes, and shows; namely occasion of frays and quarrels, evil practices of incontinency in great Inns, having chambers and secret places adjoining to their open stages and galleries, inveigling and alluring of maids, especially orphans and good citizens' children under age to privy and unmeet contracts, the publishing of unchaste, uncomely and unshamefast speeches and doings, withdrawing of the Queen Majesty's subjects from divine service on Sundays and holidays, at which times such plays were chiefly used, unthrifty waste of money of the poor and fond [i.e. foolish] persons, sundry robberies by picking and cutting of purses, uttering of popular, busy, and seditious matters, and many other corruptions of youth and other enormities.

It concludes with the most powerful objection of all, that such large gatherings encouraged the spread of the plague.

These new regulations, aimed at restraining the theatre and perhaps at closing it altogether, proved to be for the actors a blessing in disguise. In response to the strict enforcement of the Act, two players' companies took the initiative of moving outside the city limits to the north-east, away from the jurisdiction of the City Council, where they constructed their own permanent playhouses. In one of these, the Theatre, built by James Burbage on land belonging to a disused monastery, Shakespeare's *Romeo and Juliet, Richard II,* and *The Merchant of Venice* saw their first performances. On the expiration of the twenty-one year lease for the land, the owner refused to renew and threatened to requisition the building. The actors, literally taking matters into their own hands, decided to tear down the building themselves, transported the timber across the river to an area also outside city jurisdiction, and, near two other playhouses owned by rival companies, the Rose and the Swan, they erected the famed Globe in 1599.

The structure of the Elizabethan playhouse, its financial administration, and the nature of the audience for which it catered had their impact upon the plays which were presented there. The precise form of the stage remains to some extent conjectural. The only sources are an unreliable sketch of the

Swan theatre by a visiting Dutchman named De Witte, a pen-and-ink drawing of London by Wenceslas Hollar in 1640 which includes a distant view of the Globe as it was rebuilt after a fire, and an extraordinarily frustrating contract for the building of the Fortune theatre in 1600, drawn up one year after the Globe was completed. The Fortune was to be rectangular in contrast to the 'wooden O' of the Globe, but in other respects similar, and its measurements are helpful in assessing the size and overall format of playhouses in that era. However, just as the contract reaches the vital section devoted to the construction of the stage which would have been of inestimable value to the historian, it disappointingly substitutes for details the bald statement that it is '. . . to be fashioned like unto the stage of the said playhouse called the Globe'. Nevertheless, on the basis of stage directions in Elizabethan plays, the requirements of specific scenes there, and parallels drawn from the continent, a fairly reliable picture emerges.[18]

The shape of the Globe (*Plate 13*) combined the circular form of the 'baiting-house' (a building for cockfights and bear-baiting, often hired out for play performances in this period) with the generally rectangular format of the inn, to whose two storeys Burbage added a third. Just as the earliest motor-cars simply affixed engines to horse-drawn carriages without adapting them till much later to the specific needs of the car, so on building their first permanent theatre actors in England conservatively followed the structures with which they had become familiar. On the other hand, except for the major drawback that they were exposed to the elements, necessitating daylight performances in the early afternoon and closure during heavy rains, in other respects they were well suited to the players' needs. Around the projecting 'apron stage' (*Plate 14*) the groundlings, the common people who paid least, stood on three sides, close to the actors. Burbage's decision to charge one penny for the 'pit', an extra penny for a bench in one of the surrounding galleries, and sixpence for a private room there was far-reaching. In contrast to Spain, for example, where Lope de Vega (1562–1635) wrote for an exclusively aristocratic audience, the Elizabethan dramatist needed to satisfy all levels of society in his mixed audience. Plays were avoided which might prove 'caviare for the general', and comic scenes with popular appeal were inserted into the most solemn tragedies. The result was a strengthening of that peculiarly English tendency to mingle humour with seriousness evidenced earlier by the 'baboon-eries' and facetious misericords. The interior of the playhouse was only about the size of a tennis court, but since groundlings stood packed closely together at a full house, it could hold, when filled to capacity, a surprisingly large audience of between two and three thousand people.

Little scenery was used on the stage apart from thrones and stools but the simple design offered great flexibility. On either side of the trapdoor (for the emergence of ghosts or a grave-digging scene) columns supported the 'heavens', but the awkwardness of their interrupting the stage could be turned to advantage. With a little imagination they became trees on which to pin lovers' sonnets or ship masts for clinging to in storms, and an actor delivering a soliloquy or 'aside' could move beyond one to create the impression that he was separated from the rest of the cast. The doors for entry and exit had windows or casements above to create the impression of house-fronts in street scenes. The recess between them could, with the curtains partly closed, become an inner room, such as Gertrude's bedroom, and behind it was hidden the 'tiring-house' or dressing room for the actors. Above the recess and joining the two casements was what served as the balcony for Juliet, the battlements from which the besieged Richard II could harangue the rebel Bolingbroke below, or the monument to which Cleopatra flees and into which she lifts the dying Antony. The upper gallery, a 'crow's nest' for the lookout on a ship, was more usually used as the musicians' gallery to which a king could call for 'Music, ho!' as he would in an Elizabethan banqueting hall. The gables contained cannons, fired during battle scenes (on one occasion they set the thatch alight and burnt the Globe to the ground, but it was rebuilt on the same foundations). Cannon balls would be rolled over the oak floor inside to produce the sound of thunder, and other 'noises off' emanated from there. Topping all was the flag whose unfurling informed citizens across the river that a performance was due to begin shortly.

The stage thus offered a number of acting areas, but it did demand a greater effort of imagination on the part of the audience. A line such as 'This castle hath a pleasant seat . . .'

as Duncan enters Macbeth's abode, often seeming superfluous
in modern productions, was a necessary piece of information
in the original performance telling the audience what the scene
was supposed to represent at the same time as it introduced
an image necessary for the scene. Similarly, the assassination
at dead of night would have to be performed in broad daylight, and Macbeth's lines:

> Now o'er the one half world
> Nature seems dead, and wicked dreams abuse
> The curtain'd sleep.

functioned, before the advent of stage lighting, as more than
a setting of mood in preparation for the horror; as, in fact,
an indication that the audience must imagine a darkness
absent from the stage.

Some compensation for the bareness of the stage was provided by the rich robes worn by the actors, often passed on
to them for a small fee by courtiers discarding them in favour
of the latest fashions. Processions and dances were also
elaborately presented. The acting of women's parts by boys
in this period did not mean that the standard was amateurish.
The boys were carefully selected and highly trained. Samuel
Pepys, who attended one of the last performances in which
female parts were acted by boys commented that the leading
boy '. . . made the loveliest lady that ever I saw in my life!' —
a substantial tribute from one who prided himself on his
success with women.

The actors' companies were generally composed of some
four or five main actors (increasing to twelve in the later
period) with additional temporary actors hired for specific
performances. Considerable doubling of parts with quick-
changes behind the scenes ensured coverage of all the roles,
which were designed with that purpose in mind. A dramatist,
particularly if he was connected with a company, would often
write roles with the specific talents of the actors in mind.
Philip Henslowe, the manager of the Admiral's Men, the
main rival of Shakespeare's group, was a shrewd non-acting
business man whose diary has been preserved (with its flair
for imaginative spelling). He kept his players and playwrights
on a tight rein by ensuring that they remained financially in
his debt — 'Lent Bengemyn Johnson, the 5 of Jenewary 1597

in redy money the some of Vs.' — and he brought the leading actor of the company, Edward Alleyn, into the family by marrying him to his daughter. James Burbage's Lord Chamberlain's Men, later renamed the King's Men, decided when they moved to the Globe after his death to create a corporation of 'sharers', in which the five main members, one of whom was Shakespeare, would purchase a share in the company and its profits; and the innovative system seems to have worked very smoothly. Where a playhouse was not owned by the company, the general admission price went to them while the extra payment for the galleries belonged to the owner. During periods of plague, they would leave on tour of the provinces, and some companies existed only in the provinces, but there was no doubt that London was the vibrant centre of dramatic activity. There successful companies would enhance their reputations by being invited to perform at court.

The potential London audience in those days (once children, the elderly, and those disapproving of the theatre are subtracted) was probably around thirty thousand. With playhouses able to take up to 3000 spectators, each play could run for some ten performances before exhausting the potential; hence there were no long-running box-office attractions such as keep theatres solvent today. A play would normally run for four or five nights and then, if successful, be re-run some time later. With five or six competitive companies performing daily, as well as private indoor theatres using boy-actors for all parts, there was a keen and unremitting demand for new plays or for reworkings of old ones. Thomas Heywood claimed that he had had a hand in writing no less than 220 dramas, and Shakespeare's output of well over thirty full-length plays testifies to the need. Companies held on to their stock of dramas as their most valuable asset, resisting pirating by other companies and selling off plays only when their financial situation was desperate, as some did in the plague year of 1593. That continual demand for plays in the final decades of the century helped to create a new phenomenon in England, the professional writer relying on his pen for his livelihood.

6

'Grub Street'

UNTIL the 1570s, literature had been in the main a noble-man's pastime, an amateur art to which an aristocrat could apply himself in leisure moments as one facet of the all-round accomplishments expected of the courtier. The proliferation of titles among the leading writers earlier in the century — Sir Thomas More, Sir Thomas Wyatt, the Earl of Surrey, Sir Thomas Norton, Sir Thomas Sackville — is sufficient indication that literature was then largely the preserve of the upper class. As students at the Inns of Court or the universities, they wrote plays for performance by their fellow students, circulated sonnets among their friends, and as maturer states-men and scholars produced elegant translations of classical and Italian authors for the edification of future 'governors' of the country. Publication was disdained as unfitting for a nobleman, particularly publication for payment, and when their writings did find their way into print, the purpose, the author earnestly explained, was to forestall the threat of piracy by some unauthorised printer, real or imaginary. Towards the end of the century, however, the situation altered. Although courtiers such as Sir Philip Sidney, Sir Walter Ralegh, and Sir Francis Bacon continued to make their contribution to the art of letters, a new type of author appeared whose motives for writing were more urgent.

The growing concern with education at this time had trans-formed the colleges of Oxford and Cambridge from medieval-type institutions catering primarily for the unworldly scholar into thriving educational centres at the focus of religious and political thinking. New colleges had been founded, old colleges consolidated and expanded, bursaries endowed, and oppor-tunities offered there not only for the sons of aristocrats but also for promising young minds drawn from the lower echelons of society. By the 1560s Caius College, Cambridge, had a student body of which two-thirds came from the middle and working classes. The Inns of Court, too, where in London young lawyers trained for their profession, had begun to throb with a new vitality. Their doors had been opened to a wider spectrum of students who, as in all generations, in addition to their more serious activities, flung themselves avidly into a life of vivacious debate, amateur theatricals, unruly pranks, and frequent brawling. But when their student years drew to an end, the time had come to consider a livelihood. For sons of the landed aristocracy the path was clear, but not for the indigent scholar who had managed to make his way to the university. The training he had obtained there, with its sharpening of his wits and accumulation of learning, had made him unfit for the humbler craft followed by his father, without furnishing him with an admission card to any remunerative profession. The few professions which did exist, such as reading for the bar, demanded firm family connections for any reasonable income to be assured. In brief, the award of a university degree conferred upon the lower-class recipient an automatic social elevation to the rank of 'gentleman', but did not supply him with an income to support that status.

Accordingly, a new figure emerged on the scene (with profound implications for the future direction of English literature), the middle-class writer arising out of the social sub-stratum of the urban tradesmen. Spenser was born to a journeyman, Marlowe to a cobbler, Greene to a Norwich saddler, and all had made their way as poor scholars or 'sizars' to Oxford or Cambridge. On completion of their studies, the world of letters beckoned, for it demanded use of the gifts they had acquired and seemed likely to lead to patronage and eventual court appointment. Unfortunately, as the bitter complaints of poets confirm in this period, the path to court preferment was at best slippery and perilous, with few reaching the sparkling prizes it promised. The number of hopeful aspirants, swollen by the flow from the universities, had far outgrown the limited offices at the patrons' disposal and, while a candidate strove to attract the eye of a potential sponsor, he desperately required some ready cash to supply his immediate needs. Such authors could not subsist on the meagre income from their writing alone. Spenser enrolled in government service in Ireland, Marlowe became a political informer to supplement his earnings, and Greene, who remained faithful to his trade, like so many fellow scribblers, ended his life in dire poverty.

Yet under the pressure of need they managed to produce, with extraordinary versatility and seemingly unlimited energy, a stream of poems, plays, epitaphs, prose romances, ballads, translations, adaptations, political tracts, and lurid confessions of the prodigal's repentance. The latter (or at least those sections devoted to the period of profligacy which preceded remorse) were often based on first-hand experience, for the life of the hack-writer, as in all eras, encouraged Bohemianism. The struggling artist, beset by debts and unappreciated by the public, drowned his frustrations in pots of ale and nightly carousal and, partly by his own testimony, the hack-writer became associated in the public mind with brothels, taverns, and the criminal underworld (none of which prevented him from composing pious moral tracts if there was any prospect of remuneration). As the inimitable Nashe admitted, when '. . . the bottom of my purse is turned downward and my conduit of ink will no longer flow for want of reparations . . . I prostitute my pen in hope of gain.'

Like the actors who were also a new phenomenon on the social scene, the professional writers lacked a trade guild to protect their rights. The players could at least appeal directly to their audiences and could themselves determine the admission price for performances. When control became irksome, they could move across the river or leave London temporarily on a tour of the provinces. The writer, on the other hand, was at the mercy of the printer who stood between him and his public. Apart from Oxford and Cambridge which already had their own scholarly presses, London was by royal decree and for reasons of political control the only city authorised to publish. Consequently, there were no other centres to which the writer could move when work was hard to come by. The commercially-motivated publisher alone decided what should be published and he determined the fee. Payment was not normally, as today, a percentage of sales, but an outright purchase of copyright. If the work caught the public's fancy and sold well, the author had the frustrating experience of watching the profits fill his publisher's coffers while he himself went hungry. Furthermore, since any official acknowledgement of hack writing would endanger the status of gentleman which his university degree had granted him, he was inhibited from organising a body or guild to protect the rights of his profession. He was therefore doubly exposed to the economic exploitation of his talents.[19]

From the financial straits of the writer, literature was to benefit. Apart from the astonishing quantity of writing produced under the pressures of economic survival, there was a qualitative change too. The calm, measured prose of the humanists, of More, Ascham, Elyot, and North, was replaced by a new outpouring of exuberant invective, of strident polemic, of scurrilous innuendo. The hack-writer strove above all to catch the public ear, to make his name known to all, to blare forth his literary wares in order to ensure that the publisher, having sold his stock, would come back for further material. He would deliberately stir up controversy, fling insults at his colleagues, and charge into counter-attack with relish as long as the public was eager to watch the fight or, what mattered more, prepared to purchase the pamphlets in which battle was joined. The style becomes boisterous, brimming over with dramatic similes and extravagant vocabulary. The wording may be exaggerated but it is never dull; for to the paid hack, dullness spells doom. Nashe, for example, attacks:

> . . . vainglorious tragedians who contend not so seriously to excel in action as to embowel the clouds in a speech of comparison, thinking themselves more than initiated in poets' immortality if they but once get Boreas by the beard and the heavenly Bull by the dewlap. But herein I cannot so fully bequeath them to folly as their idiot art-masters that intrude themselves to our ears as the alchemists of eloquence, who, mounted on the stage of arrogance, think to outbrave better pens with the swelling bombast of a bragging blank verse. Indeed, it may be the ingrafted overflow of some kill-cow conceit that overcloyeth their imagination with a more than drunken resolution, being not extemporal in the invention of any other means to vent their manhood, commits the disgestion of their choleric incumbrances to the spacious volubility of a drumming decasyllabon.[20]

George Gascoigne (c.1538—77) was in one respect an exception to the general pattern as he was born into a financially secure, aristocratic home; but it was an advantage of which he swiftly divested himself. Enrolled by his father, Sir John

Gascoigne, as a law student at Gray's Inn in preparation for his entry into court circles, he cut short his studies, joined the court at about the time of Elizabeth's accession, and flung himself enthusiastically into the life of a fashionable gallant. Within a short time he had run through his inheritance, and sunk himself into debt, a situation exacerbated by his embroilment in numerous lawsuits, all of which were decided against him. An attempt to restore his fortunes on the battle-field ended with his capture by the Spaniards, and he returned to England destitute with no alternative but to rely on his pen rather than his sword. If we are to believe his repeated protestations, he consistently refused payment from publishers in order to preserve his status as a gentleman, and restricted himself to writing which might help solve his financial difficulties while yet being consonant with his standing. He composed works to catch the eye of patrons, devised a masque for the Montague family, and obtained a royal commission to prepare an eyewitness account of the siege of Antwerp. He did succeed in obtaining some support from Lord Grey of Wilton, but the few years remaining before his early death in 1577 were insufficient to remedy his affairs and he died in poverty.

Artistically, Gascoigne's writing career proved to be as ill-starred as his hope for court advancement, and his prolific output never won him the status of a major writer. But he was an extraordinary innovator, chalking up an impressive list of literary 'firsts'. His fertile inventiveness produced the first novella in English, the first prose comedy, the first translation of an Italian tragedy, the first masque, the first blank-verse satire, and the first treatise on English poetry. In addition, his *One Hundred Sundry Flowers* constituted in embryonic form the first sonnet sequence and, to round out the list, his report on the siege of Antwerp has a claim to being the first instance of war journalism. In the variegated range of his writing he became a prototype for the new professional writer, eager to put his hand to anything which could be turned to immediate advantage, sensitive to subtle changes in public taste, and swift to exploit new fashions, if necessary creating them himself if he could be first in the field.

As a poet he had the endearing notion of modestly dividing

his verse in descending order of merit into 'Flowers' (which he felt were his better efforts), 'Herbs' (useful, if not beautiful), and 'Weeds' (neither profitable nor beautiful, yet containing some virtue). His advice to the reader for choosing between these categories introduces to English prose the swashbuckling mode of the University Wit, a tongue-in-cheek moral solemnity in which the grave didacticism is belied by the flamboyance of style:

> To speak English, it is your using (my lusty Gallants) or misusing of these posies that may make me praised or dispraised for publishing the same. For if you (where you may learn to avoid the subtle sands of wanton desire) will run upon the rocks of unlawful lust, then great is your folly, and greater will grow my rebuke. If you (where you might gather wholesome herbs to cure your sundry infirmities) will spend the whole day in gathering of sweet-smelling posies, much will be the time that you shall misspend, and much more the harm that you shall heap on my head. Or if you will rather beblister your hands with a Nettle than comfort your senses by smelling the pleasant Marjoram, then wanton is your pastime, and small will be your profit.

In his brief treatise on poetry, *Certain Notes of Instruction* (1575), he applied to English verse the critical principles being developed abroad. He pointed to the need for 'fine invention' to counteract the clichés of *crystal eyes* and *cherry lips* which had begun to clog contemporary verse. In this he was responding perceptively to the need for the 'conceit', that sharp imaginative twist of thought which was to typify the best of English poetry until the close of metaphysical verse in the seventeenth century. His own poems were often dulled by his use of the jog-trotting 'poulter's measure' — a term, incidentally coined by him in this treatise — but when he deserts it in favour of the sonnet he illustrates if in minor form the 'invention' which he advocates. A lady accuses him of ignoring her, and a sonnet is at once produced explaining gracefully that he is merely avoiding those dazzling eyes which have already caused him so much damage. The advice he offered the poet was timely, for much Petrarchan-style poetry in this period had been ending lamely, merely reiterating in the final lines the lament or plea for mercy expressed earlier. This new insistence upon inventiveness helped to create the energised final couplet of the later Elizabethan sonnet which draws the quatrains together and gives point to the sonnet as a whole, as in Shakespeare's concluding lines to Sonnet 138:

> Therefore I lie with her, and she with me,
> And in our faults by lies we flattered be.

Gascoigne's innovative prose tale *The Adventures of Master Ferdinando Jeronimi* is a story in which little of importance occurs, and for that very reason in its account of day-to-day affairs it offers a sharply-etched vignette of the leisured upper class in his day, sonneteering, gaming, love-making, and conversing. It provides an early example of the social realism which was to distinguish the novel during its growth in the eighteenth century. Originally set in contemporary England, his novella was transposed to an Italian background to deflect criticism that the author was casting aspersions on the moral standards prevailing at home. In the revised form, now presented under the guise of being a translation, it tells of a young Venetian visiting Lombardy who wins the love of his host's charming and eligible daughter but, as young men often will, prefers the illicit favours of the host's daughter-in-law. After the affair has run its course, interspersed with poems sent back and forth by the lovers, Ferdinando returns home little the worse for his adventure. The concluding paragraph warning the youthful reader not to indulge in such 'wicked lusts' does little to counteract the indulgent mood of the narrator towards the morally relaxed world of the aristocracy and the maturing experiences of a young man's initiation into the traditions of courtly love. The moral seems to have been an after-thought appended to conciliate his critics.

His interest in drama had found expression even before he was pressured to write by pecuniary needs. During his student days at Gray's Inn, he prepared the text of *Supposes* (1567) for performance there, and it was an immediate success with repercussions beyond the confines of the student world. Although a translation of Ariosto's fine comedy *I Suppositi* (1509) in which characters impersonate each other in the cause of love, the adaptation nevertheless demanded considerable ingenuity and creative skill on Gascoigne's part. At a time when Ariosto's work was little known in England, he conflated two extant versions by the author, selecting the best of each, and wove them into a free-flowing, naturalistic prose dialogue, while preserving the Italian locale. Its effectiveness on the stage paved the way for the use of prose in English comedies and created a new vogue for dramas set in Renaissance Italy — a vogue which Shakespeare adopted in many of his plays, using this specific comedy by Gascoigne as a basis for his *Taming of the Shrew*.

Gascoigne's second play *The Glass of Government* (1575) belongs to the period of his moral 'conversion'. The sincerity of that repentance remains open to doubt, particularly as lurid accounts of such sin and penitence became a stock-in-trade of professional writers in subsequent years. Attacked on his return from Holland for the lasciviousness of the poems he had recently published, he hastened to announce the change wrought in him by an awakening conscience and prefixed a letter blandly explaining that he was now republishing them to '. . . serve as an example to the youthful gentlemen of England that they run not upon the rocks which brought me to shipwreck.' He then published a number of pious tracts apparently intended to repair his reputation and thereby to improve his prospects for professional advancement, and at the same time began work on a drama introducing into England the 'prodigal-son' plays he had witnessed in the Low Countries. The history of such drama forms an interesting by-way in literature.

The comedies of Plautus and Terence, used as a means of enlivening the teaching of Latin translation in schools, were based on accounts of a mischievous servant indulging in such escapades as turning his master's house into a brothel during the latter's absence. Such high-spirited ruses served to relieve the tedium of classroom instruction but scarcely accorded with the moral principles to be imparted to the young in a Christian society. Accordingly, schoolmasters on the continent turned to the Bible for guidance, and found in the Gospels the story of the prodigal son, who had wasted his inheritance in riotous living before repenting and returning to the fold. The period of prodigality provided the scenes of carousal and waggery to parallel the ruses of Terentian comedies, while the renegade's repentance supplied the ethical lesson required for the overall moral tone. These pseudo-Terentian plays were widely adopted in the schools, Gnaphaeus' *Acolastus* reaching thirty-one editions in less than fifty years. Gascoigne's *The Glass of Government*, again employing prose, takes a severer line than his continental models, the wayward boys being either executed or banished at the conclusion instead of being greeted with a fatted calf, or, as in certain contemporary versions, merely birched and forgiven. In brief, Gascoigne's attempt to convince his readers of his own moral conversion settled like a pall on his later writings, stifling the native vigour, inventiveness, and humour visible in his earlier work. But in the short period in which he did write in that freer style, he contributed significantly to changing the direction of English literature, signposting new paths which others were to explore after him, and expanding the variety of literary forms available to the writer.

The Euphuistic style

John Lyly (1554–1609), the son of a minor ecclesiastical official, needed to make his own way in the world but, through his grandfather who had been a friend of Erasmus and More, he was born into the humanist tradition. The period he spent at Oxford left him with a contempt for the swaggering drunkenness of student life there, which he lambasted in later years under the thin disguise of the schools at 'Athens' — '. . . such playing at dice, such quaffing of drink, such dalliance with women, such dancing, that in my opinion there is no quaffer in Flanders so given to tippling, no courtier in Italy so given to riot, no creature in the world so misled as a student at Athens. Such a confusion of degrees that the scholar knoweth not his duty to the Bachelor, nor the Bachelor to the Master, nor the Master to the Doctor.' Nevertheless, he himself managed to obtain a sound classical education which served him well in his subsequent literary career.

The latter began more impressively than it was to continue. At the early age of twenty-four, he burst upon the scene with *Euphues: the Anatomy of Wit* (1578), a prose piece of wide influence in the era which at once captivated court fashions to become their touchstone. As a contemporary recalled in later years: 'All our ladies were then his scholars . . . that beauty at court which could not parley Euphuism was as little regarded as she which now there speaks not French.'[21] The work itself was flimsy in plot, the tale of a young man, Euphues, who steals the affections of his best friend's betrothed and, when he in his turn is jilted by her, proceeds rather unfairly to lecture his friend on the ways of the world. The attraction of the piece lay less in the story than in the style, with its carefully balanced phrases, its alliterative repetitions, and its wealth of similes drawn from abstruse classical or botanical sources:

> This young gallant, of more wit than wealth, and yet of more wealth than wisdom, seeing himself inferior to none in pleasant conceits, thought himself superior to all in honest conditions, insomuch that he deemed himself so apt to all things, that he gave himself almost to nothing but practising of those things commonly which are incident to these sharp wits, fine phrases, smooth quipping, merry taunting, using jesting without mean and abusing mirth without measure. As therefore the sweetest rose hath his prickle, the finest velvet his brack, the fairest flower his bran, so the sharpest wit hath his wanton will and the holiest head his wicked way ... Venus had her mole in her cheek which made her more amiable; Helen her scar on her chin which Paris called *Cos amoris*, the whetstone of love; Aristippus his wart, Lycurgus his wen. So likewise in the disposition of the mind, either virtue is overshadowed with some vice, or vice overcast with some virtue.

This style, developed from techniques existing embryonically in the prose of his immediate predecessors, remained in vogue for more than a decade before being discarded by later writers. In our own era it has generally been attacked by critics as no more than 'a perversely elaborate style . . . a faddish aberration',[22] but to condemn it in such terms is to miss its very real significance as a necessary stage in the development of the English language in general and of English prose in particular. The eagerness with which it was accepted at court suggests that there did exist a need to be filled. It will be recalled that in the earlier part of the century the poverty of the English tongue had been sorely felt. Purists may have protested against the importation of 'inkhorn' terms from France, Italy, Spain, and classical languages, but they could not block the flow. By the last decades of the century, the English language had become incomparably expanded, the foreign words having been absorbed and domesticated and a wide range of native words resuscitated from their previous disuse and brought back into daily currency. As Richard Carew remarked in *The Excellency of the English Tongue* (1595), the language could now supply words to suit all possible styles of writing:

> ... the long words that we borrow, being intermingled with the short of our own store, make up a perfect harmony, by culling out which mixture with judgement you may frame your speech according to the matter you must work on, majestical, pleasant, delicate, or manly, more or less in what sort you please.

In this period, one senses a new delight in the sound of words, an intoxication with the richly variegated vocabulary now at the writer's disposal. There is a love of erudite display, of subtle discrimination between apparent synonyms, of intricate alliterative inter-weaving. An intelligent adolescent usually passes through a phase of indulging in atrocious puns. He is really flexing his verbal muscles, testing out his widening vocabulary, his increased command of connotations, his new-found skill at evoking the apt word or phrase whereby to prove his wit. Later his need for such ostentatious word-play will subside and a maturer judiciousness will modify that exuberance; but it is a valuable stage in his development. England itself passed through such an adolescent phase in the later sixteenth century, and Shakespeare, particularly in his earlier plays, formed part of it. As Samuel Johnson justifiably complained, a pun for him was often the fatal Cleopatra for which he was content to lose the world, and if that fashion prevailing in his day has proved less palatable to later generations, it formed nonetheless an intrinsic part of that superb command of language which was to distinguish his maturer writings. In *Love's Labour's Lost*, it is true, he may poke fun at such linguistic extravagances, and in a later play parody the inflated vocabulary of the courtier represented by the unfortunate Osric:

> HAMLET: Sir, his definement suffers no perdition in you, though, I know, to divide him inventorially would dozy the arithmetic of memory, and yet but yaw neither in respect of his quick sail. But in the verity of extolment, I take him to be the soul of great article, and his infusion of such dearth and rareness as, to make true diction to him, his semblable is his mirror and who else would trace him, his umbrage nothing more. [*V*, ii, 112]

Yet even in such parody there is a zest and amusement which betrays in Shakespeare himself a joy in the art of verbal pyrotechnics and elaborate formalism.

In that broader context, we may appreciate more fully the success of Lyly's *Euphues* which appeared ready-to-hand for the orgiastic outburst of linguistic self-indulgence in the latter part of the century. With its witty antitheses, its play on similar-sounding words, and its plethora of similes, it offered an incentive for bravura and virtuoso display. The severer classical models were now being deserted in favour of a greater freedom to elaborate at will in a manner particularly suited to the growing sophistication and individualism at court, and in prose the regular Ciceronian triplet was being replaced by more independently designed echoes and repetitions. That personal, idiosyncratic 'fancy' in prose style had its contemporary parallel in music as Thomas Morley, the doyen of English composers, suggested that a composer of music '. . . taketh a point at his pleasure, and wresteth it as he list, making either much or little of it as shall seem best in his conceit.'[23]

After the publication of a sequel, *Euphues and his England*, written in the following year, Lyly turned to the stage as a source of livelihood – not, however, to the professional stage but to the so-called 'private' theatre which had been developing alongside. In 1576, the same year as Burbage built his permanent Theatre, Richard Farrant, Master of the Children of the Chapel Royal, had leased as a private playhouse a former monastery at Blackfriars standing empty since the Dissolution. The boys of the Chapel Royal were primarily choristers, but were trained also to perform plays interspersed with songs before the royal court. The playhouse was originally intended by Farrant as a site for rehearsals, but in time he traded on its royal connection by opening its supposed 'rehearsals' to the public. The theatre was only private in the sense that it charged a higher admission fee, namely fourpence instead of one penny; however, since one penny at the professional theatre admitted only to the pit, and more was demanded for the gallery, the price was in fact competitive. The building was smaller and more intimate, with the great advantage over the playhouses that it was roofed, protecting its audience from inclement weather. Moreover, the lighting required for an indoor performance encouraged more elaborate

visual effects, and as the plays were also frequently preceded
by musical concerts, they offered a strong counter-attraction
to the professional companies, at times drawing audiences
away from the Globe, with the boy actors, as Shakespeare
wryly admits, being 'most tyranically clapped' for their
performances.[24]

Although a gifted boy actor can impersonate women
remarkably well, no matter how accomplished he may be,
his voice range remains limited, incapable by nature of match-
ing the mature masculinity of a Richard Burbage or Edward
Alleyn. As a result, the plays written for performance at the
private theatres, tailored for such boy companies, were
dramatically less ambitious. They were more artificial and
limited in scope, often a form of didactic debate on some
moral theme, with choral interludes serving to vary the fare.

Lyly wrote a number of plays for the Chapel Royal and
for the boys of St Paul's, the best-known being *Campaspe*
(1583). Alexander the Great, infatuated by a captive girl,
orders the artist Apelles to paint her portrait, and on discovering that the painter and model have fallen in love, he nobly
renounces her in favour of her lover. The debate tradition is
preserved, with minor characters discussing in the opening
scene whether Alexander is to be admired more for his
courage or for his magnanimity, and the answer is provided by
the latter's final proud comment on relinquishing Campaspe:
'It were a shame Alexander should desire to command the
world, if he could not command himself.' Particularly interesting is the rise in the status of the artist, paralleling that
'divinity' accorded to Michelangelo and others in Italy.
Although the moral victory in the play is Alexander's, it is
the creative artist who wins here the love of Campaspe —
perhaps a little wishful thinking on the part of Lyly.

Once the initial popularity of *Euphues* had begun to wane,
Lyly's financial struggles reasserted themselves. His affairs
had seemed to take a promising turn when Queen Elizabeth
hinted that the lucrative post of Master of the Revels might
soon be his. Unfortunately for him, she had a knack for
extracting years of loyal service on the basis of some vague
promise never fulfilled, and Lyly fell victim to her parsimony.
In a petition he sent her in 1601 he complained bitterly:
'Thirteen years Your Highness's servant, but yet nothing . . .

a thousand hopes, but all nothing; a hundred promises, but yet nothing.' This was the melancholy refrain chanted by so many fellow-hopefuls in this era, and like most of them he was fated to end his days in the poverty he had so hoped to escape.

The most prolific of Lyly's imitators, Robert Greene (1558—92), could serve as a paradigm of the professional writer in the Elizabethan era, both in his successes and his failures. Little is known of his life except through the supposedly autobiographical pamphlets he produced which, for all their claim to authenticity, remain suspect because of their obvious exaggeration. He was born in Norwich, the second son of a saddler, and enrolled at Cambridge as a sizar or poor scholar (who paid his way by serving at table), obtaining there his BA and MA degrees. Having risen in rank through his academic attainments, he was on his return to Norwich able to marry a gentleman's daughter, and had a son by her; but having squandered her dowry, he abandoned her there to try his fortune in London. If his own testimony is to be believed, he lived dissolutely, associating with the cheats, cutpurses, and brothel-keepers about whom he was later to write, and maintaining himself by turning out a stream of pamphlets, romances, and poetry with a facility which amazed his literary friends, being able, as Nashe said, to have 'yarkt up a pamphlet' in a night and day which might have taken another writer seven years.

His early works exploited in the main the prevailing vogue for euphuistic love-tales and, with the skill of a hack-writer dependent on his pen for a living, he was quick to catch the languid refinement of style, the learned aphorisms and chaste similes which would ensure good sales among those following the fashion. His works won him wide popularity, and though, because of the economic situation of the writer in his day, he received meagre monetary returns, he became during his brief career one of the best-known authors of his time. After the early imitative works, Greene began introducing his own techniques, notably a toning down of the elaborate ornamentalism of style and the attaching of greater weight to plot. Among his most successful romances was *Tully's Love* (1589) which, while it retained the basic scheme of lovers competing for the hand of a fair lady, cleverly broadened the appeal. Instead of an unknown 'Philautus', he selected as his hero the renowned Roman orator Cicero, familiar to his readers at the very least from their studies at school and therefore of interest in his own right. In this fictional tale, Cicero undertakes to plead the cause of his friend Lentulus, whose love has been firmly but gently rejected by the beautiful Terentia. Cicero's suit on behalf of his comrade cannot evoke love where it does not exist, but does elicit from her the inviting reply: 'But I marvel, Cicero, that being young and of such eloquence, we hear not of your loves. I fear you reach so high that you think no maids in Rome honourable enough for your paramour. Were I a man and had Tully's grace and his tongue, I would plead for myself.' Cicero is not slow to grasp the hint nor to reciprocate her love, but feels he cannot betray his friend. Yet all ends happily, when Cicero's love is ·discovered, and his friend withdraws his claim. The plot in such narratives is still little more than an excuse for debates about love, for the exchange of witty poems between the lovers, and for exercises in stylistic elegance, but it has begun to possess an interest of its own, drawing those elements together in a more effective and even dramatic form. It was, in fact, at this period that Greene began writing for the stage. According to his account, an actor overhearing him bewail his lack of funds during a period when his finances were at a low ebb and recognising that he was an indigent university scholar, suggested that he try writing plays '. . . for which you will be well paid, if you will take the pains.' Now that the actors had moved into permanent playhouses, the demand for fresh dramas had grown, and the needy university graduate was a natural choice as their supplier.

His first plays, such as *Alphonsus, King of Aragon* (1588) added little to the development of the stage, but *Friar Bacon and Friar Bungay*, probably written during the following year, may well have provided the impetus for Marlowe's *Dr Faustus*. It takes as its theme the legend that the medieval philosopher Roger Bacon practised magic and devilish arts, and it weaves around that theme a complex plot combining competitions between magicians, a doubly fatal duel between two fathers and their two sons, a test of lovers' fidelity and finally Friar Bacon's renunciation of his black arts and his determination to devote himself to prayer and good works:

FRIAR BACON: ... it repents me sore
         That ever Bacon meddled in this art.
         The hours I have spent in pyromantic spells,
         The fearful tossing in the latest night
         Of papers full of nigromantic charms,
         Conjuring and adjuring devils and fiends
         With stole and albe and strange pentaganon ...

His verse lacks the power and splendour which Marlowe was to introduce to the stage, but it does display a wider range of interest than the work of his predecessors, a concern with the esoteric, and with the introduction of terms drawn from the world of learning with which few but the scholar would have been familiar. The play was well received and performed a number of times by Henslowe at the Rose. His pseudo-historical play *James the Fourth* (1590) mingles a tale of the king's attempt to seduce a virtuous court lady with fairy-tale scenes of Oberon king of the elves, the latter forestalling his more famous appearance in *A Midsummer Night's Dream* a few years later.

At this period, Greene's writings took a sharp turn in direction. He declared publicly that he had reformed his ways and that henceforth he would produce only morally instructive works. In 1589, he composed together with Thomas Lodge a play entitled *A Looking-Glass for London and England* in which London was compared to the corrupt Nineveh of biblical times, denounced by the prophet Jonah. After scenes of incestuous love and attempted murder, a choric figure warns the audience:

       London look on, this matter nips thee near;
       Leave off thy riot, pride, and sumptuous cheer,
       Spend less at board, and spare not at the door,
       But aid the infant and relieve the poor.

The play won immediate popularity (there were five editions before 1617 and numerous contemporary references to its performance), and it was followed by Greene's *Vision* written the following year in which he dedicated his future works to the cause of virtue.

Greene's repentance has, despite the sensationalism with which he trumpeted it forth, for the most part been accepted by historians as genuine, but in fact there are strong reasons for viewing it with suspicion. At the very time he was writing his famed pamphlets *A Groatsworth of Wit Bought with a Million of Repentance* and *The Repentance of Robert Greene* (1592), begging God to forgive him for his past debauchery and warning all readers to learn from his dreadful sins (including his desertion of his wife), he was continuing unperturbedly to live together with his mistress in London leaving his wife to fend for herself; and for all his public declarations of new-found piety, there is not the slightest hint either from his own writings or from the reports of his contemporaries that he had actually changed his way of life.

A new audience

At the risk of being cynical, we may suspect that there were more practical reasons for his literary change of direction. Greene's predecessor Lyly had aimed his romances at the court and, more specifically, at the fashionable ladies there, and he declares in the preface that he would rather his work '. . . lie shut in a lady's casket than open in a scholar's study.' The wealthy members of a literate aristocracy, both male and female, were by tradition the obvious target audience for books which the poor scholar would be unlikely to afford. Now, however, a new reading public was beginning to emerge which possessed both the means and the desire to purchase pamphlets and books, and whose growing numbers attracted the attention of the professional writer. England's expanding economy in the last decades of the century had offered substantial opportunities to the merchant, investor, and entrepreneur, and the social gap between the upper and lower classes was becoming filled by prosperous burghers. Their commercial contracts and book-keeping required them to be literate, and in order to bolster their families' enhanced social status they took care to provide their sons and daughters with a sound education. They began to assemble their own collections of books — Thomas Bodley, who established at this time the foundations for Oxford's famed library, was the son of a merchant — and they wished to keep abreast of the latest literary vogues. They were to be seen, together with the courtier, frequenting the book-stalls in St Paul's Walk where freshly-published volumes, ballad-sheets, poetry, religious tracts, romances treatises on husbandry, jest-books, medical handbooks, and astrological almanacs were displayed for sale.

The members of the rising middle class were already developing Puritan leanings, even if they did not always enrol formally in that sect. They had a practical reason for embracing the doctrines of Protestantism with greater enthusiasm and severity than others. The unhesitating condemnation of worldly wealth by the medieval and the later Catholic church could scarcely accord with the new urge to invest in overseas ventures, to open up fresh markets, and to accumulate capital. In contrast, the Protestant justification of honestly gained riches as being a mark of divine blessing (on the basis of the Old-Testament Abraham, rewarded for his goodness by flocks and herds) was soothing to the burgher. Moreover, the more extreme stance of Calvinism with its insistence on industriousness proved a useful tool for chiding lazy workers and idle apprentices in the name of God rather than personal profit. And finally, their need for a settled, law-abiding society as the framework for their economic activities inclined them to support a stricter form of Christian behaviour, and hence to encourage regular church-going and the dissemination of morally edifying works. There was an extraordinarily large sale in this period of sermons and religious tracts, which may often have been purchased less out of a desire for reading-matter than the wish to place them prominently on the book-shelf as a sign of the sober Christian principles to which the household subscribed.

On the other hand, such citizens were still human, with a natural desire for something more lively to read. Greene's discarding of romances in favour of prophetic denunciation was probably a shrewd recognition of the new audience's needs, one of the first instances of a tactic preserved by the modern Sunday tabloid — the 'exposure' of vice and debauchery which provides for the reader a lurid account of the forbidden world within a reassuring framework of stern moral condemnation. *A Looking-Glass for London*, which fulfilled these requirements in its indignant condemnation of incestuous love after a careful depiction of it, was followed by a series of pamphlets describing, with obviously first-hand knowledge, the corrupt practices of the London underworld, ostensibly as warnings for the '. . . young gentlemen, mer-

chants, apprentices, farmers, and plain countrymen' who
were the potential victims, and together with these works
appeared the strident, breast-beating confessions of the
author's own past wallowing in sin, all calculated to appeal
to the ambivalent interests of this new middle class.

The 'cony-catching' pamphlets of 1591–2 were decked
out with a glossary of contemporary criminal slang, detailed
accounts of cozening which exposed the tricks of the trade,
and for good measure an eye-catching frontispiece illustrating
a cony or rabbit (the accepted symbol of the dupe) surrounded
by the dice, pick-locks, playing cards, or tankards by which
he is to be lured to his doom. In these publications, the
underworld figures are roundly condemned in virulent terms
for their '. . . most loathsome and detestable sins', yet the
headings of these accounts of theft and deception such as
'A merry tale how a Miller had his purse cut in Newgate
Market' reveal the author's sympathy with the thieves and
tricksters, so that he can end a tale of cozening: 'At this, all
the hearers laughed, but not so merrily as the foist and his
fellows that then were sharing the money.' One such pamphlet
presents a debate between a male and female cony catcher,
each claiming superiority in the profession as they relate their
skills, and another, paralleling Greene's own confessional
works (and thereby strengthening the impression that both
were really commercial ventures) purports to be a notorious
criminal's account of his own life, in which '. . . he telleth
very pleasantly in his own person such strange pranks and
monstrous villainies by him and his consorts performed, as
the like was yet never heard of in any of the former books of
cony-catching.'

As literary works, they mark the beginnings of journalism
in England. The clearly etched prose accounts of contemporary scenes advance well beyond Gascoigne's *Siege of
Antwerp*, which had in any case been a governmentally commissioned report not intended for the wider public. Greene's
change of theme can be viewed, in this respect, as part of the
overall scene we have been examining. That idyllic world of
romance with noble heroes and heroines, which he had
inherited from Lyly, satisfied only one part of the Renaissance
temperament. Missing was the response to the actual, and his
sudden swing towards the depiction of the underworld in all

1. This ornate gateway to St John's College, Cambridge founded, as part of the humanist emphasis on education, by Lady Margaret Beaufort, mother of Henry VII, pays tribute to her in the daisies ('marguerites') and Tudor rose incorporated in the design.

2. The art of printing, depicted in this contemporary engraving, stimulated a swifter dissemination of knowledge and an improvement in the general level of literacy.

To the right honorable Lorde, John Dudley, Lorde Lisle, Earle of Warwicke, and maister of the horse to the kynges maiestie: your assured to commaund Thomas wilson.

When Pyrrhus Kynge of the Epirotes made battayle agaynste the Romaynes, & could neither by force of Armes, nor yet by anye Policye wynne certayne stronge holdes: he vsed commonly to send one Cineas (a noble Oratour, and sometimes scholer to Demosthenes) to perswade with the Capitaynes & people that were in them, that they shoulde yelde vp the sayde holde or townes without fyght or resistaunce. And so it came to passe, that through the pithye eloquence of this noble Oratoure, diuers stronge Castels and Fortresses were peaceablye geuen vp into the handes of Pirrhus, whyche he shoulde haue founde verye harde and tedious to wynne by the sworde. And this thynge was not Pirrhus himselfe ashamed in his commune talke to the prayse of the sayde Oratoure, openlye to confesse: allegynge that Cineas throughe the eloquence of his tongue, wanne moe Cityes vnto him, then euer him selfe shoulde els haue bene able by force to subdue. Good was that Oratour

A.i.   which

3. A page from Thomas Wilson's *The Art of Rhetoric* (1553) printed in the black Gothic letters generally used until the 1570s, when they began to be replaced by roman letters similar to those in use today.

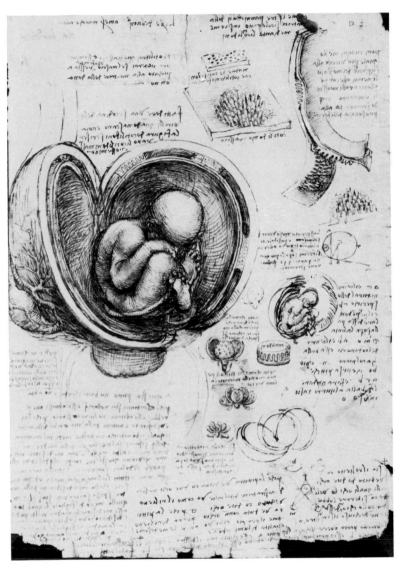

4. Leonardo da Vinci's anatomical drawings based upon his dissection of cadavers reflect the spirit of empirical enquiry and meticulous attention to detail forming one aspect of Renaissance culture.

5. 'Sir Thomas More' by Hans Holbein the Younger. In addition to his manifold
activities as lawyer, humanist, and theologian, More was a patron of the arts,
assisting Holbein in obtaining portrait commissions.

6. The lady's hand placed companionably upon the lutanist's shoulder in Lorenzo Costa's 'Concert' suggests the harmony of spirit which music was in that age believed to inspire.

7. Michelangelo's 'Creation of Adam' breaks with earlier tradition by depicting Adam in Renaissance terms as a potentially powerful figure, intelligent and unafraid, waiting only for the final touch of the divine.

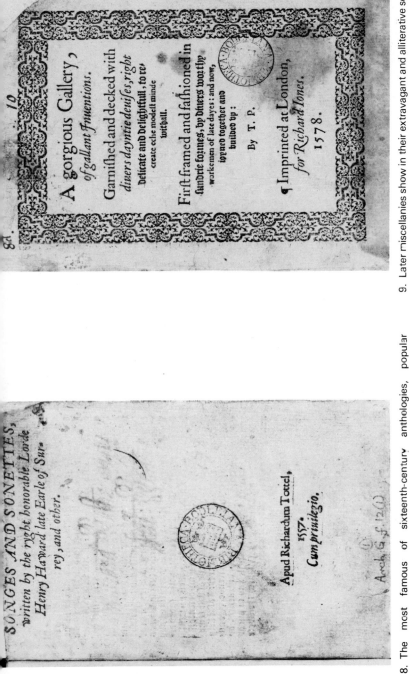

8. The most famous of sixteenth-century anthologies, popular beyond Shakespeare's day and generally known as *Tottel's Miscellany*, preserved many poems which have not survived elsewhere.

9. Later miscellanies show in their extravagant and alliterative self-advertisement an attempt to catch the reader's eye, as publishing becomes commercially competitive.

10. The hall at Hatfield House, built by Queen Elizabeth's advisor, Robert Cecil. Plays, interludes, and masques were performed in such halls, usually against the far wall with the doors serving for entrances and exits and the musicians' gallery for balcony or battlement scenes.

11. A miniature by Nicholas Hillyard (*c*. 1590) presents the mournful pose of an Elizabethan sonneteer beneath a Latin motto proclaiming the pangs of unrequited love.

12. A portrait of Queen Elizabeth by Marcus Gheeraerts reflects her love of symbol and heraldic formality. The pearls denote virginity, the globe her command of the world, and the paintings behind her the recent victory of her fleet over the Spanish Armada.

13. The Globe Playhouse: a reconstructed model based on contemporary drawings reveals its reliance on the general format of the inns, where travelling players frequently performed before building a theatre of their own.

14. The Globe Playhouse: the projecting 'apron' stage and the use of recesses and casements at the rear provided, with a little imagination from the audience, a remarkably flexible acting area.

its stark reality, the direct confrontation with the swindlers, cut-throats, and whores of London, endowed his writing with a fresh zest and vigour, a clarity of portrayal absent from his earlier works. Now often offered as first-person narrative, it pointed forward to Defoe's *Moll Flanders*. In one such work, a reformed prostitute recalls her past:

> I never would go to the church and sermons. I utterly refused, holding them as needless tales told in a pulpit. I would not bend mine ears to the hearing of any good discourse, but still delighted in jangling ditties and ribaldry. Thus to the grief of my friends, hazard of my soul and consuming of my body, I spent a year or two in this base and bad kind of life, subject to the whistle of every desperate ruffian, till on a time, there resorted to our house a clothier, a proper young man, who by fortune coming first to drink, espying me, asked if I would drink with him.

In Greene, these two aspects, the ideal and the actual, the romance and the real remained polarised, for they were given no time to develop. In the same year as the cony-catching and confessional pamphlets were published, Greene was dead at the age of thirty-four. He ended his life in miserable poverty, and his doublet, hose, and sword had to be sold for three shillings to cover the cost of burial. Even allowing for the drain on his resources which his reputed riotous living must have constituted, his success as a writer, and his prolific output (some thirty-five works in the few creative years at his disposal) had not brought him an income in any way commensurate with his talents.

His friend Thomas Lodge (1558–1625) fared better in life, mainly because in maturer years he left the ill-paying profession of writer to become a well-established physician, where he could afford to indulge a taste for elegant translation instead of battling against destitution. Born into a wealthy merchant family — his father became Lord Mayor of London soon after Thomas's birth — he nevertheless attended Merchant Taylors' school as a poor scholar since the family affairs collapsed suddenly into bankruptcy. By the time he had proceeded to Trinity College, Cambridge, and from there to law studies at Lincoln's Inn, the family's fortunes had revived, but the young man's insistence on dabbling in writing together with his decision to become a Catholic aroused such strong parental disapproval that he was disinherited by his father and thrown on his own resources. He became involved with Gosson in a pamphlet warfare on the morality of the stage, not particularly distinguishing himself in the skirmish, collaborated with Greene on *A Looking-Glass*, wrote a sanctimonious tract *An Alarm Against Usurers* (1584) exploiting his own considerable experience of money-lenders to create a 'prodigal-son' tale, and ran through the usual gamut of literary forms to produce a substantial body of writing. In general, it is standard fare, but his reputation rests, as it did in his own day, primarily on one work, for which he is deservedly famed.

His romance tale *Rosalind* (1590) looks both backwards and forwards. Subtitled *Euphues' Golden Legacy*, it acknowledges its debt to Lyly, but it also was to serve as the main source for Shakespeare's *As You Like It*. Stylistically, the tale is only mildly euphuistic. Freeing itself from the more tiresome repetitions and learned allusions, it reverts only occasionally to the vogue of balanced, alliterative similes, and then more in amused parody than imitation. Indeed, one of the charms of the romance is its refusal to take itself too seriously, either stylistically or in its adoption of the idyllic Arcadian setting. In the midst of their dangerous flight, the two heroines preserve their good humour. Rosalind, disguised as a page to elude her pursuers, rails against women's inconstancy, and when teasingly reproved by her girl-friend as a traitress to her sex, replies:

> I speak now as I am Aliena's page, not as I am Gerismond's daughter: for put me but into a petticoat and I will stand in defiance to the uttermost that women are courteous, constant, virtuous, and what not. Stay there, quoth Aliena, and no more words!

Tightened structure

It is in plot, however, that *Rosalind* marks a major advance over all earlier romances, and Shakespeare's adoption of that plot with little change, suggests how closely the developing form of the romance was related to the dramatic excellence of the English stage at the end of the century. For until now, subtleties in plot had been minimal in all genres. Such works as Chaucer's *The Canterbury Tales* or Boccaccio's *Decameron* had offered brief, independent stories loosely strung in succession as on a thread, but never integrally related. Any story could be removed without seriously damaging the work as a whole. Alberti's Renaissance demand for the overall unity of a work by means of the integration of its separate parts into an artistic whole had been applied in its day to architecture and by extension to painting, but it took much longer for the concept to infiltrate literature. Within the sixteenth century, dramas such as *Gorboduc* or *Campaspe* and the romance tales by Gascoigne or Lyly had employed single-line plots, often as no more than a frame for moral debate or elegant speeches, and where a sub-plot did appear, usually a low-life comedy, its relationship to the main story was minimal.

Here, however, for the first time a few different stories, each capable of standing independently as the main theme of earlier works, are so closely interwoven as to become an inseparable entity. The power struggle at court with the exile of the rightful duke, the love of a faithful shepherd for the scornful Phoebe, the conflict between two brothers over the family inheritance, the reform of the villainous brother, the delightful 'wooing' of the disguised Rosalind by her unsuspecting lover, and the elder brother's adoration of her 'low-born' friend become inextricably entwined within the setting of the forest. The threads are so firmly knotted that at one stroke all misunderstandings are resolved. As Rosalind discards her masculine disguise at the climax of the story and appears as her true self, her 'wooer' is rewarded for his fidelity by finding he has been rehearsing his love all along to his real beloved, the Duke is joyfully reunited with his daughter, her girl-friend is shown to be of noble birth and therefore worthy of the reformed lover, and Phoebe becomes reconciled with her shepherd having promised to do so if her love for the page prove impossible. All that is needed to return the duke to his palace is a brief skirmish in the forest with the usurpers and the marriages of the three pairs of lovers can be celebrated in a society restored to peace and order. This intertwining of plot-strands offered for the stage a tightening of dramatic tension as well as a broadening of range. As one plot is interrupted at a climactic moment to take up the thread of another, suspense is increased, and such multiplicity of theme could eventually offer valuable analogues and contrasts to deepen the dramatic effectiveness of the main characters and of their moral dilemmas.

The rollicking prose of Thomas Nashe (1567—1601), which seems to burst at the seams with rumbustious energy, forms the climax of the Elizabethan's heady delight in language so conspicuous among these professional writers. He joyed in the act of writing itself irrespective of the specific theme, cramming into his prose whatever satiric jibes, self-mockery, and ridiculing of contemporary modes happened to occur to him at that moment, and above all supplying an inexhaustible flow of motley vocabulary in a continuous display of linguistic prowess. 'Foreigners', he informs his English reader, 'call us bursten-bellied gluttons: for we make our greedy paunches powdering-tubs of beef'; social climbers 'filch themselves into some noble man's service either by bribes or by flattery and, when they are there, they so labour it with cap and knee and ply it with privy whisperings that they wring themselves into his good opinion ere he be aware'; and having himself despaired of obtaining patronage, he flagellates those who still preface their works with flowery dedications — 'if my unable pen should ever enterprise such continuate task of praise, I would embowel a number of those wind-puffed bladders and disfurnish their bald pates of the periwigs poets have lent them.' All these passages appear in his *Pierce Penniless* (1592) supposedly a supplication to the devil; and with an engaging frankness (evocative of the style Laurence Sterne was to adopt many years later in *Tristram Shandy*) he dismisses any charge of irrelevance as being itself irrelevant:

> Whilst I am thus talking, me thinks I hear one say, what a fop is this, he entitles his book *A Supplication to the Devil* and doth nothing but rail on idiots and tells a story of the nature of spirits. Have patience, good sir, and we'll come to you by and by. Is it my title you find fault with? Why, have you not seen a town surnamed by the principal house in the town or a nobleman derive his baronry from a little village where he hath least land? So fareth it by me in christening of my book.

Nashe resembled most of his fellow professional writers in coming from a modest background (his father was a clergyman) and having studied as a sizar at university. His tendency to ribald scoffing and sharply realised depictions, as well as his attractive technique of speaking directly to the reader (as

in the above passage), as if the latter were at that moment
sitting opposite him, he inherited from his brilliant opponent
in the famed Marprelate controversy. During the conflict
between the Puritans and the establishment, an anonymous
writer began issuing polemical pamphlets aimed against the
prelates; but in order to ensure a wide reading public, the
pamphleteer deserted the usual solemn fulminations of the-
ologians in favour of a racy, journalistic prose. His thrusts
went home so effectively and proved so damaging to the
Church that the bishops saw no alternative but to respond in
kind, and they hired Lyly and Nashe to spearhead a counter-
attack. There is no scholarly agreement on which pamphlets
were actually written by Nashe, but his early involvement in
the controversy left a clear mark on his subsequent writings
in their lively, impudent, and provocative jibing at contemporary manners. Indeed, the one venture he made into a more
solemn form, his sententious *Christ's Tears Over Jerusalem*
(1593), proved a dismal failure, and he never reverted to it.

Had he been born into a later era, Nashe's talents would
no doubt have found their natural outlet in the satirical novel
or in a racy type of journalism, but with neither as yet existing as recognised genres, he was compelled to invent his own
literary form. *.The Unfortunate Traveller* (1594), which he
termed 'a phantastical treatise', possesses clear elements of
both. By employing a first-person narration for his account
of Jack Wilton's adventures, he creates an effect of immediate
eye-witness reportage, a verisimilitude enhanced by the
frequent introduction of historical personages into the story.
On the other hand, the hero's sequence of amorous escapades
and hairsbreadth rescues from hanging lend an amusing fic-
tionalism to the work, lest the reader take it all too seriously.
Nashe was probably drawing upon the picaresque tales emanating from Spain, notably *Lazarillo de Tormes*, with their
repudiation of the chivalric tradition as the hypocrisy and
cruelty of society are revealed to the central character; but
here the author is less concerned with moral problems, preferring to offer a frolicsome account of Jack's experiences in
the world, a young man endowed with an irrepressible zest
for life and not overburdened by moral scruples.

His adventures follow each other too swiftly for elaboration
— the witnessing of a plague in Rome, the massacre of Ana-

baptists in Munster, a love intrigue within 'the Sodom of Italy' — and a vividness of description is needed to imprint these fleeting scenes upon the mind. Fortunately, that was a skill in which Nashe excelled. Through the author's eye for telling detail, an English captain, duped by Jack's flattery, comes dramatically alive within a few short lines:

> Oh my auditors, had you seen him how he stretched out his limbs, scratched his scabbed elbows at this speech; how he set his cap over his eyebrows like a politician, and then folded his arms one in another, and nodded with the head as who would say, Let the French beware for they shall find me a devil . . .

The style of the work adapts itself to the episode or to the individual speech patterns of the character. When Henry Howard, Earl of Surrey, is introduced into the story, the language becomes a burlesque of the sonneteer's exotic images: 'Her high exalted sunbeams have set the Phoenix nest of my breast on fire, and I myself have brought Arabian spiceries of sweet passions and praises to furnish out the funeral flame of my folly. Those who were condemned to be smothered to death by sinking down into the soft bottom of a high-built bed of roses, never died so sweet a death as I should die if her rose-coloured disdain were my death's man.'

Nashe was at his best in the thrust and parry of literary controversy, where his fund of scurrilous invective, his ready wit, and his flair for taunting caricature proved witheringly effective. His most famous skirmish was with Gabriel Harvey, a Cambridge don drawn into argument almost by chance as a sequel to the Marprelate affair. In those days no holds were barred, and playing to the public for whom *Strange News* (1593) was intended, Nashe would as readily ridicule his opponent for being the son of a ropemaker as he would for the quality of his prose. His scorn for Harvey's experiments with English hexameters has, by its pithy accuracy, outlasted the verse itself: '. . . our speech is too craggy for him to set his plough in: he goes twitching and hopping in our language like a man running upon quagmires, up the hill in one syllable and down the dale in another, retaining no part of that stately smooth gait which he vaunts himself with amongst the Greeks and Latins'. Eventually when the controversy seemed liable

to exceed all bounds, the Archbishop of Canterbury inter-
vened, forbidding either side to continue the dispute.

Nashe now began a drama entitled *The Isle of Dogs*. No
doubt through urgent need of ready cash, he sold it in an
unfinished state to a group of players (probably the Earl of
Pembroke's Men), who, after it had been completed by Ben
Jonson, performed it in 1597. The play has not survived but
it caused a furore. The Privy Council, informed that it was 'a
lewd play' containing seditious and slanderous matter, clapped
Jonson and two of the players in gaol, but failed to find Nashe
who had been warned in advance and had fled from London
to wait for the excitement to subside. He never returned, for
two years later he was dead.

The emergence of the professional writer from the ranks of
the artisan class had introduced into literature a more raucous
note, an eager jostling for public attention which had been
missing in the urbane writings of courtier and humanist. Yet
if Greene and Nashe employed huckster techniques to promul-
gate their wares in the commercially oriented world of publication — new-minted phrases to catch the reader's eye, a
self-dramatising exhibitionism, a bantering ridicule of com-
petitors, and an adroitness in responding to the very latest
fashions — these were not qualities shared by all those
subsisting by their pens. The hack-writers were, by their own
admission, ready to prostitute their talents for money, if
necessary subordinating artistic integrity to the immediate
needs of their purse. Accordingly, the works they produced
for all their originality and boisterous vigour, remain of interest
today less for their intrinsic merit than for the light they shed
on the changing social and economic conditions prevailing for
the Elizabethan writer. Yet in their pursuit of quick cash
returns, they did introduce new literary forms, enlarge the
potentialities of the English language, and help create that
effervescent literary underworld of back-biting, gossip, deep
drinking, and cut-throat competition from which greater
figures such as Marlowe were to emerge, who refused to
compromise their art.

7

Harmony and proportion

THE melodious verse of Wyatt and Surrey had seemed to promise a new springtime for English poetry; but the blossom was long in coming. Surrey's death in 1547 was followed by a lull of over thirty years, during which time the miscellanies continued popularising the sonneteering style but added little of significance. This faltering of the new poetry after so encouraging a start has proved puzzling to historians. It may reflect a more general slowing-down in the spread of Renaissance ideas in England. The study of Greek, for example, so essential to the revival of classical learning on the continent, was here sucked into the vortex of religious controversy. After its introduction by Grocyn at the turn of the century and its rapid development at the universities during the 1520s, by 1556 its condition could only be described by Sir Thomas Pope, the founder of Trinity College, Oxford, as being 'much decay'd'. Regarded with some justice by the Catholic church as a potential threat to the authority of the Latin Vulgate, Greek learning was actively discouraged during the reign of the Catholic Queen Mary, and Sir Thomas, although eager to give renewed impetus to such studies, admitted, 'I fear the times will not bear it now.'[25]

Similarly, the damage suffered by the school system at the time of the dissolution of the monasteries in the years 1536—9 had provided a serious set-back to education. The annexation of school revenues and the dispersal of their teaching staff as the parent bodies were dismembered caused, in Ascham's words, 'the collapse and ruination' of the entire educational system, with only a few schools continuing to function. The blow to education came at a particularly bad time. Just as the aristocracy was becoming convinced of its duty to supply from its own ranks educated future governors for the country, and the incentive to send one's sons to the best schools was filtering down to the classes below, many such schools were closed down. It was to take until the 1560s before such famous schools as Shrewsbury and Merchant Taylors began to emerge, as, with the growing prestige of education, wealthy merchants began diverting their gifts from the Church in the direction of bequests and scholarships to schools, and encouraging their trade guilds to establish new schools of their own. Under such enlightened headmasters as Thomas Ashton and Richard Mulcaster, the pupils at these schools (numbering among them Sir Philip Sidney, Fulke Greville, and Edmund Spenser), became imbued with a humanist love of learning, including poetry, music, and drama. Their contribution to poetry was to make itself felt only after their graduation from university in the 1580s some thirty years after Surrey's death, thus accounting in large part for the lacuna in poetic development.

The poetic styles which Wyatt had brought back from his travels in Italy and France had at that time been introduced as novelties on the English scene, but the intervening years had already established Petrarch's sonnets, Ariosto's *Orlando Furioso* (1532) and the pastoral poems of the French Clément Marot (1496–1544) as acknowledged models for the aspiring English poet. Such veneration for continental literature was at the same time a source of chagrin, an admission that England had fallen behind and could at best be only an imitator of the excellence achieved abroad. Edmund Spenser (*c*.1552–99) felt the slight particularly keenly. In contrast to the prevailing fashion of importing French words and phrases into verse in order to flaunt a familiarity with the vogues abroad, he deliberately turned back to England's past, rooting his language in the native soil of Chaucer's England two hundred years earlier; and, while he continued to admire and even to borrow from his colleagues abroad, he remained dedicated to the creation of a specifically English verse, indigenous to the cultural tradition on which it was to draw. Poetically, he raised aloft the national flag, challenging all to acknowledge the supremacy of the English heritage. The introduction and notes to his first published poem, although signed 'E.K.', may well have been written by Spenser himself and in any case certainly reflect many of his own views. There the protest against foreign importations into the language and the claim for purity of diction were vigorously advanced. The debasers of English, it was argued, have:

> . . . patched up the holes with pieces and rags of other languages borrowing here of the French, there of the Italian, everywhere of the Latin, not weighing how ill those tongues accord with themselves, much worse with ours. So now they have made our English tongue a gallimaufray or hodge-podge of all other speeches.

The complaint had been voiced before in England, but no-one before Spenser had seriously envisaged returning to the archaic forms displaced by the new importations, nor to an antiquated spelling. The latter, 'E.K.' felt, should like grey hairs make the style 'seem grave and, as it were, reverend.' Since such usage appeared outmoded even to Spenser's contemporaries and was integral to his literary aims, quotations from his poetry will, in contrast to the practice elsewhere in this book, be offered in their original, unmodernised form.

His first published poem, *The Shepheardes Calender* which appeared in 1579, may seem to contradict his aims by introducing into English literature a classical genre, the pastoral eclogue of Theocritus and Virgil; but in fact this usage conformed to his basic conception, his purpose being not to ignore Renaissance innovations, including a return to classical models, but rather to implant them afresh within an English setting and to incorporate them as part of the national tradition. The pastoral idyll, in which companionable shepherds stretch languidly beneath a tree to sing of their loves, sometimes with a third shepherd to adjudicate the prize for the best song, had not appealed to the medieval mind with its condemnation of *otium* or Sloth as one of the seven deadly sins. The Renaissance approval of the contemplative life as the rightful complement to the active gave such scenes renewed legitimacy,[26] and while the biblical tradition regarding literature as no more than a vehicle for moral instruction had persisted for the most part through the Middle Ages, the reinstating of a classical delight in beauty for its own sake now made the literary competition acceptable once again.

Spenser domesticated the classical pastoral in more ways than one. By forming the separate laments for unrequited love into a cycle of twelve eclogues and relating them to the months of the year, he was able to integrate them with the

seasonal changes in the English landscape. In April, the shepherd tenders bouquets of flowers such as would then have
adorned the hedges, fields, and gardens in an English springtime — daffadowndillies, cowslips, and kingcups — styling
some, like the 'Sops-in-wine', by their familiar local nicknames.
The eclogue for the following month opens with a refreshing
evocation of an English May-day festivity:

> Is not thilke the mery moneth of May,
> When loue lads masken in fresh aray?
> How falles it then, we no merrier bene,
> Ylike as others, girt in gawdy greene?

The shepherd most clearly associated with the poet himself
he called Colin Clout, borrowing the name from Skelton as
a means of strengthening the sense of continuity with earlier
traditions of English poetry; and metrically he deserted the
regular lines of classical pastoral in favour of varied, experimental forms echoing Chaucer's usage or based on the English
ballad stanza.

This early work already contained a hint of the direction
his major poetry was to take. As a student at Pembroke Hall,
Cambridge, he had become exposed to the spirit of Puritanism
which Grindal had introduced there, including a demand for
a religion purified of Catholic taint and a faith which must be
made to permeate all aspects of life with a sense of religious
dedication. Poetry as a casual pastime for the courtier seemed
to have no place in such high seriousness of purpose, and in
the tenth eclogue his shepherd-poet expresses a weariness at
composing 'dapper ditties' to beguile the fancy of youth.
Instead, poetry should be restored to its ancient splendour,
re-consecrated to such long-neglected themes as knights fighting for noble causes and the solemnity of monarchal power:

> Abandon then the base and viler clowne,
> Lyft vp thy selfe out of the lowly dust:
> And sing of bloody Mars, of wars, of giusts,
> Turne thee to those, that weld the awful crowne.
> To doubted Knights, whose woundless armour rusts,
> And helmes vnbruzed wexen dayly browne.

Early in 1579, Spenser's introduction to Sidney's circle, the
Puritan faction at court led politically by Sidney's uncle the

Earl of Leicester, aroused in him hopes of obtaining the patronage he needed for advancement at court. In fact, probably through having antagonised Lord Burghley in his satirical *Mother Hubberds Tale*, he received instead a government appointment to Ireland where he was to remain away from court in various posts of increasing responsibility until the end of his life. His residence there was probably more suited to his quieter nature than the stresses and tensions of court life, and so far from chafing at his exile he came to love the Irish countryside, folklore, and people, introducing many of its scenes into his poetic world.

Spenserian allegory

The Sidney circle with which Spenser became associated, intensely patriotic as well as Puritan in its leanings, had held as one of its cherished aims the re-establishment of England among the leading literatures of Europe by creating a body of poetry excelling not only in literary merit but also in moral and Christian probity. *The Faerie Queene* was designed by Spenser to fulfil both those aims. In a letter to his friend Gabriel Harvey, Spenser had declared his avowed purpose to emulate in this poem and even to 'overgo' the famed *Orlando Furioso* of Ariosto, then at the height of its reputation, and in the poem's content he provided that ethical commitment which was intended to restore to poetry the moral function it had possessed in biblical times. That it succeeded even though the poet's death at the age of forty-seven left it in unfinished form, with only six of the twelve projected books completed, is a tribute not only to the quality of the verse but also to the imaginative conception which lay behind it, allowing each individual story within the broader sequential framework to be savoured independently. The plan had been to relate in 'darke conceit' or allegory the Faerie Queene's despatching of various knights to overcome monsters or temptations representing twelve moral vices; but the composite nature of allegory as Spenser conceived it enabled him to function with multi-level effect and thereby achieve in one work the apparently disparate aims he had before him, religious, patriotic, and literary.

Spenser has been called the most learned of English poets,

reputed, among many other languages, to have been 'perfect in the Greek tongue'. Within his poetry, the Platonic influence is strong, with its conception of an ideal world of undisturbed harmony and proportion of which this mundane reality is but a faint copy. Accordingly, his allegorical presentation of virtues such as Holiness, Temperance, and Courtesy takes on the quality of the Platonic ideal, a perfection unifying all elements of that virtue within it. From a literary viewpoint, such a technique was potentially hazardous, liable to create in his poem the fairyland of an idealised world drifting away into some vague mist. Instead, with a Renaissance facility for integrating the abstract with the concrete, linking the dream-world with the tactile, Spenser attached those idealised figures to real personages at court. The Faerie Queene herself functions, as he specifically declared, not only as a symbol of glory in general, but also of 'that most excellent and glorious person of our soveraine Queene'. Such equations, he warns us, are not fixed, but tenuous and variable, so that two different virtues may at times recall the same individual. Throughout the poem, therefore, the reader becomes sensitised to a topical allusiveness, Sir Calidore's prowess as an athlete and wrestler inevitably evoking for contemporaries associations with Sidney; and Leicester, Ralegh, and Burghley flit shadowily in and out of the fairy-tale.

The effect of that topicality is twofold, religious and nationalistic. On the one hand it ensured that the practical application of those moral lessons to real life be not forgotten, and, on the other, it invested the Elizabethan court with a legendary splendour and noble idealism, offering its members an image of moral endeavour with which they could more easily identify because it was expressed in terms of martial valour. The age in any case loved heraldry and symbol. The progresses of Elizabeth called forth elaborate pageants representing her, in praise of her virginity, as the chaste Goddess Diana reproving Cupid, and accordingly the projection of the Elizabethan scene into the mythological world of ancient British knights battling dragons in the name of Truth and Justice had a strong appeal, heightening the courtier's growing sense of his national dignity and of the challenges which lay before him in his own era.

The medieval mind had been particularly attuned to allegorical modes of thought, both in the prefigurative reading of the scriptures at two or more levels of meaning (seeing in Abraham's readiness to sacrifice Isaac a foreshadowing of God the Father's willingness to sacrifice his own son, Jesus) and in the morality plays themselves, with their dramatic personifications of the virtues and vices. *The Faerie Queene*, for all its indebtedness to that morality tradition, adds a new dimension to it, ushering it into the Renaissance world. In such morality plays as *Everyman*, the personified figures had been essentially static in character, confined within the limits of the specific qualities they represented. Fellowship drank convivially with all and sundry, Envy sneered and calumniated in accordance with the name he bore, and Sloth snored away in a corner of the stage. Within that tradition, Spenser does indeed offer some brilliantly etched vignettes:

> And by his side rode loathsome *Gluttony*,
> Deformed creature, on a filthie swyne,
> His belly was vp-blowne with luxury,
> And eke with fatnesse swollen were his eyne,
> And like a Crane his necke was long and fyne,
> With which he swallowed vp excessiue feast,
> For want whereof poore people oft did pyne;
> And all the way, most like a brutish beast,
> He spued vp his gorge, that all did him deteast.   [I,iii,21]

Yet in his poem, these are only minor characters, passing briefly across the stage. In contrast, his central figures, while symbolising virtues, are such only in potential; and with a humanist concern for man's personal achievements, Spenser presents such characters as gradually maturing, struggling laboriously towards the fulfilment of the ideals they represent. The Red Cross Knight (St George, the patron saint of England) may symbolise Holiness, his mighty arms scored with the marks of previous battles, but as the poem opens we discover to our surprise that the man within that armour is as yet untried:

> A Gentle Knight was pricking* on the plaine,   *spurring
> Y cladd in mightie armes and siluer shielde,
> Wherein old dints of deepe wounds did remaine,
> The cruell markes of many a bloudy fielde;
> Yet armes till that time did he neuer wield . . .   [I,i,1]

As he proceeds to prove himself worthy of the cross he bears
upon his shield, he reveals his human weaknesses and failures,
his despair and gradual resurgence of faith, his growth in
moral stature in the course of discovering the well-springs of
his own being. Man is no longer the victim of larger forces
working upon him, with his function, as in the morality plays,
limited to a simple choice between the advice of a good and a
bad angel. He has become instead, as the age now sees him, a
more complex creature, beset by doubts, waylaid by his own
fantasies, deceived by externals, and yet despite those inherent
weaknesses, capable of determining his own fate if his will
remain strong. Even the reward for virtue has changed. It is
no longer acquittal from the fires of hell threatening beyond
the grave, but rather the dignity of self-realisation in this
world, the manly honour of having triumphed over temptation
itself:

> The noble hart, that harbours vertuous thought,
> And is with child of glorious great intent,
> Can neuer rest, vntill it forth haue brought
> Th' eternall brood of glorie excellent:
> Such restless passion did all night torment
> The flaming corage of the Faery knight,
> Deuizing, how that doughty turnament
> With greatest honour he atchieuen might . . .   [I,v,1]

By investing the medieval tales of chivalry with allegorical
meaning, Spenser revitalised an out-moded genre, raising it
to a new level of sophistication. A medieval mind habituated
to the miraculous legends of saints might believe in a magical
ointment capable of healing fatal wounds overnight and
allowing a severely-wounded combatant weakened by loss of
blood to rise whole and refreshed next morning; but such
fantasy would have strained the credulity of the more pragmatic Elizabethan age. It would suit the needs of Puck in
comedy, but not a serious work of moral intent. However,
that ointment when presented as a symbol of inner faith
overcoming debilitating despair and transforming it overnight
into courageous hope provides no strain to credulity and the
naiveté of the original usage is made to suit a maturer response.
Such allegory permitted, in the same way, a more subtle
depiction of character. A knight would under normal circumstances fall irretrievably in our estimation were he, like the

Red Cross Knight, to tremble in the face of danger, grow deathly pale and need to be rebuked by his lady 'Fie, fie, faint-hearted knight . . . frail, feeble, fleshly wight.' But when that lady represents a part of himself, his own moral conscience bravely rebuking his weaker components for temporary backsliding, the heroic quality of the character is restored. The battle is within, in accordance with the Puritan penchant for presenting man's struggle against temptation in terms of an unceasing martial contest with the weaker elements of his own being.

The reader's search for a symbolic meaning adds zest to the series of adventures on the surface level. As in a modern detective story, Spenser delays the moment of revelation in order to increase tension and sharpen curiosity. Britomart, representing Chastity, comes upon her champion sorely beset by six knights who together demand that he swear allegiance to their mistress and betray his own. Only after the battle, when they enter the castle decorated with erotic scenes, are the six identified as personifications of sexual gratification in its various forms [III,1,45]. In such scenes, for all his censure of sensual surrender, Spenser displays, as part of his humanist response to beauty, a mature awareness of the attractions which such temptations offer. The Catholic condemnation of all physical love as a weakness of the flesh had been replaced in Protestantism by its validation there as a divine blessing conferred upon mankind. Such love, the Reformers argued, must be disciplined and restrained within the bonds of marriage, but the beauty of the flesh was acknowledged and seen as a potentially positive quality. Within the broader aesthetic awakening, typified by the introduction of the classical nude into contemporary painting and sculpture, an affirmative response to the attractiveness of this world was legitimised, and only its misapplication was to be reproved, namely immodesty and wanton seductiveness. So Spenser's Bower of Bliss, while it is a symbol of such lasciviousness, still remains a garden 'sweet and fair to see', with joyous birds in cheerful shade, divinely harmonious music, and in the bower itself, a naked lady 'in a vele of silke and siluer thin, / That hid no whit her alablaster skin' [II,xii,77]. The temptation is real, and hence the courage needed to resist the allurement all the greater.

That heightened aesthetic sensibility found its expression in the quality of the verse too. The demand for proportion and harmony in art encouraged by the revival of Platonism in Italy now entered English verse. Spenser's smooth-flowing lines create a concord of sound whatever the scene. A dawn is described in splendid terms:

> At last the golden Orientall gate
>   Of greatest heauen gan to open faire,
>   And *Phoebus* fresh, as bridegrome to his mate
>   Came dauncing forth, shaking his deawie haire.

But a few lines later a battle-scene, vivid as it may be in its clash of arms, nevertheless retains the overall musicality of tone. The alliteration of 'shining shieldes' and 'burning blades' modifies poetically the harshness of theme in much the same way as a Titian painting mutes the wildness of a bacchanalian orgy by modulating the colours and subtly balancing the figures of the revellers:

> A shrilling trompet sownded from on hye,
> And vnto battail bad them selues addresse:
> Their shining shieldes about their wrestes they tye,
> And burning blades about their heads do blesse,
> The instruments of wrath and heauinesse.   [I,v,6]

Above all, it was Spenser's invention of a new stanzaic form which ensured the proportioned harmony of the work. Where the classical epic had employed an uninterrupted sequence of hexameter lines, Spenser broke his poem into equal nine-line stanzas, each consisting of iambic pentameters with the concluding line, the so-called Alexandrine, one foot longer. The succession of small, self-contained units is pleasing both to eye and ear, and Spenser dispels any monotony in repetition by varying the movement within each stanza. At times the concluding line summarises, at times it points in a new direction; it may slow down the speed after a swift forward motion, or increase it after a steadier rhythm. And within the stanza itself there may be an undisturbed flow, a sharp division into separate quatrains, or any number of other variations. In the following stanza, for example, the third line is split, as a fresh sentence moves us from the particular to the general, and then surges forward in its condemnation of the mindless masses.

The Alexandrine then switches direction with a direct appeal to such wanderers to turn back to the narrow path:

> Strange thing it is an errant knight to see
> Here in this place, or any other wight,
> That hither turnes his steps. So few there bee,
> That chose the narrow path, or seeke the right:
> All keepe the broad high way, and take delight
> With many rather for to go astray,
> And be partakers of their euill plight,
> Then with a few to walke the rightest way;
> O foolish men, why haste ye to your owne decay?   [I,x,10]

The remarkable craftsmanship of Spenser's verse has won him the appellation 'the poet's poet'. He reveals a mastery of movement, sound, imagery, and meaning which raises poetry to a new level of achievement. At one point, the foul monster Error vomits forth her cursed spawn which swarm over the knight's legs. As he slices off the monster's head, the hateful brood try in vain to find their way back to shelter within its mouth, finding instead only the wound at its neck. A brilliantly placed run-on line — 'Their wonted entrance to haue found / At her wide mouth' creates metrically a feeling of frustration at the absence of the expected line-ending, which echoes the frustration of the brood at missing their familiar shelter:

> Her scattred brood, soone as their Parent deare
> They saw so rudely falling to the ground,
> Groning full deadly, all with troublous feare,
> Gathred themselves about her body round,
> Weening their wonted entrance to haue found
> At her wide mouth: but being there withstood
> They flocked all about her bleeding wound,
> And sucked vp their dying mothers blood,
> Making her death their life, and eke her hurt their good. [I,i,25]

The gruesome conclusion leads into the harmony of the final line, epitomising the corruption of values which Error induces, the inversion of death and life, of good and evil.

The Faerie Queene, or those parts which were completed, appeared in two sections. The first group of three books was published in 1590, winning the poet immediate acclaim as well as a life pension of £50 per annum from the Queen, and the second group of three books some six years later when he was already well established. In the interim he produced *Colin Clouts Come Home Againe*, celebrating a visit Sir Walter Ralegh paid him in Ireland, in which the poet and his visitor are charmingly portrayed as two shepherds piping their lays to each other in mutual admiration and delight. It was, incidentally, during that visit in 1589 that Ralegh persuaded Spenser to publish his great poem and thereby try his fortune at court.

Spenser's autobiographical tendency, whereby he often placed himself as a recognisable figure within his work, (in the tradition of Chaucer's pilgrim) found expression in his sonnet cycle *Amoretti*. It was written in the Petrarchan tradition, but with a significant difference. That tradition, like the tales of chivalry produced in a society where marriage had been aimed primarily at the joining of property, had glorified extra-marital love. Sir Launcelot's passion for King Arthur's wife Guinevere, Petrarch's enduring love for Laura though she was married to another had, as in the subsequent sonneteering mode, been approved however incongruously by a society ostensibly committed to the Christian ethic. For a poet of Spenser's religious sensitivity such moral ambivalence was unacceptable, and for him the only valid consummation of love was within the bonds of marriage. At the allegorical level, the victorious knight is joined in matrimony to Una, the symbol of Truth, and the sonnet sequence, reflecting Spenser's own life, is largely devoted to his love for Elizabeth Boyle (his first wife had died some years earlier) and her hesitation at marrying a man so much older than herself. The sequence ends with their parting, though he did in fact marry her in 1596. He had probably intended to provide a concluding sequel which his early death prevented. The sonnets are generally unsatisfactory, playing with conventional themes on his mistress's coldness and 'cruelty' or introducing such clumsy conceits as a list of the flowers whose smells her body recalls in its various parts (Sonnet 64). The sonnet, it would seem, was a genre for which Spenser was temperamentally unsuited, his imagination unable to move freely in its constricting form.

In contrast, Spenser's marriage-songs, his exquisite 'Epithalamium' and 'Prothalamium' would alone have earned him a revered place in literature. The first was composed in

honour of his own bride, the second commissioned by the
Earl of Worcester for the wedding of his two daughters. Such
marriage-songs had traditionally been associated with ribald
innuendo as part of the comic release of springtime fertility
rites, but Spenser endows them with uncustomary purity and
freshness. The refrains of both poems — 'The woods shall to
me answer and my eccho ring' and 'Sweet Themmes runne
softly, till I end my Song' — place the marriages within the
open countryside which, as it were, participates in the celebrations as part of the natural fulfilment of life's cycle. The
bride is awakened at dawn, garlanded with flowers to match
her own rosy cheeks, and led towards the bower with all the
apparatus of the natural world as classical mythology had
seen it, Phoebus shining upon her from above, nymphs to
escort her, and Hymen awaiting her arrival. And yet these
pagan gods and goddesses are merged into a fully Christian
sanctification of the wedding, with the 'Song of Songs' and
the 'Book of Psalms' contributing to the hallowing of the
scene:

> Open the temple gates vnto my loue,
> Open them wide that she may enter in,
> And all the postes adorne as doth behoue,
> And all the pillours deck with girlands trim,
> For to recyue this saynt with honour dew,
> That commeth in to you.
> With trembling steps and humble reuerence,
> She commeth in, before th' almighties vew . . .
> And let the roring Organs loudly play
> The praises of the Lord in liuely notes,
> The whiles with hollow throates
> The Choristers the ioyous Antheme sing,
> That all the woods may answere and their eccho ring.

This untroubled blending of pagan and Christian imagery
offered a new model for English poetry, arising from Spenser's
own humanist training. As part of the continental revival of
learning and particularly under the influence of Pico della
Mirandola a more universal view of religion had arisen, perceiving in pagan mythology parallel patterns of belief among
nations which had not yet been privileged to make contact
with the Bible. As a result, the pagan and the Christian began
to merge. Venus the goddess of Love was seen (as she appears
in Botticelli's *Primavera*) as the classical counterpart of the

Virgin Mary, the matriarch of divine love. By a process of allegory similar to the prefigurative method applied to the Old Testament, classical myths could be translated into Christian terms, Hercules, for example, becoming the archetypal partner to Samson. The tension between pagan and Christian was thereby relaxed, and the apparatus of Greek and Roman verse could be absorbed into contemporary and even religious poetry with no sense of blasphemy. Spenser's blending of the two traditions in his poetry was another facet of that overall harmony for which his writing is so distinguished both in form and content.

The perfect knight

Sir Philip Sidney (1554—86) might well have been in Spenser's mind when, in his satirical *Mother Hubberds Tale*, he presented, as a contrast to the envious backbiters he was attacking, his own as well as Castiglione's conception of the ideal courtier — honourable at all times, loyal to his monarch, despising flattery, accomplished in diplomacy, excelling in the arts of war, in horsemanship, athletics, and archery, who when wearied by his manifold activities:

> . . . doth recoyle
> Vnto his rest, and there with sweete delight
> Of Musicks skill reuiues his toyled spright,
> Or els with Loues, and Ladies gentle sports,
> The ioy of youth, himselfe he recomforts:
> Or lastly, when the bodie list to pause
> His minde vnto the Muses he withdrawes . . .

Sidney indeed became a legend in his era as the fulfilment of this humanist ideal. The urge for signal achievement in all spheres of life, which had impelled Alberti in the fifteenth century to take degrees both in law and science, to become a distinguished diplomat, to produce major treatises on art and architecture, and to build a church which was to revolutionise the aesthetic tastes of his time, had at last reached England. The fame Sidney attained in his brief lifetime scarcely included his writings, which were known only to an intimate circle of friends until their publication some years after his death, but the impetus they gave to English literature once they became known and the quality which they achieved in their own right are of the same innovative order as the contributions Alberti made to the arts of his own generation.

Noble in birth and groomed to be the heir of his uncles the powerful Earl of Leicester and the Earl of Warwick, he seemed destined for a brilliant career. His own family, though honourable, was relatively poor, his father Sir Henry Sidney having devoted himself to the Queen's service to the detriment of his own affairs with the usual niggardly remuneration from that monarch; but with the promises held out before the son, temporary lack of funds seemed a small obstacle. His personal talents were soon recognised as more than equal to the hopes placed upon him, but fate was to prove less amenable. The Earl of Leicester married unexpectedly, and the birth of an heir deprived Sidney of the succession. Even worse, despite his excellent court connections and his own acknowledged capabilities, the Queen was reluctant to advance him, probably because of his staunch Protestantism at a time when she was still toying with the possibility of a Catholic marriage. In 1577 he was at last sent on a mission to Germany and on his way back, on being received by William of Orange, made so deep an impression on that king that the latter proposed a marriage between Sidney and his daughter as a means of cementing an alliance between England and Holland, provided Queen Elizabeth would approve. She did not; and on his return to court he found himself in disfavour. It is to this period of 1578–82 that his literary activity is generally assigned. In 1583, he married Frances Walsingham, moving in to live with his father-in-law because of the poor state of his own finances, and only in 1585 did his prospects seem briefly to improve. The Queen, refusing to let him sail to the West Indies with Drake, as a compensation appointed him Governor of Flushing where he acquitted himself admirably against the Spanish forces; but shortly afterwards he was wounded in battle by a stray bullet (in a typical act of bravado he had removed his leg armour), gangrene set in, and within a few weeks he was dead at the age of thirty-one. The only tangible recognition he received was a state funeral magnificent even by Elizabethan standards, a mark of the universal grief felt by a nation which had come to see in him an embodiment of its noblest ideals.

His period of temporary withdrawal from court in 1578, when his hopes there seemed to have dimmed, was not wasted by Sidney on embittered brooding, but exploited as an opportunity for developing those literary interests for which he had previously had insufficient leisure. In this he exemplified the combination of the active and contemplative life, resorting to the arts when warfare and diplomacy no longer called. The works he produced in that comparatively brief period are extraordinary not only in their intrinsic worth but in the advance they display over anything preceding them within each of the three genres he chose. There is a new sureness of touch as he creates his own skilfully wrought works, no longer anxiously imitative of contemporaries abroad. Both in the personal inspiration he provided for such admirers as Spenser, and in the models his works afforded to subsequent writers, he marks the new independence of spirit which was to dominate English literature in the last decades of the century.

Joining his seventeen-year-old sister, the recently married Countess of Pembroke, at her home in Wilton (later a centre of literary patronage under her aegis), he composed at her request the first English romance tale which could legitimately be set beside its European counterparts, and which led in England to such subsequent works as Lodge's *Rosalind*. Widely read in foreign languages, Sidney was familiar with Jacopo Sannazaro's *Arcadia* of 1501–4 (which, though popular on the continent, had never been translated into English) as well as other such tales appearing in Spain and elsewhere. The series of pastoral poems which they offered, loosely joined by connecting passages in prose, promoted in him the idea for a reverse format, a prose romance interspersed with occasional poems and set in the idyllic yet fallen world of Arcadia. The story he devised was of a Duke who, to avoid an ominous oracle, retreats with his family into a forest, living isolated from all but a few shepherds. Two princes in love with his two daughters infiltrate into that pastoral world dressed respectively as a shepherd and an Amazon. The latter's female disguise creates confusion as the old Duke becomes infatuated with the outward form and his wife with the man she perceives within. Eventually all ends happily, but those complications together with the developing loves of the central characters and various sub-plots introduced *en route* hold the reader's attention throughout, and offer ample opportunity for philosophical discussions on honour, beauty, love, and good government.

The innovation of Sidney's *Arcadia* is far-reaching, more so than may at first sight appear. It looks forward, in fact, to the 'green world' of Lodge's *Rosalind* and, through Lodge, to that of Shakespeare's comedies. As a fallen land still enjoying the after-glow of the golden age, Arcadia offers a setting of heightened imaginative awareness, a land like the forest in *As You Like It* in which heroes can be more heroic, fools more obviously foolish, and lovers both more passionate and more absurd than in real life. It is the world induced today by the psychiatrist's couch, where frustrations can be sublimated and fantasies acted out. Its purpose, however, is not escapism, as some have thought, but moral exploration and re-assessment. Temporarily freed from the immediate pressures of social and ethical norms, we may in that realm of the fancy examine afresh the vexed problems of age, love, parenthood, or social responsibility, before returning to this world bearing the knowledge such vicarious experience has gained for us. This 'green world' of legendary forests and magical woods is the instance *par excellence* of that ever-present link between the ideal and the real which exemplifies the Renaissance imagination at its best, the idyllic setting in which can be perceived the workings of the actual and the mundane.

To add a note of self-parody as well as realism he places within the book, a melancholy lover named Philisides (a transparent pseudonym for *Phili*p *Sid*ney) and the mildly amused tone which he employs in the narration is intended to prevent the reader from taking the plot too seriously, and ensures that the work be regarded as an artefact, patently employing the variegated tales and interwoven sub-plots as vehicles for lessons on valour, courtesy, and moral sensibility. The series of ship-wrecks, love-potions, and commuted death-sentences so beloved by that era would otherwise have verged on melodrama, but they are kept in control here by the slightly humorous presentation as well as the elegance of language.

Stylistically, the romance marks the culmination of the gradual refinement of the English language perceptible through the sixteenth century. Sidney relies neither on imported

vocabulary nor on a return to the archaic forms advocated by
Spenser, but, employing the simpler diction of the language
of his own day, creates a gently modulated flow of words, a
flexibility of tone, and a sweet-sounding ripple of movement.
There are echoes of the antitheses which Lyly's *Euphues* had
recently made popular but they are never there gratuitously,
only to qualify a description or heighten a contrast. The scene
as one of the princesses is about to bathe, unknowingly in
the presence of her disguised lover (an evocation of Ovid's
description of Diana, watched by the hidden Actaeon) provides the perfect setting for the amorous episode, with nature
participating in the eroticism of the scene. The river:

> . . . ran upon so fine and delicate a ground, as one could not easily
> judge whether the river did more wash the gravel or the gravel did
> purify the river; the river not running forthright but almost continu-
> ally winding, as if the lower streams would return to their springs or
> that the river had delight to play with itself. The banks of either side
> seeming arms of the loving earth that fain would embrace it, and the
> river a wanton nymph which still would slip from it.

This dreamy world of fantasy is, as always, sharply focused
by a realistic detail. The ladies, confident that they are un-
observed, are about to disrobe:

> . . . yet for the more surety they looked around about and could
> see nothing but a water-spaniel who came down the river showing
> that he hunted for a duck, and with a snuffling grace, disdaining that
> his smelling force could not as well prevail through the water as
> through the air, and therefore waiting with his eye to see whether
> he could espy the ducks getting up again. But then a little below
> them, failing of his purpose, he got out of the river and shaking off
> the water, as great men do their friends, now he had no further cause
> to use it, inweeded himself so as the ladies lost the further marking
> his sportfulness.

The ironic comment on human morals which Sidney deftly
slips into the description — 'shaking off the water, as great
men do their friends' — typifies that worldly-wise distancing
from the scene which lends the romance its sophistication.

Literature was beginning to be viewed with new seriousness
even by the courtier who still disdained publication. Although
written originally for his sister's private enjoyment — 'only
for you, only to you', as he wrote in an accompanying

letter — the romance intrigued Sidney as an art form, and on its completion, he began a fundamental rewriting, greatly expanding the plot to highlight the heroic and moral elements. This 'New' Arcadia broke off in the middle of a sentence in Book III and after his death was published in 1590 under the Countess of Pembroke's supervision. The abrupt ending proved troublesome to readers and in 1593 a composite version appeared which tacked on the conclusion from the earlier version; and such was the form in which it was frequently republished in subsequent years. Only as late as 1907 was a manuscript copy of the 'Old' Arcadia discovered by a London bookseller, which permitted comparison between the two versions and showed the care which Sidney had bestowed on the reworking.[27]

However, his growing concern with literature as a serious art form and not merely as a courtier's pastime would have been known to us from another source. The rapid growth of secular drama at this time had aroused the opposition of the more conservative sections of the population. The City aldermen, representing the interests of the merchants, saw in such play performances a threat to the sober, hard-working life they were attempting to inculcate in their apprentices and in 1574 they banned all servants and apprentices from attending the playhouse, probably with limited success. The religious opponents were more concerned with the threat the theatre posed to morality, both in the intrinsic quality of the plays themselves and in such concomitants of the theatre as its serving as a meeting place for prostitutes and gamblers. Stephen Gosson, who, after studying at university, was drawn to London as a playwright and possibly also as an actor, subsequently repented of his ways and issued *The School of Abuse* (1579) in which, with an obvious affection for the calling he had left, he attacked what he now saw as the corruption of the stage. Admitting that the players '. . . seek not to hurt, but desire to please', he castigated in the lively contemporary language of the professional writer the abuse to which play-acting leads: 'In our assemblies at plays in London, you shall see such heaving and shoving, such itching and shouldering to sit by women, such care for their garments that they be not trod on . . . such ticking, such toying, such smiling, such winking, and such manning them home when the sports are ended.' On the assumption that Sir Philip Sidney, as a Puritan, would approve of his sentiments, Gosson dedicated the work to him without requesting prior permission. Probably in order to dissociate himself from it, Sidney produced in reply his *Apology for Poetry* (known also as the *Defence of Poesy* from the titles of the two separate editions published in 1595) which constituted the first serious treatise on literary theory in England employing humanist concepts.

The term *poetry* he uses here in its original Greek sense, to denote not verse alone but all forms of imaginative literature including drama. The principles it enunciates are not startlingly new but the treatise served the important function of lending to literature a new dignity and gravity of purpose. The assumption that poetry and drama were idle occupations had received added force from the revival of Platonism. In a philosophical system where the real world was a faint reflection of an ideal truth, fiction, as a mere imitation of that real world, seemed even further removed from the ideal, the shadow of a shadow; and therefore Plato, for all his affection for his 'sweet sister Poetry', had reluctantly excluded it from his model republic as serving no useful purpose there. Sidney's *Apology* is in large part an attempt to answer that charge, by arguing for the moral purposiveness of literature in persuading towards some high and excellent truth. The writer, Sidney maintains in words which themselves illustrate his theme of the fascination of literature, comes '. . . with a tale which holdeth children from play, and old men from the chimney-corner; and pretending no more, doth intend the winning of the mind from wickedness to virtue.' The poet makes no claim to a literal or objective truth, readily acknowledging the fictitious nature of his work but (as in Sidney's own *Arcadia*) he creates a golden world superior to the brass of actuality, a rich tapestry of rivers, trees, and flowers more abundant and sweet-smelling than nature itself can create. His argument for the moral function of literature, buttressed with examples drawn from the biblical prophets, is weakest in dealing with the problem that literature may also use its persuasiveness to corrupt moral values, the very charge that the Puritans were beginning to level with such ferocity at the stage; but at least he had established that the fictitious element in literature was not in itself a negative quality but an intrinsic part of its creative force for good. His treatise concludes with a glance at the development of drama in his own era, praising *Gorboduc* for its stately speeches and recommending comedy for its part in ridiculing the pompous, the dandified, and the pretentious.

The third genre for which Sidney set new standards was the sonnet which, under his hand, responded to a major change on the English scene. In his discussion of literature, he had commented that the poet '. . . cometh unto you with words set in delightful proportion, either accompanied with, or prepared for, the well-enchanting skill of music.' The amateur music-making which Henry VIII had begun to make fashionable at court in Wyatt's day had now spread to all sections of society, and in the last quarter of the century England seemed to have burst into song. In 1588, John Case wrote '. . . manual labourers and mechanic artificers of all sorts keep such a chanting and singing in their shops, the tailor on his bulk, the shoemaker at his last, the mason at his wall, the shipboy at his oar, the tinker at his pan, the tiler on the house-top.' The printing of music, which had been in its infancy when Surrey wrote, had now become commercially profitable and songs were no sooner written than they appeared on sale at the book-stalls to be purchased, taken home, and tried out with friends in the four or five-part harmony favoured in England, or alternatively as a solo, accompanied on the lute or virginals. As the princesses in the *Arcadia* go to bathe in the river, they do not forget to '. . . take with them a lute, meaning to delight them under some shadow'; and even the Elizabethan barber-shop kept a musical instrument available for customers to entertain themselves with while they waited their turn.

This was the period when English music reclaimed its place in the forefront of Europe. It was the time of William Byrd, Thomas Tallis, John Dowland, and Thomas Morley, and the Queen herself fostered the fashion at court with her own accomplished playing of the virginals and her irrepressible love of dancing. In such a setting, poetry and music fostered each other in a form of symbiosis. On the one hand, poets composed lyrics to fit melodies which had already caught the popular fancy, so that William Webbe could record in 1586, '. . . neither is there any tune or stroke which may be sung or played on instruments which hath not some poetical ditties framed according to the numbers thereof'; and in the opposite direction, poets began writing their verses on the assumption that they would probably be set to music and thereby gain wider currency. The theory of a cosmic harmony produced by the spheres and echoed in all the arts provided a fresh sensitivity to the concord of sound in poetry, and to the proportion and decorum required in all its parts. George Puttenham summarised the view in 1589 by the definition: 'Poesy is a skill to speak and write harmonically; and verse a kind of musical utterance by reason of a certain congruity in sounds pleasing the ear.'[28]

Sidney had included some twenty poems in his *Arcadia*, but the turning-point for the poetry of the century proved to be his sonnet-sequence *Astrophel and Stella* ('The Star-lover and his Star') which, like his other writings, circulated only in manuscript during his lifetime. It was published posthumously in 1591 in an unauthorised edition and a corrected form appeared in 1598. The sequence contained over a hundred poems, mostly in the form known today as the sonnet (in that period the term included any brief lyrical poem), and the sequence was immediately acclaimed as ranking England with its European peers in the realm of poetry too. Individually, these sonnets exemplified the harmonious flow of sound which was to become the hall-mark of sonnet-eering verse in this era, the smooth integration of theme, image, and mood into a melodious whole, with a graceful turn of wit in the final lines. In Sonnet 39, the speaker, bemoaning the futility of his love for Stella, begs sleep to relieve him of his grief, offering as the most tempting bait the privilege of obtaining through his dreams a vision of Stella herself. The opening lines, foreshadowing Shakespeare's 'Sleep that knits up the ravell'd sleeve of care . . .', reveal in their mature grasp of human experience and the evocative range of imagery the qualities which were to distinguish the 'golden' era of Elizabethan poetry:

> Come sleep! O sleep, the certain knot of peace,
> The baiting place of wit, the balm of woe,
> The poor man's wealth, the prisoner's release,
> Th' indifferent judge between the high and low;
> With shield of proof shield me from out the press
> Of those fierce darts despair at me doth throw;

> O make in me those civil wars to cease;
> I will good tribute pay, if thou do so.
> Take thou of me smooth pillows, sweetest bed,
> A chamber deaf to noise and blind to light,
> A rosy garland and a weary head;
> And if these things as being thine by right,
> Move not thy heavy grace, thou shalt in me,
> Livelier than elsewhere, Stella's image see.

Quite apart from the improved quality of the individual sonnets with their masterly control of a genre which had always seemed experimental till now, the work as a whole marked a much firmer artistic discipline in structural form. The dominant medieval tradition had been to join separate stories such as legends of the saints loosely together in a collection. The mystery cycles had been presented as individual plays often performed simultaneously at various 'stations' with the audience wandering from one to another, not necessarily in the correct order, partly because that order was itself fragile when Noah was seen typologically in terms of Christ the Redeemer and Sarah hearing the news of Isaac's future birth represented the Annunciation. In the same way, within the sonneteering tradition Petrarch's *Canzoniere* had offered a series of sonnets consisting of variations on the theme of his love for Laura, in which, apart from the break which occurs at the news of her death and the consequent change to a more etherial love, there is little to suggest any integral development of theme. The sixteenth century began to reject that looser format, replacing it by a preference for a linear forward movement, a firm plot-line in drama, romance tale, and even poetry, which should proceed through a clearly defined sequence of events. It marked a literary counterpart to the concern with spatial and chronological perspective in Renaissance painting, a desire for a fixed placing of each event in time and locality.

In Sidney's *Astrophel* the sonnet sequence consists not of variations on the love theme, but an exploration of a lover's emotional experience as he progresses from the first sight of his mistress, through his gradual surrender to her spell, his anguish at the coldness of her response, his ecstatic achievement of a kiss, and on to his quieter sorrow at their enforced separation. The series of poems becomes individualised and

dramatically alive, often with a wry self-parody. Struck by
the beauty of his mistress's eyes shining at him beneath their
dark lashes, he cries out in mock warning to others:

> Fly, fly, my friends, I have my death wound, fly;
> See there that boy, that murdering boy, I say,
> Who like a thief, hid in dark bush doth lie . . .

The cliché of Cupid's darts is genially revitalised, yet the
genuineness of the love experience is preserved nonetheless,
and the immediacy of the emotion vividly conveyed.

With that rare ability to turn everything he touched to
gold, even his disappointment in love became transformed by
him into material for poetry. Penelope Devereux, the daughter
of the Earl of Essex, had been proposed to him for future
betrothal when she was only thirteen, but he had declined.
A few years later she blossomed into a beauty totally captivating his heart, but by then she had already been promised
to Lord Rich. Her marriage gave rise to the anguished self-
condemnation of Sonnet 33 for his having failed to seize the
glorious opportunity when it had been first offered to him,
though he admits that then he '. . . could not by rising morn
foresee / How fair a day was near.' That she is the object of
this sonnet sequence he acknowledges both in this sonnet and
in an earlier and rather spiteful attack on her husband which
contemptuously puns throughout on the name 'Rich'. On the
other hand, there can be no assurance how far the sequence is
autobiographical, particularly in view of the strong tradition
of artificial Petrarchan posing in contemporary poetry. Most
probably, Sidney used his own experience of frustrated love
as an emotional reservoir upon which to draw, without necessarily remaining faithful to the details of that relationship.
Whatever the degree of fidelity to his own life, the poems as
literary artefacts do create a powerful emotional and psychological realism. Whether he did in fact succeed in extracting
from her a kiss and was asked by her to remain silent or
whether it is all a figment of the imagination is immaterial, as
the passion and wild joy of the moment leap into life from
the concluding lines of Sonnet 81:

> Then since (dear life) you fain would have me peace,
> And I, mad with delight, want wit to cease,
> Stop you my mouth with still still kissing me.

As the final line suggests, Sidney, for all the heady excitement of love's rewards, had not forgotten the need for 'fine invention' in poetry, the witty turn of phrase or idea which Gascoigne had recently called for; and throughout these sonnets the melancholy of unrequited love is modified and enlivened by sudden shafts of humour or 'conceit'. Envious of the attention his mistress pays to her lap-dog, he ruefully complains:

> Dear, why make you more of a dog than me?
> If he do love, I burn, I burn in love . . .
> Bidden, perhaps he fetcheth thee a glove,
> But I unbid, fetch even my soul to thee.

One reason for the freshness of Sidney's sonnets is his rejection of the platitudinous images and stock terms which had come to bedevil contemporary verse. He scorns 'You that do dictionary's method bring / Into your rhymes,' and thereby merely echo 'poor Petrarch's long-deceased woes / With new-born sighs.' Instead his own muse instructs him to 'look in thy heart and write.' The result is not a rejection of the Petrarchan mode nor even of its conventional forms which continue to appear in his poems, but an attempt to personalise them, to revitalise the worn images by a new application or fresh tone, as in the Cupid passage above. In one of the loveliest of his poems, Sonnet 90, he extends to his beloved a delicate compliment, renouncing all claim to poetic fame because, as the last lines wittily explain, she herself is the source of his inspiration. Yet here too, the wit in no way detracts from the genuineness of the devotion, and indeed reinforces it. The broken rhythms of the second line, the enjambement of 'to frame / A nest . . .' and 'there should be / Graved . . .' testify to a poetry which has freed itself from the more rigid bonds of metre hampering so much English verse at that time, and which now conveys across the line-endings the throb of emotional or intellectual involvement, till the sonnet reaches its close in the quiet confidence of the final couplet:

> Stella, think not that I by verse seek fame,
> Who seek, who hope, who love, who live but thee;
> Thine eyes my pride, thy lips mine history;
> If thou praise not, all other praise is shame.
> Nor so ambitious am I as to frame

> A nest for my young praise in laurel tree;
> In truth, I swear I wish not there should be
> Graved in mine epitaph a poet's name.
> Nay, if I would, I could just title make
> That any laud to me thereof should grow,
> Without my plumes from others' wings I take;
> Since all my words thy beauty doth indite,
> And love doth hold my hand and makes me write.

Even when most obviously within the Petrarchan mode, the rejected lover complaining of the coldness of heart he has discovered in his mistress, he enlarges the dimension. Surrey had used the sonnet to admire the beauty of nature but Sidney's Sonnet 31 is one of the first instances in literature of the establishment of an emotional rapport between man and nature, the clothing of nature in the mood of the spectator. Sidney's speaker discerns in the pale face of the moon the mark of a fellow-sufferer from love's pains:

> With how sad steps, O moon, thou climb'st the skies!
> How silently, and with how wan a face!
> What, may it be that even in heavenly place
> That busy archer his sharp arrows tries?
> Sure, if that long-with-love-acquainted eyes
> Can judge of love, thou feel'st a lover's case;
> I read it in thy looks; thy languished grace
> To me, that feel the like, thy state descries . . .

The mingling of seriousness and wit which characterises Sidney's love poetry elevates it far above the platitudinous verse and complaints of so many contemporaries. The equation with the moon's lot may not be intended seriously and yet through that conceit the languid sorrow and melancholy longing of the frustrated lover come through with powerful effect, reinforced by the slow movement of the verse, its frequent pauses for thought, and the sympathy for the moon's sad lot applied by transference to his own condition.

A group of poems by Sidney for which he is less famed but which in his own eyes were no doubt of greater worth than his sonnets was his verse translation of certain *Psalms of David*, in which, like Wyatt and Surrey before him, he sought to poetise the literal English rendering. In his *Apology* he had, in defending poetry, pointed in justification to the 'divine poem' of David's psalter which '. . . is fully written in metre,

as all learned Hebraicians agree, although the rules be not yet
fully found.' The prose rendering of the psalms in the Authorised Version of 1611 was still to come, with its closely
literal rendering which conveyed the rhythmic doubling-back
of the original; but in Sidney's day something seemed sadly
lacking in a text whose superb imagery testified to its divine
origin yet whose rhythms moved clumsily along in the English
versions then available. There seemed here to be a challenge
for the poet to restore what had so obviously been lost in the
transfer. Unlike Sternhold and Hopkins whose aim had been
merely to adapt the text to a regular metre suitable for hymn-
singing, Sidney experimented with a variety of metrical forms
as he strove to capture the lilting movement which the content
of the psalm suggested. If for a moment we can forget those
later rhythms of the Authorised Version which have become
so much a part of our language, then the version which Sidney
provides is indeed distinguished, expressing the sentiment of
the biblical text with grace and delicacy in the cadences of
English poetry:

> The Lord, the Lord my shepherd is,
>   And so can never I
>   Taste misery.
>
> He rests me in green pastures His,
>   By waters still and sweet
>   He guides my feet.
>
> He me revives, leads me the way
>   Which righteousness doth take,
>   For His name's sake.
>
> Yea, though I should through valleys stray,
>   Of death's dark shade I will
>   No whit fear ill.

Each of the three genres in which he experimented, the
romance tale, the literary treatise, and the sonnet, Sidney
succeeded in raising to a new level, infusing them with a fresh
vitality, an enhanced sophistication, and an independence
from slavish imitation of continental models. He thereby
encouraged others to develop for England a new body of
Renaissance forms, inspiring Lodge, for example not only

to write his own romance tale but also a sonnet sequence. What he might have achieved had he lived beyond his brief years, particularly had he set his hand to the drama in which he displayed an interest within his *Apology*, must be left open to conjecture.

A fallen favourite

Sir Walter Ralegh (*c*.1552—1618) had one of the most colourful careers of any Elizabethan, rising from comparative obscurity as the son of a country gentleman to being the Queen's special favourite at court. Even when the Earl of Essex began to supplant him in her affections, he retained a position of eminence. A daring soldier and adventurer, he was knighted in 1584, and in the following year granted a royal patent to colonise Virginia; and he used his manifold activities to amass a large personal fortune. By the age of forty he was at the height of his powers, but then in 1592 he committed what was (next to treason) the most unforgivable crime known at court — he transferred his affections from the Queen to one of her maids of honour, who apparently lost her honour in the process. The Queen commanded him to marry the young lady, Elizabeth Throckmorton, and with the fury of a woman scorned, clapped both of them in the Tower. Although released by the end of the year, understandably Ralegh never regained his former position at court, and in the realignment of political forces at the accession of King James, was arrested and convicted of treason on an obviously trumped-up charge. He remained imprisoned for thirteen years and then in 1616 was briefly released to lead an expedition against certain Spanish settlements. On his return, the political situation had changed and a *détente* with Spain was being sought. Ralegh was at once arrested and publicly beheaded, ostensibly on the charges levelled against him in 1603 but really as a sacrificial victim intended to appease Spain.

In his day, Ralegh enjoyed an excellent reputation as a poet, and moved in literary circles. He was a friend of Sidney, Marlowe, and Spenser, being responsible for persuading the latter to publish the first instalment of *The Faerie Queene*. Unlike Sidney, however, he had no sister of literary bent to care for the posthumous publication of his poems, and since, in the custom still prevailing among the aristocracy, he disdained to publish his own verse, only a few of his poems have survived, mostly by chance, and those few cannot always be attributed to him with certainty. Even their dating is obscure, and the long-established tradition that certain poems were written in prison the night before he was beheaded, although it may add poignancy to their reading, has itself become suspect.

Within those extant poems we are offered an occasional glimpse of the vigorous, confident adventurer he must have been in his youth. *Serena*, probably written to his wife soon after their marriage, has the surge of passion associated with one who responds with vitality to the opportunities life holds out:

> Let's, then, meet
> Often with amorous lips, and greet
> Each other till our wanton kisses
> In number pass the days Ulysses
> Consumed in travel, and the stars
> That look upon our peaceful wars
> With envious luster. If this store
> Will not suffice, we'll number o'er
> The same again, until we find
> No number left to call to mind
> And show our plenty . . .

Yet even that affirmative call for love is set within the frame of a lament for the swift onset of death and decay; and the dominant mood of these surviving poems is disillusionment and world-weariness, suggesting that they belong to the period after his fall from power. His famed 'Reply' to Marlowe's pastoral poem 'Come live with me and be my love . . .' was not simply a witty rejoinder exposing the impracticality of the idyllic vision, as it might seem in isolation, but a deeper expression of his own loss of faith in the promises of youth:

> The flowers do fade, and wanton fields
> To wayward winter reckoning yields;
> A honey tongue, a heart of gall,
> Is fancy's spring, but sorrow's fall.

A peculiar charm of his poety is the ease with which his melancholy slips into the forms and cadences of the sonnet-

eering tradition. The lover's protest at the cruelty of his
mistress becomes here the sufferer's complaint at the cruelty
of fortune, and for all his bitterness, as in the Petrarchan
mode, a sweet melodiousness prevails, his laments suggesting
that even they are intended for accompaniment on the lute.
One such complaint, his 'Farewell to the Court', employs a
rare poetic form, a sonnet conforming in all points to the
normal pattern except that each quatrain concludes on the
same line — 'Of all which passed, the sorrow only stays' —
evocative of the recurrent refrain beloved in Elizabethan
song. Even in his most scornful moods, the use of a stanzaic
refrain such as 'And give the world the lie' modifies the
sharpness of his attack by preserving the poetic harmony of
the whole:

> Say to the court it glows
> And shines like rotten wood;
> Say to the church, it shows
> What's good, and doth no good.
> If church and court reply,
> Then give them both the lie.

From within this sense of blighted hope there gradually
emerges a source of comfort, a spiritual transcendence of the
disenchanting material world and a faith in the eternal world
beyond the grave. There he foresees, in obvious contrast to
the experience of his own false trial '. . . heaven's bribeless
halls / Where no corrupted voices brawl'; and the opening
of the poem from which that comes is a masterly interweaving
of the medieval morality tradition and the sophisticated world
of the Renaissance courtier, with the soul spurning the
gorgeous robes and envious strife of court in favour of the
old calm and simplicity of the pilgrimage towards heaven:

> Give me my scallop-shell of quiet,
> My staff of faith to walk upon,
> My scrip* of joy, immortal diet,   *wallet
> My bottle of salvation,
> My gown of glory, hope's true gage,
> And thus I'll take my pilgrimage.

Ralegh had also used his time within the Tower to compose
his prose work *The History of the World* (1614), whose care-

fully wrought cadences testify to the compelling rhetorical effects which could now be achieved in the language. He will pause at the account of a king's fall to offer the memorable apostrophe: 'O eloquent, just and mighty Death! whom none could advise, thou hast persuaded; what none have dared, thou hast done; and whom all the world hath flattered, thou only hast cast out of the world and despised.' His work stands, together with Richard Hooker's *Of the Laws of Ecclesiastical Polity*, as a monument to the new-found confidence and authority of English prose at the turn of the century, but where Ralegh's more impassioned writing is often close to a poetic prose, Hooker (1553–1600) writes with the more sober dignity of reasoned scholarship. In an age when religious disputation could be vicious in its acrimony, as in the Marprelate controversy, Hooker generously acknowledged that his adversary, the Puritan William Travers, was a good and sincere man, and rather than become embroiled in any personal animosity, he withdrew to the quiet of his study to compose his massively learned defence of Anglicanism and the Elizabethan religious settlement. Steering a middle course between the papal infallibility claimed by Rome and the right to individual interpretation of the Scriptures demanded by the Puritans, he argued majestically for that concept of order and rationalism within the state which forms the basis of Elizabethan hierarchy. The style, predominantly Ciceronian, is not captivating or brilliant, but relies upon the cumulative force of its solid argumentation. Occasionally, however, a more gentle and personal note enters, as in his warm plea to the Puritans to reconsider their position: 'The best and safest way for you therefore, my dear brethren, is to call your deeds past to a new reckoning, to re-examine the cause ye have taken in hand, and to try it even point by point, argument by argument, with all the diligent exactness ye can; to lay aside the gall of that bitterness wherein your minds have hitherto over-abounded, and with meekness to search the truth . . .'.

Court literature in the final decades of the century, notably in the poetry and prose of Sidney, Ralegh, and Spenser (who was admitted to those circles), displays, therefore, a rich maturity in both style and content, a more cultivated taste, a sweet melodiousness of sound, a widening range of imagery, and a more formal structuring. In contrast, the hack-writer's world during the same period had produced a vigorously strident tone, a wealth of new-coined phrases, lively innuendo, mordant satire, and a lusty showmanship dictated by the urgent need to catch the public's ear. Such apparently polarised literary forms were to merge and cross-fertilise in the one area which had by necessity to appeal to both social levels, the Elizabethan stage. It required on the one hand the patronage of the courtiers for its protection and on the other the regular attendance of the populace for its economic survival. The leading dramatists, moreover, were admirably suited to combine these divergent forms. Marlowe and Shakespeare, emerging from the hurly-burly of tavern life and the competitive world of the paid writer were yet, through their university or grammar school training, the heirs to a cultivated classical tradition. They were blessed, therefore, with a sensitivity both to the delicate nuances of the sonneteers and to the rumbustious gusto and colourful ribaldry of the Grub Street pamphleteers, and could draw upon that dual responsiveness in achieving the range and variety of their own dramatic creations, the stirring rhetoric of Tamburlaine, the languid poetising of Richard II, and the swaggering bawdiness of Sir Toby Belch.

8
Marlowe's mighty line

THE year 1564 saw the birth of both Marlowe and Shakespeare; but of the two, Marlowe was to mature more swiftly. By 1592, the date of the first recorded reference to Shakespeare as a playwright, Marlowe's career was almost over. He had burst unheralded upon the English stage some five years earlier at the age of twenty-three, completed the five great plays which were to transform the theatre, and was about to depart suddenly from it leaving the disturbing question of what more he might have done had he been granted more years.

By background Christopher Marlowe (1564—93) belonged to the world of the Grub Street writers. Born into the lower middle class to a fairly well established shoe-maker in Canterbury, he had by the age of fifteen attracted sufficient attention to be awarded a scholarship to the King's School there, and in the following year a further scholarship to Corpus Christi College, Cambridge. The six years he spent in college remain something of a mystery. From his subsequent writings we may deduce that he read deeply in the classics, yet, if the scholarly detective work by Dr Leslie Hotson is correct, part of that time he spend abroad in the English secret service, probably spying for the government upon the Catholic recusants in Rheims. As a result of his lengthy absences, he was nearly refused his degree and, perhaps for the same reason, seems to have attained to no academic distinction during the period of his studies. On being granted his degree, however, he moved to London and there achieved immediate acclaim with his play *Tamburlaine* which in its leading role launched the famed Edward Alleyn on his acting career, and which proved so successful that Marlowe was impelled at once to compose a sequel in order to capitalise on the play's popularity. Three further plays followed, probably with *Dr Faustus* as the last (the order of the plays following upon *Tamburlaine* has never been firmly established) and then at the age of twenty-nine his career was cut short in a tavern brawl.

His death may have been no more than the result of tempers inflamed by drink as the coroner's inquest declared, but his connection with the secret service, together with the fact that a few days earlier a warrant had been issued by the Privy Council summoning him to appear before them on a charge of atheism casts some suspicion on the circumstances of his death.[29] In connection with the latter charge, it is known that he became a member of Sir Walter Ralegh's little 'academy', a group of friends meeting for philosophical and scientific discussion which had been branded by pamphleteers 'The School of Night' or 'The School of Atheism' (even though Ralegh's writings testify to his own deep religious faith, and he was later cleared of such charges). Against Marlowe himself witnesses had declared before the Privy Council that he jested at the scriptures, suspected homosexual relations between Jesus and St John, and '. . . into every company he cometh, he persuades men to Atheism, willing them not to be afeared of bugbears and hobgoblins, and utterly scorning both God and his ministers.' Such testimony, important though it may be, cannot be taken entirely on face value. One witness, Kyd, was under threat of torture at the time and probably only too eager to deflect attention away from himself by incriminating others, while the latter quotation from Richard Baines sounds like an over-zealous response to Marlowe's disdain of foolish superstitions. Yet the charge was levelled, and presumably was based upon a reputation he had gained for some degree of religious scepticism.

He seems to have composed his *Dido, Queen of Carthage* while still at university, possibly in co-operation with Nashe. The title-page of the quarto edition announces that it was acted by the Children of the Chapel, and such performance by a boys' company would account for the large number of women and children in the cast. Attempts have been made to revive interest in it as drama, but it is so far removed from the vigorous theatre he inaugurated on leaving college that it has remained only a literary curio. Based upon the opening books of Virgil's *Aeneid* which relate Dido's desperate attempts to retain Aeneas' love, it is primarily a poetic piece with set speeches to be relished for their lyrical quality rather than their dramatic force. Marlowe's career as a playwright began in earnest only when he settled in London. With the supreme self-assurance of youth, he declared in the prologue to *Tamburlaine the Great* (1587) that his purpose was to break with prevailing traditions of the English stage, which he scathingly dismissed as merely '. . . jigging veins of rhyming mother wits, / And such conceits as clownage keeps in pay,' in favour of a new type of tragedy:

> We'll lead you to the stately tent of war,
> Where you shall hear the Scythian Tamburlaine
> Threatening the world with high astounding terms,
> And scourging kingdoms with his conquering swords.

We are, he informs us, to view his hero in a 'tragic glass'. But that term, it transpires, is a misnomer; for the first of the two plays to which this is the prologue (and which stood independently until his later decision to add a sequel) contains no hint of Tamburlaine's fall or death. In that regard alone it marked a significant innovation. *The Mirror for Magistrates*, which until Marlowe's day had constituted the main literary form of the chronicle, had continued the medieval concept of the wheel of fortune by presenting a collection of verse narratives devoted solely to the fall of princes. It claimed as its acknowledged moral purpose '. . . by example of others' miseries, to dissuade all men from all sins and vices.' Here, however, the moral seemed inverted, offering by example the achievement of kingship by a commoner, through ruthless and vigorous determination. Drawing upon a Spanish account, translated into English in 1571, of Timur the Lame (known commonly as Tamerlane), Marlowe presents the spectacular rise to power of a humble shepherd whose martial prowess and brilliant generalship eventually win him the command of the entire Mongol empire. His hero possesses a confidence and driving ambition, a desire for self-aggrandisement as well as the public humiliation of his conquered enemies which, in the previous morality tradition, would have served as classic instances of human *hybris*, the pride which inevitably calls down the thunderbolts of heaven. Entering after victory, he boasts in language which must at its first performances have sent ominous shivers down the spines of an Elizabethan audience:

> The god of war resigns his room to me,
> Meaning to make me general of the world:
> Jove, viewing me in arms, looks pale and wan
> Fearing my power should pull him from his throne . . .
>
> [Part I: V,i]

Yet so far from being dashed to his doom in punishment for setting himself above the gods, he proceeds to further victories, adding wider and richer territories to his already vast empire. Understandably perhaps, the romantics saw in Marlowe a Promethean rebel against divine authority, and in subsequent years he was widely regarded, partly on the basis of the charge of atheism, as a man inwardly committed to Machiavellianism and only outwardly conforming for safety's sake to the requirements of Christian belief (as in the final scene of *Dr Faustus* when the scholar is dragged down to hell for his sinful pact with the devil). In fact, as has since been shown,[30] *Dr Faustus* is in a very real sense a Christian morality play, with the final scene serving not as a sop to the Privy Council but as the consummation of the drama as a whole. We are therefore left with the strange phenomenon of a dramatist apparently challenging the moral assumptions of Christian belief and yet at the same time basically conforming to them.

As so often, the broader context of the era may help to set the problem in perspective. Michelangelo's fresco *The Creation of Adam* (*Plate* 7), painted at the height of the Italian Renaissance early in the century, also marked a break with tradition. As God stretches out his hand to infuse life into a recumbent Adam, there awaits him not the pale, thin creature familiar from medieval paintings, helplessly expecting God to raise him into life. Instead Adam is here a resplendently powerful figure, rippling with muscles and, as it were, graciously extending a hand only for the final touch of divine energy. His muscular torso represents iconologically the artist's new awareness of man's potential in this physical world. The Christian framework of the story remains, as the subsequent scenes in the ceiling fresco depict. Man will fall by sin and require heavenly redemption. Nevertheless, the artist, emerging from a medieval sense of man's subservience and impotence, sees with increasing wonder the creative strength that does lie within human control, the possibilities for individual achievement during his earthly existence. In England, Marlowe was the first to give expression to that fascination with human power in its magnificence and its temptations, its splendour and its corrupting influence. His major plays, in fact, explore in sequence four aspects of such power — imperial power in *Tamburlaine*, acquisitive in *The Jew of Malta*, monarchal in *Edward II*, and demoniacal in *Dr Faustus*. His purpose, it would seem, is not to subvert the established order. It is rather that in his imaginative conjuring up of such awesome might, swept along by the excitement of the vision, he transgresses at times the narrower bounds imposed by conventional religious or hierarchical norms.

The effect of this larger vision upon the English stage was immediate. By the magniloquence and the sense of infinity he conveyed, Marlowe outstripped the limited debates on political expediency which had served as the theme for serious drama, to enlarge the very concept of man presented there. Blank verse had already been used in the theatre but, partly by its enhanced subject-matter, it now became infused with a fresh vitality and vigour, creating what Ben Jonson was to call Marlowe's 'mighty line'. Beside his majestic verse, that of *Gorboduc* (praised by Sidney as the most impressive play yet written) is limp and cold. It seems by comparison to deal with petty dukedoms and spiteful, personal recriminations:

> PORREX: Shall I give leisure by my fond delays
> To Ferrex to oppress me all unware?
> I will not, but I will invade his realm
> And seek the traitor prince within his court.
> Mischief for mischief is a due reward.

In contrast, Marlowe's verse has a spaciousness and richness which tease the imagination. Tamburlaine lays at his mistress's feet the entire world in all its variegated wealth and sensuous delights, and thereby our vision of both the man who can command such opulence and the love which inspires the sacrifice becomes greatly enlarged:

TAMBURLAINE: A hundred Tartars shall attend on thee,
Mounted on steeds swifter than Pegasus;
Thy garments shall be made of Median silk,
Enchased with precious jewels of mine own,
More rich and valorous than Zenocrate's.
With milk-white harts upon an ivory sled,
Thou shalt be drawn amidst the frozen pools,
And scale the icy mountains' lofty tops . . ..

[Part I: I,ii]

The poetry is charged with the thrill of discovery and conquest. Kingship for Tamburlaine is not merely the honour of being seated upon the throne but the ability to wield power creatively, to strive ceaselessly for knowledge of the heavens and the earth in quest of all that lies within the reach of man. For that reason, the subduing of each realm, the defeat of previously potent kings, and even the ritualistic recital of exotic place-names added to his rule succeed, by erecting kingdom upon kingdom, empire upon empire, in producing an amplified sense of man's possible attainments:

TAMBURLAINE: Our souls whose faculties can comprehend
The wondrous architecture of the world,
And measure every wandering planet's course,
Still climbing after knowledge infinite,
And always moving as the restless spheres,
Will us to wear ourselves and never rest,
Until we reach the ripest fruit of all,
That perfect bliss and sole felicity,
The sweet fruition of an earthly crown.

[Part I: II,vii]

In that setting, the scenes of Bajazeth, the vanquished emperor of the Turks, confined within a cage and fed with scraps of food discarded by the victor, or of the enslaved kings forced to drag Tamburlaine's chariot serve less to depict his cruelty than to display the eminence of one who uses kings for his footstools. The very fact that the conquered monarchs are not cowed, but resist defiantly until death even in captivity, itself redounds to his greatness, displaying the regal dignity of those whom he has succeeded in overcoming.

In addition to the enhanced subject-matter, the play provided a powerful visual impact which helped gain Marlowe his popularity in the theatre. Bajazeth beating out his brains on the bars of his cage, the pathetically incoherent madness of his wife on discovering him dead (a scene imitated repeatedly by subsequent dramatists), the captured Olympia who, preferring death to disloyalty, tricks her enamoured captor into unintentionally slitting her throat before the audience's eyes, all these helped to move drama away from wordy debate into powerful theatre. We know something of the realism with which such scenes were enacted from the account of a mishap during an early performance. As the Governor of Babylon, for refusing to surrender to Tamburlaine's forces, is by his order hung in chains from the city wall to be shot at by the soldiers, one of the actor-soldiers misaimed '. . . and killed a child and a woman great with child and hurt another man in the head very sore.' In other words, the Senecan tradition of off-stage action reported by a messenger was clearly being deserted, while the goriness of those Senecan off-stage scenes, heightened to blood-curdling effect by the need to recreate them verbally, was retained now that they were being performed in full view.

Christian or Machiavel

The question of Marlowe's degree of identification with the ruthless and un-Christian self-interest of his main characters is less acute in *Tamburlaine*; for although firm in his commitment to his military principles the hero there rarely is vicious by Elizabethan standards of warfare. Before each battle, he offers his enemies the choice of joining him as honoured kings or governors under his command. Only when they persist in defiance does he gradually but irrevocably harshen the terms, knowing that any reversal would weaken the effectiveness of that stratagem for the future. The massacres he commits on determined resisters, loathsome as they may be to us, were normal concomitants of conquest in that era (witness the bloody compaigns of Cortez). *The Jew of Malta*, however, poses a different problem. Its central character, Barabas, is a figure of unredeemed evil, poisoning wells, destroying the sick, and deliberately driving men into bankruptcy and suicide. Yet he exerts a powerful fascination as we watch him at his machinations, free from the trammels of conventional moral sanctions.

In fact, the prologue, delivered in the person of Machiavelli, may provide the clue, although as in all drama much depends on how that prologue is read. Since plays in that era were intended not for publication but for performance, Marlowe would himself have instructed the actor in the method of delivery and he therefore adds no stage directions to the text. The idea that Marlowe was at heart a rebel against religious authority has received much support from the lines in that prologue:

> I count religion but a childish toy,
> And hold there is no sin but ignorance.

We should recall, however, that any attack on religion under Elizabeth, the supreme head of the Anglican church, constituted treason and, had that passage been delivered seriously, both playwright and actor would have been clapped into jail for sedition. In the following lines the prologue even couples with the 'fooleries' of religious belief the contemporary faith in the divine right of kings, yet this speech was never referred to in the investigations by the Privy Council just before his death, and seems to have aroused no protest at performances. The speech as a whole, therefore, must have been delivered in a tone of gloating villainy (in the tradition of the devils from the mystery plays), hence evoking from the audience a feeling of amused indulgence. In the same way, the Jew himself must not be romantically sentimentalised in modern terms as the suffering under-dog. For the Elizabethan, living in a country which had expelled all Jews some three centuries earlier, the Jew was synonymous with Judas. He was the figure of AntiChrist, here even bearing the name of the hated Barabas, the thief for whom Jesus, according to the Gospels, had been exchanged. His name and religion alone, therefore, would mark him out at once for the scorn and contempt of the Elizabethan. And from a reference in the text it is clear that he even wore in this play the 'snout' or false nose traditional for the villainous Judas figure of the mystery plays.

On the other hand, the evil within the play undoubtedly exerts a certain attraction; for as the prologue explicitly acknowledges in Machiavelli's name: 'Admired I am of those that hate me most.' If the philosophy of ruthless self-interest was morally abhorrent to the audience, the uninhibited power to which it could lead was compelling to the imagination.

The mixed feelings it evoked paralleled perhaps a modern audience's response to a film about a Mafia mobster or 'godfather', feared by his subordinates, loathed by his enemies, yet wielding through his very callousness and his amassing of untold wealth a sinister command over other men's lives.

There was also a contemporary motivation behind Marlowe's selection of this theme. As he was writing this play, England was experiencing a late awakening to the challenges of exploration and the search for new sources of wealth. Vasco da Gama, opening up the Cape route, had won for Portugal the fabulously rich spice trade of the East Indies. Spanish galleons were plying the seas laden with spoil from Cortez's conquest of the Aztec empire, and Marlowe's friend Ralegh was now urging Elizabeth to empower him to achieve similar wonders for England. He was planning to search, as he did a few years later, for the golden city of El Dorado and the Inca treasure reputed to be there. If *Tamburlaine* had .made the English stage aware of the new spaciousness of empires, *The Jew of Malta* was responding to the infinite riches such expansion could pour into the coffers of the adventurer and the merchant. The play opens, therefore, to reveal Barabas in his counting-house with heaps of gold coins before him and yet, like Tamburlaine, disdaining such paltry acquisitions compared with the untapped sources yet to be exploited, the 'infinite riches' that could be imported from overseas, from the Indian mines and wealthy Moors, from Greece, Malta, Alexandria and Spain:

> BARABAS: Give me the merchants of the Indian mines,
> That trade in metal of the purest mould;
> The wealthy Moor, that in the eastern rocks
> Without control can pick his riches up,
> And in his house heap pearls like pebble-stones,
> Receive them free, and sell them by the weight;
> Bags of fiery opals, sapphires, amethysts,
> Jacinths, hard topaz, grass-green emeralds,
> Beauteous rubies, sparkling diamonds . . ..

The Christians in the play are little better than Barabas himself, reneging on treaties when it suits their turn and arbitrarily confiscating the Jews' wealth and property when money is required for the state; yet their false dealing is in no way made to mitigate his own evil, which is of long standing. Finding in his recently purchased slave Ithamore an amusing yet equally heartless villain (a relic of the Devil's comic Vice from earlier drama), and making him his confederate in his plans, he confesses to him his own insatiable appetite for cruelty. If Marlowe's language exhilarates, his imagery elevates, and his scenes carry great theatrical force, his weakness as a dramatist lies primarily here in his characterisation; for the heroes and the villains of his plays lack the subtler shading and complexity we expect from great drama. Barabas is a figure of unrelieved diabolism, whose occasional flashes of caustic wit do little to deepen his portrayal. His daughter Abigail he uses callously as a mere pawn to further his intrigues, whether to recover the monies hidden in his requisitioned home or to play off her suitors against each other in order to lead them to their deaths. When she finally deserts him to join the nunnery, he displays neither regret nor grief, but like a stock villain of later melodrama, malevolently concocts a plan to poison her together with her fellow nuns, a plan which he unhesitatingly puts into execution. In that respect, Marlowe's plays show little advance over their predecessors, but the vitality of movement distracts from that failing, notably the sequence of spectacular scenes of violence culminating in the moment when Barabas is made aptly to fall into the boiling cauldron he had prepared for others — the traditional Elizabethan punishment for poisoners.

Edward II, as an exploration of monarchal power misused, a king's lack of wisdom in directing and controlling his realm, is ultimately a play about weakness. There are no daring flights of imagination, no conquests of vast territories or treasures, and for that reason the verbal exuberance with which Marlowe had captivated his audiences is muted. Yet in its depiction of the political repercussions of such weakness it presents with telling effect the magnitude of regal responsibility and the chaos that can ensue to the kingdom as a result of mismanaged rule. Moreover, by focusing upon a king succumbing to his homosexual impulses at the expense of the order of the realm, Marlowe was turning drama away from universal lessons on the fall of princes towards a concern with the individual, the conflict of a man torn between the demands of his office and his own sensuality. If Marlowe's characters still remain comparatively shallow, this work, produced at a time when Shakespeare was also experimenting with the genre helped to inaugurate the use of the chronicle play as a dramatic form closely allied to tragedy yet suited also to the patriotic needs of a country newly aware of its national heritage as it was preparing to challenge the supremacy of Spain.

The reduction in range of theme, while it produced a corresponding moderation in rhetorical force, also created a more flexible style which promised well for the future of drama. In the same way as euphuism had marked the 'adolescent' phase in prose, an intoxication with words before writers settled down to a more sober usage, so on the stage *Tamburlaine* had displayed the immense possibilities of blank verse in a burst of flamboyant rhetoric, like a plane roaring its engines to test them out before the carefully controlled take-off. The gory spectacles now become less frequent in the drama, the soaring imagery more subdued, and the stage is set for the more intimate perception of character interplay, as in Shakespeare's *Richard II* which in all likelihood took this play as its model. There is, therefore, a fresh naturalism of diction as Gaveston here plans his future manipulation of the newly crowned king:

> GAVESTON: . . . these are not men for me.
> I must have wanton poets, pleasant wits,
> Musicians that with touching of a string
> May draw the pliant king which way I please.

Marlowe himself was reputed to have had homosexual tendencies, and there are passages both in his *Dido* and in *Hero and Leander* which would seem to confirm the supposition. If it is true, then he is strangely unsympathetic both to Gaveston, the King's 'minion', and to the King himself. His disapproval is unambiguous as we watch the self-seeking upstart use his emotional hold upon the king to extract titles and appointments which allow him to flaunt his superiority over the legitimate earls and barons, and drive them reluctantly to rebellion.

In the first half of the play, only the Queen wins our regard, caught as she is between her genuine love for her husband and her knowledge that he has spurned her publicly in favour of a male. After Gaveston's murder, the King continues to alienate our sympathies as he persists in his ways, stubbornly substituting a new minion for the old, though he knows the peace of his kingdom is at stake. It is only at his deposition from the throne and his humiliating imprisonment in the cellar of a castle up to his knees in sewage that the polarity between his past splendour and his present degradation arouses compassion:

> EDWARD: And there in mire and puddle have I stood
> This ten days' space; and, lest that I should sleep
> One plays continually upon a drum.
> They give me bread and water, being a king;
> So that for want of sleep and sustenance
> My mind's distempered, and my body's numbed,
> And whether I have limbs or no I know not . . .
> Tell Isabel, the queen, I looked not thus,
> When for her sake I ran at tilt in France.
> And there unhorsed the Duke of Cleremont.

Absorbed by the political implications of a realm in disarray, Marlowe does not end the play with the King's murder but with the closing of a circle, the punishment of Young Mortimer. Whatever his justification, he had transgressed the rule prescribing the sacrosanctity of kings. In the final scene, he duly meets his death, but with dignified words evocative of the new age:

> YOUNG MORT.:   Farewell, fair queen; weep not for Mortimer,
> That scorns the world, and, as a traveller,
> Goes to discover countries yet unknown.

Forbidden knowledge

The Elizabethan playwright had a knack for selecting unpromising source-material and spinning from it a dramatic creation of incomparably superior quality. The legend of John Faustus, a medieval scholar who sold his soul to the devil in return for magical powers, had been popularly recorded in ballad and prose, either as a folkloristic lesson not to dabble in devilry or for the entertainment offered by the farcical tricks he plays on others when in possession of supernatural powers. For Marlowe the story offered different possibilities. He saw within the tale a parable epitomising a central spiritual dilemma of his time and one to which his own character made him particularly prone. In *Tamburlaine*, caught up by the surging conviction that nothing lay beyond man's power if only he willed it, Marlowe had made his hero boast of his equality with the gods as he proceeded from conquest to conquest. Yet within the Christian conscience could still be heard the ancient call for humility, the warning against eating from the forbidden tree of knowledge, and the threat of eternal torment beyond the grave for whoever fell into the sin of pride. In an age on the threshold of empirical enquiry, already questioning the authoritative assumptions of the past, the temptation to taste of such forbidden fruits was strong, and *The Tragical History of Dr Faustus* gave voice on the one hand to the power of that temptation to explore uninhibitedly the new areas of knowledge and, on the other, to the dread of damnation which Christian doctrine accorded to the transgressor. Whatever his personal leanings, Marlowe's ultimate commitment in this play is to the orthodox religious view, not only in the final scene of Faustus' agony. Throughout the play's earlier scenes too, the fearful implications of his pact with the devil are fully acknowledged and the reality of hell, by means of Mephistopheles' actual presence upon the stage, is left in no doubt. Yet within that traditional Christian framework the yearning for free intellectual enquiry and for the power which knowledge may bring is compelling, providing a dramatic ambivalence in which the play's appeal resides.

The splendid opening scene here, as in Marlowe's previous plays, creates the sense of man's unbounded potential by spurning as paltry all human achievements to date. Within a few compressed lines, man's intellectual, practical, and spiritual accomplishments are alternately relished and discarded. Philosophy has 'ravished' Faustus with its sweetness but, he discovers, it aims only at disputation; medicine's wondrous cures merely prolong earthly life, the majesty of law only settles petty divisions of property, and theology, which seems so far the best, teaches that man is doomed by original sin. Within the swift movement of thought, Faustus (and perhaps we, for the moment) forget the Christian alternative of salvation by faith, a fatal error which he will recognise only when it is too late. With theology disqualified, he turns with admiration to the forbidden world of magic and necromancy:

FAUSTUS: O what a world of profit and delight.
Of power, of honour, of omnipotence
Is promised to the studious artisan!
All things that move between the quiet poles
Shall be at my command. Emperors and kings
Are but obeyed in their several provinces,
Nor can they raise the wind or rend the clouds;
But his dominion that exceeds in this
Stretcheth as far as doth the mind of man.

Significantly, the knowledge he discards represents the attainments of the past classical or medieval heritages — the contributions of Aristotle, Galen, Justinian, and Jerome — while the vistas opening so attractively before him, although attainable only through necromancy, are associated by imagery with the limitless expanses, the untold opulence and puissance revealed by the Renaissance spirit of exploration.

With all its dramatic tensions and wide-ranging vision, the play remains a flawed masterpiece, quite apart from the triviality of certain scenes in which Faustus exercises his newfound power. The slapstick of the Pope's humiliation, the duping of the horse-dealer, and the supply of ripe grapes in winter were in any case probably the work of an inferior collaborator. They are certainly counterbalanced by the vivid account of his interstellar flight, the learned questioning of Mephistopheles on the nature of hell, and the noble apparition of Helen of Troy eliciting from him the enraptured cry, 'Here will I dwell, for heaven is in these lips, / And all is dross that is not Helena.' Those do indeed suggest the intellectual and aesthetic quality of his enquiry. The fault lies rather in Marlowe's failure to convey convincingly the inner struggle of Faustus, for here too, the characterisation remains twodimensional, insufficient for its task. An Old Man altruistically attempts to persuade him to repentance, assuring him that salvation is yet possible and Faustus, deeply moved, asks time to ponder. Mephistopheles threatens, and at once, within a few lines and with no emotional transition, Faustus swings to the opposite extreme, ordering 'that base and aged man' who had dared to dissuade him from Lucifer to be tortured with the greatest torments that hell affords. However superb the opening and close of the play as well as the moments of true greatness between, the grandeur of its theme cannot be sustained as long as the central figure lacks the dramatic refinement and subtlety to persuade us of his spiritual predicament.

On the other hand, in a reading of the text, the opportunity it offered for stage spectacle must not be forgotten, for that forms an integral part of its presentation. The play was enormously popular in its day, holding a leading place in the repertoire of Henslowe's company until the Puritan closure of the theatres. The scene of Mephistopheles' first appearance in too terrifying a guise for Faustus to bear, the apparitions of historical figures from the past, the parade of the Seven Deadly Sins were all, we know, accompanied by full theatrical paraphernalia, as '. . . shaggy-haired devils run roaring over the stage with squibs in their mouths, while drummers make thunder in the tiring house.'[31] The scene referred to in that account of a performance in 1620 is in all probability the climax of the play, as Faustus, in one of the supreme moments of Elizabethan theatre, makes his desperate plea for mercy while the chimes mark the passing quarters of his final hour. Even today such scenes retain their effect, but in a century still unsure of its rejection of the occult, diabolism was no game for the squeamish. In 1597, before his accession to the throne, James I had written a warning against dabbling in witchcraft or magic in his book *Demonology*. It is a tribute to the dramatic effectiveness of Marlowe's play and an indication of the feelings it must have aroused at that time that one group of players was reported during a public performance to have been struck with the eery sensation that there was 'one devil too many amongst them.' They broke off the scene, the audience fled in panic, and the players themselves understandably spent the night (quite out of character) in reading and prayer.[32]

Within the last great speech, the infinity that captivated Marlowe's imagination remains dominant. The measureless expanses which Faustus had contemplated so confidently as his future empire have now by inversion become the measureless aeons of eternal torture and damnation, to which he vainly pleads for some end, however distant:

> FAUSTUS: O God!
>> If thou wilt not have mercy on my soul,
>> Yet for Christ's sake whose blood hath ransomed me
>> Impose some end to my incessant pain:
>> Let Faustus live in hell a thousand years,

A hundred thousand, and at last be saved!
O, no end is limited to damned souls!

[V,ii,163—9]

Within the five brief years of his dramatic activity, Marlowe had charged the Elizabethan theatre with a new sense of grandeur, an enhanced awareness both of human magnificence and of human depravity. Moreover, to match that expanded imaginative range he had forged a blank-verse line resonant in force yet sufficiently flexible to convey the subtler nuances of poetic thought. If the plays he produced reveal, despite their achievements, the flaws of a dramatist not yet fully matured, the fault lay less with him than with fate, which seemed so perversely determined to cut short the lives of promising young writers throughout that century.

Other dramatists

Marlowe's associates in the theatre, friends and enemies alike, were making their own contributions to the stage, many of which have failed to survive. Among the most interesting which did is *The Spanish Tragedy* written some time between 1582 and 1592. It has been attributed with some certainty to Thomas Kyd (1558—94), who believed that Marlowe had betrayed him to the Privy Council and who attempted to return the favour with interest. The play had a checkered career, achieving great popularity in its day but serving at the turn of the century as an object of derision for its extravagance and lack of finesse. Taking the Senecan blood-tragedy as its theme with a ghost crying out for vengeance in the prologue, yet placing its scenes in contemporary Spain, the play develops a complex revenge plot filled with surprises and sudden twists which nonetheless holds together remarkably well. The ghost is, in fact, only the first of a series of interconnected revenge motifs, of which the central one is the murder of Horatio, to be avenged by his mad father by means of a play within a play. The hints of *Hamlet* have not gone unnoticed, although it is likely that Kyd wrote another play entitled *Hamlet* which failed to survive and which formed the more direct source for Shakespeare.

In language it falls far below Marlowe's plays, the monot-

onously end-stopped lines making the drama seem mannered
and contrived:

HIERONIMO:	Where shall I run to breathe abroad my woes,
	My woes, whose weight hath wearied the earth?
	Or mine exclaims, that have surcharg'd the air
	With ceaseless plaints for my deceased son?

[III,vii,1—4]

In two areas, however, it did mark a significant advance, in
plot and character. Where Marlowe's plays are episodic (the
order of Faustus' experiments with his power being quite
arbitrary), here the events are integrally related, creating a
firm sense of structural cohesion. The characters are still far
from subtle, but they are at least psychologically interesting
— a heroine indulging in clandestine love, a scheming murderer,
and a crazed father whose madness grows gradually upon him
after the discovery of his dead son and thus allows him to
develop effectively before our eyes.

The life of George Peele (1556—96), another contemporary
dramatist, probably outdid in excitement and variety anything he wrote for the stage. A man of singular poetic powers
and wide scholarship, he proved an inveterate spendthrift and
wastrel, continually scrounging and swindling his way out of
gaol or destitution until he died, reportedly of the pox. To
keep himself in pocket, he poured out an unending stream of
pageants, poetic addresses, and occasional pieces, together
with some works for the stage. His *Arraignment of Paris*,
performed before the Queen by the Children of the Chapel,
was a pastoral play concluding with the Judgement of Paris.
Three goddesses compete for a prize to be awarded to the
most beautiful. In Peele's version, at the vital moment Diana
the goddess of chastity enters, interrupts the contest and to
the acclaim of the competing goddesses, awards the victory
to the Virgin Queen seated in the audience. Even she seems
to have thought the compliment excessive, and never invited
him to present further plays before her. *The Old Wives' Tale*,
although entitled a comedy, was in fact, like the above, more
of a pageant, a charming hodge-podge of fairy-tales and folkloristic legends blended into an evening's entertainment. The
only true play he wrote was *The Love of King David and Fair
Bethsabe* (an old spelling for Bathsheba), registered in 1594.

It was a more sombre play than the title suggests for, despite the Ovidian opening exulting in the romantic love of the two, it is really a grim tragedy adopting the stern morality of the Old Testament. It moves from that adulterous love through the incest of Amnon and Tamar to the rebellion and death of Absalom which marks the final punishment for David's sin. Although generally careless of plot, here Peele uses the symbol of hair to unify the sequence of sin and retribution. With echoes of the 'Song of Songs', David declares in the opening scene:

> DAVID: Now comes my lover tripping like the roe
> And brings my longings tangled in her hair.

In the concluding section the metaphor becomes fact. Absalom is literally entangled in the boughs of a tree by the hair on whose beauty he prided himself. As he hangs helplessly before the dagger of his enemy Joab, the latter's words bring the wheel full circle:

> JOAB: Now Absalom how doth the Lord regard
> The beauty whereupon thy hope was built,
> And which thou thoughtst his grace did glory in?

What prompted the dissolute Peele to choose a biblical theme is open to conjecture. Perhaps he was shaken by the recent death and repentance of his close friend Greene. At all events his is the last extant biblical play written for the stage in England for the next three hundred years, when the inhibitions about mingling the sacred with the profane were finally overcome.

9

Early Shakespeare

THE first recorded reference to Shakespeare (1564—1616) as a man of the theatre, although intended as an insult, points to a quality immediately distinguishing him from most dramatists of his day and undoubtedly constituting a major source of his achievement — that he was a true professional. Unlike Lyly, Greene, Marlowe, or Peele who, as university wits, wrote for the stage mainly through force of circumstance while they were waiting to catch a patron's eye or obtain court preferment, Shakespeare arose from within the ranks of the players themselves. He was a full-time member of an acting troupe who, in addition to his duties as a performer, produced plays to be presented by his own company. Living within the world of the playhouse rather than as an outsider hired to provide dramatic texts, performing at court, touring the provinces, he could exploit his first-hand experience of stage and audience in constructing his scenes, rely upon his actor's knowledge of intonation and rhythm in penning a speech, and even tailor the roles of his plays to suit the specific talents of each member of his group. The clownish Dogberry was designed by him for William Kempe, the more subtle Feste for Robert Armin, the great tragic roles for Richard Burbage, and Hamlet's Ghost for himself. Understandably, therefore, Greene warned his fellow-dramatists from the universities to beware of this 'upstart crow', this Jack-of-all-trades who, although only an actor, '. . . supposes he is as well able to bombast out a blank verse as the best of you.'

The term 'bombast' which Greene instinctively used to characterise the drama of the university wits is itself suggestive of the difference in approach. Marlowe, as a scholar poet wishing to impress, could thunder up a magnificent blank-verse line in *Tamburlaine*, but he lacked the actor's finesse, the finely attuned ear for extracting from the variety of intonations those nuances of speech out of which can be created the specific individual that must be brought credibly alive upon the stage. Shakespeare possessed that quality to a remarkable degree even in his earliest plays where, instead of allowing the blank-verse form to dominate the speech and thereby produce a more stylised dramatic artefact, he gives precedence to the ripple of thought, the natural pauses and spurts which break up metrical regularity to create the living speech of a young girl, warm, eager, and bright, whose femininity no male disguise can hide:

> JULIA: . . . for at Pentecost,
> When all our pageants of delight were play'd,
> Our youth got me to play the woman's part,
> And I was trimm'd in Madam Julia's gown,
> Which served me as fit, by all men's judgements,
> As if the garment had been made for me.
>   [*Two Gentlemen of Verona* IV,ii,163—8]

That actor's sensitivity, valuable as it was in the advantage it gave him over other dramatists, would not alone have created the unmatched power of his maturer plays. Such skill demanded a psychological comprehension of human motivation astonishing in its profundity, an unrivalled poetic imagination, and a sense of structure which could unify these elements into a dramatically cohesive whole. And in listing such achievements, it must not be forgotten that Shakespeare possessed a further quality extremely rare in theatrical history, a dual pre-eminence in the disparate spheres of tragedy and comedy, at times interweaving the two in a manner which deepened and enriched the effectiveness of each.

In background, Shakespeare's social standing was in fact no lower than that of the university men, despite his description as an upstart. His father was a successful glover in the small market-town of Stratford-on-Avon who, although illiterate (signing documents with a mark rather than his name), attained to the respected position of high bailiff, the equivalent of mayor in the town. His prosperity, however, was short-lived and, although he was never reduced to selling their large family home, he was compelled to mortgage other property, before long was relieved of his position as alderman, and eventually was even excused from contributing to the fund for poor relief. This drop in fortune does not explain, however, why his son William never proceeded to university, since scholarships were, as we know, available for promising youngsters. The school at Stratford was of good standing, and it is generally assumed that he obtained there his acquaintance with the classics, but there are no records extant to confirm his attendance. On the other hand, there is clear documentation for the next step in his life, that on 23 November 1582, at the unusually early age of eighteen, he was married by a special licence to the daughter of a neighbouring family, Anne Hathaway, who was eight years his senior. Such early marriages were socially acceptable where a large dowry was involved, but in this instance the sum recorded was nominal. An entry in the parish register only six months later recording the birth of a girl, Susanna, to the couple would seem to explain the haste; and less than two years later in 1585 Anne presented him with twins, a boy Hamnet (who died young), and a second daughter Judith.

The next seven years in his life are blank and have given rise to much speculation. He may have been a schoolmaster, a soldier, a lawyer's clerk, an apprenticed actor; and there is nothing but guess-work to rely upon. By 1592, the year of Greene's attack, he must already have been established in London as a rising actor and playwright, particularly as Greene parodied there a line taken from one of his early plays, which readers, it was assumed, would easily recognise. Greene's attack was professional, not personal, and it is significant that in an age of venomous backbiting and professional jealousies not a single comment has been preserved from that era which was aimed maliciously at Shakespeare as a man. Greene died shortly after the attack, and when Shakespeare approached the printer with a mild remonstrance, the latter at once published an apology regretting that he had had any part in offending one of such civil demeanour, such excellence as an actor, and so fine a reputation for honesty and uprightness. It says much for the evenness of the dramatist's temper than Ben Jonson, who quarrelled bitterly with almost everyone he knew, and even killed an actor as a result of a dispute, remained, despite their literary competitiveness, a firm and loyal friend to Shakespeare, declaring after his death (with a hint at the new divinity of the creative artist), '. . . I loved the man, and do honour his memory on this side idolatry as much as any.'

Modern dramatists, at least since Ibsen, have become associated with the challenging of accepted norms, with a questioning of social patterns and moral assumptions in their desire for radical change; but Shakespeare was remarkably conservative in his views. In cosmology, he adopted the old Ptolemaic universe untouched by Copernicus, socially he supported the need for a clearly defined class order, and morally, although little concerned with the formalities of the Christian religion, he remained a firm upholder of its basic tenets, its insistence upon charity, love, and mercy, epitomised in his heroines Cordelia and Desdemona. Moreover, in contrast to the commonly held picture of artistic genius as highly neurotic, solitary, or suffering from extremes in mood, his friends repeatedly applied to him the term 'gentle'; praising his open and free nature and the pleasantness of his wit.

Shakespeare's dramatic career began inauspiciously. In 1592, just as he was beginning to make his name in the London theatre with his early *Henry VI* plays, a severe outbreak of plague closed down all the playhouses there, and was to keep them closed for two years. The players were even unwelcome in the provinces, which they usually toured when the London playhouses were shut, presumably lest public gatherings there should encourage similar outbreaks. The Earl of Pembroke's men, according to Henslowe, unable to cover their travel expenses, were '. . . fain to pawn their apparel for their charge', and there is evidence that they were eventually forced to sell their most treasured possession, the playbooks themselves. As a result the acting groups simply disbanded until the plague should abate. If the university men used the stage as a stopgap while they sought for patronage, Shakespeare reversed the process and now sought patronage to tide him over until the playhouses should re-open. In 1593, he published his non-dramatic poem *Venus and Adonis*, with a clear invitation for support in its dedication to Henry Wriothesley, the nineteen-year-old Earl of Southampton. The appearance in the following year of a second poem *The Rape of Lucrece* with a much warmer and more personal dedication to the same Earl suggests that his first poem had met with favourable response.

Non-dramatic poems

In the same year as Shakespeare published the first of those poems, Marlowe's *Hero and Leander* was, four months after its author's death, entered by a printer in the Stationer's Register with a note that the unfinished portion of the poem had been supplied by George Chapman. Although it was probably not published until later, the poem was widely known from that time, presumably circulating in manuscript, and, together with *Venus and Adonis*, it created a vogue for mythological verse narrative. Marlowe's poem particularly was immensely popular, being imitated and echoed by poets for at least two generations, partly for its elegant retelling of Ovid's tales and partly for its sly and amused undercutting of the classical myths. With an eroticism evocative of the tapestries now being hung prominently on the walls of Elizabethan homes, he recounts, for example, Mercury's attempt to seduce a pretty young shepherdess, in the process reducing the god to the very mortal level of any lusty young man:

> The while upon a hillock down he lay,
> And sweetly on his pipe began to play,
> And with smooth speech her fancy to assay,
> Till in his twining arms he lock'd her fast,
> And then he woo'd with kisses, and at last,
> As shepherds do, her on the ground he laid,
> And tumbling in the grass, he often stray'd
> Beyond the bounds of shame . . . .

Venus and Adonis, although sharing the honours with Marlowe's poem and itself widely praised in its day, has not retained universal admiration. Taking as its theme the love of the goddess Venus for a reluctant and bashful young boy and containing some vivid descriptions of the countryside, it suggests nevertheless that the poet was as yet more at ease in dramatising scenes for stage presentation than describing them through the mouth of a narrator, and the imagery here is often clumsy, to say the least. As the goddess embraces the boy against his will, the description scarcely encourages sympathetic identification:

> Forc'd to content, but never to obey,
> Panting he lies and breatheth in her face;
> She feedeth on the steam as on a prey,
> And calls it heavenly moisture, air of grace.

The picture of a mature female pursuing a tender young boy, and even at one point absurdly tucking him under her arm, is so lacking in amorous interest that a topical allegory has been suggested to explain the choice of theme — that it constituted an oblique encouragement to the young Wriothesley to continue to resist (as he did at the cost of a heavy fine) his guardian Lord Burghley's efforts to marry him to an apparently willing granddaughter.[33] The caricature of a handsome young man in flight from an amorously inflamed female would then have made a good deal more sense; but there is unfortunately no evidence from contemporary responses to the poem to suggest that any such topical reference was recognised. In contrast, *The Rape of Lucrece* makes no attempt either at coyness or eroticism, solemnly recounting the tragedy of the chaste Lucrece who was ravished by Tarquin and committed suicide after her disclosure of the crime. It is a competent poem but no more, offering little indication of the untapped powers of its author. Indeed, such a strained conceit as

> Even here she sheathed in her harmless breast,
> A harmful knife, that thence her soul unsheathed.

although intended seriously here, reads more like the comic suicides of Pyramus and Thisbe in *A Midsummer Night's Dream* than the noble deaths of Romeo and Juliet, indicating once again (since all three works were produced at approximately the same time) how much more at home Shakespeare was in managing his stage-work than in constructing narrative pieces.

The publication of Sidney's splendid sonnet-sequence *Astrophel and Stella* in 1591 had fired the imagination of the age, with every self-respecting poet trying his hand at the genre in the years following, until around 1596 the fashion died down as suddenly as it had arisen. Shakespeare, it is assumed, composed at least the major portion of his sonnet-sequence during that period, and we know from a reference by Francis Meres in 1598 that some of the poems must have been in circulation by then. Shakespeare himself apparently took no steps to have the sequence published as he did for his two narrative poems, and it was only in 1609 when the vogue was long past that an unauthorised edition was issued. The printer, Thomas Thorpe, was by then trading on Shakespeare's reputation rather than any current demand for such collections, and in fact no further edition appeared for over thirty years.

The collection contains some of the loveliest poems in the language, although the quality is not consistent throughout, some of the sonnets seeming to be merely exercises or variations on a theme. Sidney's innovation, adopted eagerly by his imitators, had been to thread the individual sonnets into a whole by weaving the poet's expressions of longing, hope, frustration and joy into a unified narrative fabric. The developing relationship between the poet and his mistress was thus perceived through the sequence of changing moods, with the obliquely-told story adding interest to the forward movement. Shakespeare's sonnets break with that convention in two respects, first in addressing the major portion of the love poems to a young male in place of a mistress, and secondly in broadening the cast to include four participants. He adds a raven-haired mistress, addressed mainly in the latter poems, as well as a second poet who proves to be a rival of the sonneteer not only in the literary sphere but also for the loved one's affections.

The emotional intensity of these sonnets as well as the unity of the speaker's character throughout make it difficult to resist some degree of autobiographical reading. As Thorpe prefixed to his edition the enigmatic dedication: 'To the only begetter of these ensuing sonnets, Mr. W.H.', a scholarly treasure-hunt has been continuing for many years in search of the young male aristocrat who inspired Shakespeare's affection, the 'dark lady' who aroused his jealousy, and the rival poet who was the cause. None of the candidates put forward so far has won any degree of scholarly consensus. Among the more popular suggestions have been the Earl of Southampton (whose initials would need to be reversed and title dropped in order to fit the Thorpe dedication), a court lady-in-waiting, Mary Fitton, as the dark lady, and perhaps Marlowe as the rival. The entire search, however, may well be less a treasure-

hunt than a wild-goose-chase. It is, after all, the finished poem
which counts, the literary transformation of experience into
art rather than the raw material out of which it is created,
and the identity of the participants in the double love-triangle
can have little bearing on our appreciation of the sonnets
themselves, belonging more to literary gossip than literary
criticism.

Although not the inaugurator of the sonnet-form which
bears his name (it had first been used by Wyatt), the use
he makes of the final couplet is entirely his own, endowing
his sonnets with their exquisite balance and structural integrity. The main body of the poem, the series of three quatrains
often broken by a slight shift of direction after the octet,
conveys the personal emotion, the speaker's involvement in
his own fears, joys, or discontent. Then at the conclusion
there comes a momentary distancing, an ability to observe
the experience in a wider context which elevates the poem
from personal introspection to resonant universality:

> Weary with toil, I haste me to my bed,
> The dear repose for limbs with travel tired;
> But then begins a journey in my head,
> To work my mind, when body's work's expired:
> For then my thoughts, from far where I abide,
> Intend a zealous pilgrimage to thee,
> And keep my drooping eyelids open wide,
> Looking on darkness which the blind do see:
> Save that my soul's imaginary sight
> Presents thy shadow to my sightless view,
> Which, like a jewel hung in ghastly night,
> Makes black night beauteous and her old face new.
>   Lo! thus, by day my limbs, by night my mind,
>   For thee and for myself no quiet find.

Within this sonnet can be perceived the wealth of imagery
which Shakespeare brought to poetry. Where earlier poets
had used simile or metaphor primarily as comparisons to
illustrate their local themes — the mistress's eyes likened to
Cupid's arrows or the lover himself to a foundering ship — he
employs them to create an exploration of human experience
at large, however narrow the specific topic may be. Here, the
disturbed sleep of the lover becomes a journey, then the pilgrimage of a soul searching, as in the religious tradition, for

illumination in the darkness, and finally that search is rewarded as the beauteous vision is imaginatively imposed upon the blackness of the night. Throughout the poem, a contrast is drawn between, on the one hand, the physical world, the wearied limbs after a day's long travel or the darkness perpetually before the blind man's eyes, and on the other the emotional or inner response, the journey in the mind, the thoughts that conjure up imaginary sights. Yet what might have concluded on a note of exhilaration as the gratifying image appears is instead modified by a rueful admission, the more universal axiom in graceful tribute to the beloved, that true devotion permits rest neither by night nor day.

As these sonnets explore their central themes of time's destructiveness, the eternity of art, or the jealousies of love, the richly variegated metaphors and similes draw into the poem the multitudinous aspects of human life. A mood of sad reminiscence:

> When to the sessions of sweet silent thought
> I summon up remembrance of things past . . . .

evokes the setting of a lawcourt; a sense of life's brevity (Sonnet 73) conjures up a wintry avenue of trees bare of feathered choristers and, by association with their overarching boughs, the vaulted choirs of some deserted abbey here prefiguring the eventual silencing of his own poetic voice; the union of two kindred souls, 'Let me not to the marriage of true minds / Admit impediments,' echoes the wedding service from the *Book of Common Prayer*; and the thought of a lover 'too dear for my possessing' in ironic contrast introduces talk of financial bonds, and commercial estimates (Sonnet 87). All this with a subtle exploitation of linguistic ambivalence and connotation which creates a deeply satisfying and multilevel response. Sonnet 146, for example, a moving meditation on man's spiritual responsibilities in this world begins:

> Poor soul, the centre of my sinful earth,
> Thrall to these rebel powers that thee array . . . .

Through the duality of the word 'earth', the soul is seen simultaneously as the spirit or angel directing the terrestrial

globe in accordance with Elizabethan ideas of planetary movement and also as the human dweller trapped within a lump of
clay, the mortal flesh which will after its many sins return to
dust and soil. In the next line, the surprising discrepancy
whereby the soul has suddenly become a king captured by
rebellious troops 'lined up' before him is magically resolved
by the secondary meaning of 'array' as 'clothe'. The soul in
this composite image is thus seen as wearing a garment of
perishable flesh which rebels against its own divinely appointed
ruler. It is then urged by the speaker to starve that outward
self in order to nourish the inner, and the sonnet concludes
with a couplet vividly consummating and unifying the complex metaphors of the earlier quatrains, and now opening out
its triumphant message to all mankind:

> So shalt thou feed on Death, that feeds on men,
> And Death once dead, there's no more dying then.

The poetic quality of these sonnets has some bearing upon
the achievement of Shakespeare's poetic dramas, but it is not
directly transferable, for the stage works were not simply
plays employing verse. They employ instead a distinctively
dramatic poetry; that is, verse which in addition to its wide-
ranging imagery and sinewy connotative force, exploits also
the dramatic context in which it is spoken. Read in isolation,
the following passage might be thought pleasantly written,
but little more:

> Peace, peace!
> Dost thou not see my baby at my breast
> That sucks the nurse asleep?

Yet its setting transforms it. Murmured by Cleopatra as she
puts the fatal asp to her breast, it is inexpressibly powerful
in its effect. The quiet maternal scene becomes instead a
haunting metaphor, unusually associating death with the rich
satisfaction of contentment and fulfilment as the queen goes
willingly to join her Antony beyond the grave. Similarly, out
of context the lines

> O thou weed,
> Who art so lovely fair and smell'st so sweet
> That the sense aches at thee . . .

might seem part of an ode to the flowers of the field but
addressed to Desdemona by an agonised Othello, they throb
with his passionate conflict between tender love and destruc-
tive jealousy.

In such poetic dramas, the images function not only to
heighten the immediate effect but also to suggest obliquely
the submerged themes of the drama as a whole, and modern
scholarship has become sensitised to the 'clusters' of such
images within each play which cumulatively create the specific
ambience of that drama and can serve as valuable pointers
to its underlying concepts. *Macbeth* includes reiterated metaphors of clothes too large for the wearer to fill, symbolising
the usurper's unsuitability to the robes of majesty; the poetry
of *Hamlet* abounds with references to putrefying weeds and
festering ulcers; and dispersed throughout *King Lear* are
metaphors of eyes perceiving inner truth, underscoring by
contrast the spiritual blindness that is afflicting the king.[34]
With that rare ability to make his text perform at any single
moment a number of different tasks, such images serve at the
same time to suggest to us certain hidden traits of the speaker,
whose instinctive choice of such metaphor may reveal qualities
of which he himself is unaware. Richard II's extravagant conceits betray the weakness for self-dramatisation that will cause
his downfall, Iago's animalistic descriptions of love his own
crude lustfulness and contempt for romantic illusion. And in
elevating his themes to universal splendour Shakespeare will
place within the mouth of a leading character cosmic images
which make the limitless heavens participants in the drama
being enacted before us:

> OTHELLO: Methinks it should be now a huge eclipse
> Of sun and moon, and that the affrighted globe
> Should yawn at alteration.
>
> [V,ii,99]

Yet however elevating the tragedies may be through this sweep
of verse imagery, the speech intonations he developed as an
actor ensure that the drama remains securely in the world of
human experience. Catering not only for the courtiers but
also for the groundlings unfamiliar with rarefied verse-forms,
Shakespeare produced a dramatic verse so easily assimilated by
the ear that, except for the heightened awareness it produces,

it is comprehensible and natural in movement and, unlike
Marlowe's figures, the characters seem scarcely to be speaking
in metre. That quality is highlighted in *Hamlet* where the
play-within-the-play needs by contrast to the enveloping
drama to sound artificial, and there Shakespeare resorts to
predominantly end-stopped lines reminiscent of the 'bombast'
beloved by most university men:

> PLAYER KING: 'Faith, I must leave thee love, and shortly too;
> My operant powers their functions leave to do:
> And thou shalt live in this fair world behind,
> Honour'd, belov'd; and haply one as kind
> For husband . . ..   [III,ii,184—8]

Set beside that passage, the verse of the outer play, in a similar
moment of farewell, is markedly supple and unstrained:

> LAERTES: My necessaries are embark'd: farewell:
> And, sister, as the winds give benefit
> And convoy is assistant, do not sleep,
> But let me hear from you.
>   [I,iii,1—4]

As a man of the theatre, Shakespeare took little care over
the preservation of his texts, and even the Quartos of the
individual plays (so named after the more convenient size of
the printed pages intended for the actors' use) seem to have
been produced without his close supervision. As a leading
member of the only company authorised to perform them,
he could be present at rehearsals to provide any necessary
stage directions, to rewrite a speech to suit some change or
direct what cuts to institute for a shortened version, and to
correct any errors which might have crept into the printed
text. On the other hand, some Quartos are so badly produced
and so obviously corrupt that they are presumed to be pirated
texts used by rival companies, '. . . diverse stolen and surrep-
titious copies, maimed and deformed by frauds.' They were
probably recorded by a combination of short-hand notes
taken during a performance and the later recall from memory
by one of the outside actors hired by the Lord Chamberlain's
Men for one of their own performances. Only eighteen out of
the thirty-seven plays firmly attributed to Shakespeare have
been preserved in Quarto form, and they alone would have

survived for later generations were it not that a few years after his death two members of his company, John Heminge and Henry Condell, undertook to collect and publish his dramatic works, obtaining permission from others who had managed to purchase ownership of individual plays. In 1623, they together issued what has come to be known as the First Folio, because of the larger format of its printed page. In general, it is carefully and conscientiously produced, but since in the system of those days pages were printed off as soon as they had been set and corrections made later by the proof-reader were inserted only after a number of copies had already come off the press, no two copies of the Folio are identical. Hence the need for textual footnotes comparing discrepancies between Q2 or F1 in most modern editions of the plays.

The early comedies

The earliest of Shakespeare's plays are clearly indebted to the traditions he found on entering the theatre. The series of three plays on *Henry VI* follows the genre of the chronicle play, and *The Comedy of Errors* is a reworking of Plautus, with two pairs of twins creating amusing situations of mistaken identity but little beyond that. *Love's Labour's Lost* is a more subtle play developing Lyly's courtly drama and, like his, clearly aimed at an aristocratic audience. It makes sophisticated fun of the fashionable sonneteering tradition at which Shakespeare was then trying his hand, the plethora of new words pouring into the language from abroad, the ornateness of euphuistic prose and other topical themes many of which are no longer identifiable. But it also contains in embryonic form what was to prove a central theme of his later comedies, the recognition that whoever walks with his head in the clouds is liable to trip over a footstool. A group of four noblemen, one of them the King, determine (with echoes of Ficino's Platonic academy) to withdraw from the world and devote themselves to philosophical study, thereby making their court 'a little Academe'. Solemnly forswearing the company of women for a period of three years in pursuit of their lofty ideal, they forget in their scholarly preoccupation that an embassy of four charming young ladies led by the Princess of France is due to pay a formal visit. The ladies soon captivate their hearts, outwitting the supposed scholars in humour and wisdom so that the hapless young men wander about ludicrously pinning sonnets on trees with great secrecy lest their colleagues discover them to have betrayed their oaths. The message is clear, the healthy reminder for his era that philosophy and life must never be divorced. A further hint of things to come, often ignored by feminists protesting at male dominance in literature, is the way that here, as in his later comedies, Shakespeare, though himself a male, generously accords pride of place to his heroines in wit, perceptiveness, and sheer intelligence, as they outclass the men in the love-game and, indeed, direct them by their greater insight to the true standards by which mankind should live.

In *A Midsummer Night's Dream*, (*c.* 1595) Shakespeare introduced a new dimension into his art, the exquisite fairy-land forest or enchanted 'green world' of the imagination which as so often in his subsequent plays serves as the contrast to the harsh realities of human existence, represented by the city. Four lovers, who might so easily have paired off happily, have perversely (for such is the way of the world) become enamoured of the wrong partners. Helena loves Demetrius who loves Hermia who loves Lysander; and Lysander's reciprocation of Hermia's love is blocked by her father's bitter opposition, who threatens to invoke the death penalty if his daughter persists in filial disobedience. The two lovers, with the rejected suitors trailing behind, flee into the wood on midsummer's night when the elves and fairies come out to play, and there is a sense of relief as they leave the city's threats and the rigid laws of society behind them.

The fairyland which Shakespeare creates is a triumph of word over matter. Upon the stage, in contrast to cinema montage, the elves and fairies must appear in human size. Only the language of the play, the verbal images and light texture of the verse can conjure up the requisite illusion of minuteness, of diaphanous shapes in swift, airy flight. The fairies talking of tiny spiders, beetles, newts and snails which inhabit their little world, seem themselves to shrink in size as they speed off to perform such microscopic tasks as hanging a pearl of dew in a cowslip's ear, with a song whose darting movement is evocative of the quick, weightless flight of small winged creatures:

> Over hill, over dale,
>   Thorough bush, thorough brier,
> Over park, over pale,
>   Thorough flood, thorough fire,
> I do wander every where,
> Swifter than the moon's sphere . . . .
>
> [II,i,1—7]

Yet this lovely dream-world is not escapist, as it might first appear. The bewitched forest is in fact a projection of actuality into dream, an imaginary world in which the mind can float freely, untrammelled by the restrictions of society, space or time; and yet, while doing so, explore the complexities, of life itself. There too, it transpires, love has its problems, with Oberon the king of the elves quarrelling with his fairy queen Titania for neglecting him in favour of the young boy to whom she has transferred her affection. Puck's magic potion, which produces in exaggerated and parodying form that very perversity of love's affections afflicting both her and the fleeing lovers by making them fall passionately in love with the first creature they set eyes upon on waking, presents us with Titania ridiculously enamoured of an ass-headed fool. The human lovers who had, until now, been eagerly pursuing each other in one direction, promptly turn about to pursue each other equally vainly in the opposite direction. From his perch on a bough above, Puck pronounces chorically the message of the play: 'Lord, what fools these mortals be!' As dawn rises and they awake from their trance, spirits and humans alike see in broad daylight the injudiciousness of their ways; and the lovers, now paired off more appropriately, can return to the real world bearing with them the lessons of their long night's dream, restored as they now are to spiritual well-being:

> DEMETRIUS: The object and the pleasure of mine eye
>   Is only Helena. To her, my lord,
>   Was I betroth'd ere I saw Hermia:
>   But, like in sickness, did I loathe this food;
>   But, as in health, come to my natural taste,
>   Now do I wish it, love it, long for it,
>   And will for evermore be true to it.
>
> [IV,i,174—180]

Bottom the weaver is one of a number of delightfully comic figures drawn, like Dogberry, from England's lower class.

Puffed up with an unfounded pride in his own histrionic powers, he also crosses the border into the enchanted wood, only to be proved an ass. Too obtuse to benefit from his lesson, he proceeds on his return to present with his rustic crew the hilariously inept performance of 'Pyramus and Thisbe' before Theseus and Hippolyta, whose wedding celebration forms the outer frame for the entire play. After his masterly creation upon the stage of the illusory world of enchanted forest handled with such delicacy and charm, Shakespeare could afford to make fun of the clumsy dramatic amateurism which must still have persisted in many strolling companies at the time he himself joined the professional stage.

History and romance

In no period of Shakespeare's career did he confine himself to any one genre, and parallel with these early comedies he was producing a series of chronicle plays which, although originating with the didactic tradition of 'fortune's wheel' and the fall of kings, was developing well beyond that theme. He was aware that the English monarchy was more precariously poised than many were prepared to admit; for the throne rested on two contradictory principles. There was not only the belief in an inalienable divine right conferred by hereditary succession as part of the hierarchical pattern of the universe, but also a more practical element often underplayed in criticism of these plays, the necessary consent of the people, expressed not by direct vote but through the leaders of the shires. Where Greek tragedy had explored the conflict between a pre-ordained fate and man's determination of his own destiny, Shakespeare was fascinated by a similar paradox implicit in sovereignty; on the one hand the profound belief: 'There's such divinity doth hedge a king / That treason can but peep to what it would', and on the other the knowledge, proved repeatedly by history, that a monarch must prove morally and politically worthy of governing his kingdom or risk forcible removal by his people.[35] Sacrosanctity had to be inter-locked with political reality. How close he came to touching the sensitive nerve of Elizabethan politics is indicated by Queen Elizabeth's angry rejoinder when it was mentioned to her that his *Richard II*, the drama of a king deposed by his people, had been widely quoted at the Earl of Essex's trial for treason: 'I am Richard II,' she said, 'know ye not that . . . this tragedy was played forty times in open streets and houses.' The only reason that Shakespeare himself was not charged or even frowned upon by the Queen was that he had written the play well before the attempted rebellion, and its aptness to the new conditions was only exploited later by the followers of Essex to rouse public support. This incident, at the very least, shows how his treatment of those historical themes was perceived as directly relevant to the contemporary problems of kingship by his audiences and, not least, by the monarch herself; particularly as, in general, it offered strong support to her position as a sovereign succeeding to the throne by right of birth and proving in the eyes of the overwhelming majority of her subjects supremely worthy of her crown.

These history plays, therefore, investigate the workings of these contradictory claims to kingship, and the qualities demanded from the monarch in order to win both divine and popular justification for office. In *Richard III* (c.1592), for example, he provided a powerful study of one who ruthlessly clambers to the throne over the murdered bodies of all who stand in his way. By eliminating all contenders, he does eventually ascend by rightful succession; but by then his crimes have disqualified him either for heavenly or for lasting political approval. Accordingly, he meets his end after a dreadful nightmare symbolising divine condemnation and in a battle instigated by popular revolt against him. Here, in Shakespeare's first great presentation of villainy, he displays the power of penetrating into a character to perceive the human qualities even of a monster. Richard's opening speech surprises us by winning our sympathy. However momentary that conscious sympathy may be, it remains submerged within us throughout the play; for stepping forward in his misshapen form, he disarmingly points directly to that hunchback with which he was endowed at birth, as the source of his malice. If, through no fault of his own, he is barred by nature from succeeding as a handsome lover or courtier, then he must of necessity find some more devious path to self-fulfilment:

RICHARD: I, that am rudely stamp'd and want love's majesty
To strut before a wanton ambling nymph;
I, that am curtail'd of this fair proportion,
Cheated of feature by dissembling nature,
Deform'd, unfinish'd, sent before my time
Into this breathing world, scarce half made up,
And that so lamely and unfashionable
That dogs bark at me as I halt by them . . . .

Such reasoning cannot excuse, but it can explain, creating that ambivalence of audience response resulting from Shakespeare's refusal to oversimplify, which so distinguishes his art.

In the subsequent *Richard II* (*c.*1596) he moved back in time to inaugurate a series of four plays intimately concerned with these themes of monarchy. The first of them presents, like Marlowe's *Edward II*, a king whose weakness makes him unfitted for the throne; but where Marlowe depicted that weakness in simpler terms, the factually political ineptness of advancing favourites over the heads of the barons, here the fault is internalised, becoming a much subtler blemish of character. Shakespeare makes Richard a sensitive, poetic, brooding king, an early version of Hamlet, missing his opportunities as he philosophises on the sadness of his own lot. Like many of Shakespeare's later tragic heroes, Richard falls through qualities which in other circumstances might be admirable, but which disqualify him for the specific task in hand. Bolingbroke, the future Henry IV, a practical man of affairs, deposes him and, by uttering before his noblemen the wish that he could be rid of the imprisoned Richard, ensures his murder in Pomfret castle. Written during Shakespeare's lyrical period, the play has some remarkable soliloquies, increasing in richness as Richard weakens in power, but it was in the two parts of *Henry IV* which followed, and the concluding *Henry V* that the full implications of this royal deposition were investigated.

However unworthy of kingship Richard II may have been, Henry IV, by having shed the sacroscant blood of a king even indirectly is thereby disqualified from sitting securely upon the throne, and after a rule racked by care and distress at home and abroad, he dies in symbolic atonement in a room named 'Jerusalem'. Only the next generation, his son Prince Hal, free from that stain, has the right to succeed as natural heir; and the focus of these two plays is on the second prop of kingship, his growth and maturity towards personal worthiness for office and the right to his people's full confidence. Many earlier dramas in the century had dealt with the choice between virtue and vice, but Shakespeare has far outstripped such commonplace treatment. The virtues to which Hal must eventually attain are honour, heroism, dedication to his cause, and the courage to risk his life unhesitatingly in the service of justice, truth, and country. Into that very setting Shakespeare introduces the lovable Falstaff, uproariously representing the gratification of the body's needs, the satisfaction of appetite, the pleasure of living for the moment and postponing the reckoning to tomorrow which may never come. He is the Seven Deadly Sins of the Middle Ages rolled up into one enormous ball of flesh. He is Gluttony, Lust, Sloth, what you will, yet so humorously attractive that he threatens repeatedly to undercut the very moral values which the play is asserting. As the gross materialist, the creature of meat and drink, of whores and carousal, he reminds us at moments of splendid dreams and high endeavour that man is for all his aspirations a body demanding victuals and the slaking of thirst. At a climactic moment in the play, as the heroes prepare to face death or injury on the battle-field in the cause of patriotic duty, Falstaff, alone on the stage, articulates for the audience the very question that each of us must ask himself at such times, however inwardly and however silently — does honour pay? Against the noble ideal is placed the disconcerting reality:

PRINCE HAL: Why, thou owest God a death (*Exit*).
FALSTAFF: 'Tis not due yet: I would be loth to pay him before his day. What need I be so forward with him that calls not on me? Well, 'tis no matter; honour pricks me on. Yea, but how if honour prick me off when I come on? how then? Can honour set-to a leg? no: or an arm? no: or take away the grief of a wound? no. Honour hath no skill in surgery, then? no. What is honour? a word. What is in that word, honour? What is that honour? air. A trim reckoning! — Who hath it? he that died o'Wednesday. Doth he feel it? no. Doth he hear it? no. Is it insensible, then? yea, to the dead. But will it not live with the living? no. Why? detraction will not suffer it: — therefore I'll none of it: honour is a mere scutcheon: and so ends my catechism. [*I Henry IV*,V,i]

Hal's dissolute carousing with Falstaff, although contrasted with the dedicated fervour of the firebrand Hotspur, is so fun-filled and carefree in its humour as to outshine the solemnity of court. Eventually, the prince must discard Falstaff as, at the end of the second play, he takes upon himself the responsibilities of kingship; but the pang of regret we feel in that scene of rejection is a tribute to Shakespeare's broad humanity, the perception he has given us that, whatever the stern moralists may say, Henry V will be a finer man for his knowledge of the two worlds, a king who will succeed more fully in understanding his subjects and, indeed, himself, because he has tasted the pleasures of self-indulgence and therefore knows its attractions as well as its evils.

With those lessons learnt, *Henry V* can now concentrate upon the stirring call to arms for king and country, and Laurence Olivier's judicious choice of this play for filming in World War II boosted the courage of the British, also fighting against superior odds. In theme, it presented a nation's self-reliance under God, determined in the justice of its cause, and the scenes of the monarch wandering in disguise among the camp fires before battle to test the temper of the people suggested a deep bond between throne and populace which must have been heartening to Elizabeth.

In stagecraft, the play offers a rare opportunity to catch an artist at a moment of change. We have seen how in all the arts the medieval subordination of time and space to the concept of eternity had gradually weakened, to be replaced by a sense of spatial and chronological perspective. The old convention of the mystery plays, whereby Joseph in Egypt stood on the stage three feet away from his brothers in Palestine could no longer function, as the need for visual accuracy grew stronger. In the prologue to *Henry V*, Shakespeare revealed both his discomfort with the physical limitations of his stage and, less obviously, his solution. He apologises to his audience for daring to present the huge battlefields of France on the small scaffold stage within the wooden 'O' of the Globe playhouse:

CHORUS: But pardon, gentles all,
The flat unraised spirits that hath dared
On this unworthy scaffold to bring forth
So great an object: can this cockpit hold
The vasty fields of France? or may we cram
Within this wooden O the very casques
That did affright the air at Agincourt?

Ostensibly, he asks for his audience's co-operation. Mentally, he says, they must fill the gap, imagining that they see whatever the stage is incapable of presenting before their eyes, and suppose that they see a thousand soldiers when only one appears before them. However, as in all art, it is not the spectator who creates the illusion, but the artist; and included within this very apology can be perceived the technique he will employ to overcome the deficiencies of his medium. For as he pleads for assistance, the verse itself changes its form, moving from a quiet, prosaic admission of the technical difficulties to a sudden soaring in verbal splendour, an exhilarating richness of language and imagery which creates imaginatively the vivid scenes which must expand the more meagre presentation upon the stage:

> . . . let us, ciphers of this great accompt,
> On your imaginary forces work.
> Suppose within the girdle of these walls
> Are now confin'd two mighty monarchies,
> Whose high, upreared and abutting fronts
> The perilous narrow ocean parts asunder . . ..

In later plays, Shakespeare was to dispense with such apologetic prologues, and by the time of *Antony and Cleopatra* he achieved such masterly control of his stagecraft that he moved back and forth from Rome to Egypt with consummate ease. But we see him at the moment of hesitation, aware of the physical limitations of his stage, and the demand for accuracy of perspective, and determined to compensate artistically for the inadequacies of his theatre.

Shakespeare never allowed himself to be bound by any precise division into genres, at one time placing in the mouth of Polonius a listing of the absurd compartmentalising to which such division leads. The players, Polonius says, are the best in the world '. . . either for tragedy, comedy, history, pastoral, pastoral—comical, historical—pastoral, tragical—historical, tragical—comical—historical—pastoral, scene individable, or poem unlimited.' In addition to the tragedies, histories, and comedies he produced at this time, there was also that borderline category which, for want of a better name, may be called romance. *The Merchant of Venice* (1596–7) although it is full of vitality and wit and ends happily, also projects the

darker shadows of our existence. Even more than Marlowe's
Jew of Malta, the play has suffered on the modern stage,
particularly after the Nazi holocaust, by attempts to tone
down what might be regarded as its anti-semitic aspects, the
racist persecution of a minority group. Such attempts may be
morally and socially laudable, but from the viewpoint of
dramatic integrity they are distortions of the play, contradict-
ing the text and emasculating its significance. For Shakespeare
is not concerned here with the Jew as a contemporary social
phenomenon (since they had long been excluded from
England) but with the clash between Old Testament morality,
at least as the Christian saw it, and that of the New.

Once Christianity had subtracted from the God of the Old
Testament the qualities of mercy and love which He had in
fact possessed there and had transferred them to Jesus, that
Old Testament God was left with the functions only of
vengeance and a stern application of the letter of the law.
Beneath the surface of this play, with its light-hearted love
themes in the golden world of Belmont, there lies a profoundly
serious dramatisation of this central Christian theme, with
Shylock representing those harsher attributes of the Old
Testament, the insistence upon an eye for an eye and a tooth
for a tooth, the demand for the precise letter of his bond and
with Portia bringing at the climactic moment of the play the
Christian message of love and generosity, that the quality of
mercy is not strained but droppeth as the gentle rain from
heaven. The main peg upon which the sentimentalised Shylock
has been hung since that interpretation first arose during the
eighteenth-century sympathy for the downtrodden minorities
of the earth has been his famous speech: 'Hath not a Jew
eyes? . . .' But if, as usual with Shakespeare, there is a momentary sympathy with Shylock at that point, a human concern
with his inner world of suffering, it must not be forgotten
that the culmination of that speech is an uncompromising
insistence upon vengeance, which for an Elizabethan audience,
particularly within this Christian setting, must disqualify him
from any lasting moral approval or justification.

Indeed, below the bright surface can be perceived the
archetypal story of the Crucifixion. Of all the leading characters, only Antonio ascetically withdraws from any pursuit of
women, a sad, serious figure almost isolated from those

around him except for his selfless generosity, his willingness to bind himself to suffer the shedding of his blood in order that another may live. He is the shadowy figure of Christ in the play, even describing himself once as the lamb going to the slaughter the '. . . wether of the flock / Meetest for death'. Shylock, who until the eighteenth century always wore the red wig and large nose familiar from the Judas figure of the mystery plays, is bitterly determined to shed the Christian blood of Antonio in vengeance, and in the name of the judgement for which he stands. It is Portia who in the trial scene vainly pleads with him in Christian terms to mitigate the justice of his plea, since in the course of justice none of us should see salvation; and only when she finds him adamant, does she catch him brilliantly by the very letter of the law he has been invoking. At the conclusion of that trial scene, even the punishment meted out to Shylock follows the Christian pattern of mercy. Although he is by law deemed deserving of the death penalty and the confiscation of all his property, the Duke at once volunteers:

> DUKE: That thou shalt see the difference of our spirit,
> I pardon thee thy life before thou ask it.

The half of his wealth which is given to Antonio, when Portia asks what mercy the latter can render Shylock, is returned to him; and the demand that Shylock convert to Christianity, which may appear harsh to us today, was for the Elizabethan an act of grace, the Jew's only hope for eternal redemption. The subplot of the magic caskets reflects this theme, as Bassanio, with the humility due from a Christian, chooses the meagre leaden casket, proving thereby as in the conflict over the law, the value of inner rather than outer truth. Seen in this larger context, the text takes on its full force in a way it cannot in the versions customary upon the stage today. As he pauses before choosing, Bassanio draws together the variegated threads of the play:

> BASSANIO: So may the outward shows be least themselves:
> The world is still deceived with ornament.
> In law, what plea so tainted and corrupt
> But, being season'd with a gracious voice,
> Obscures the show of evil? In religion,

What damned error, but some sober brow
Will bless it and approve it with a text,
Hiding the grossness with fair ornament.

[III,ii,73—80]

Here is the richness of a dramatist not only in superb command of his stage, but also aware of the complex situation of man. There is the need for firm law in Venice, the world of financial reality where the bending of law would destroy the city's commercial credibility, and with it, from the golden fairyland of Belmont flowing with generosity, wealth, and love, the message of Christian charity which must somehow be incorporated into the reality of Venice for the sake of man's moral and spiritual salvation.

By this period of his life, Shakespeare was well established as the leading dramatist of the day and sufficiently wealthy to purchase for his family in 1596 an impressively large house in Stratford. Three years later, when the Lord Chamberlain's Men moved to the Globe and re-organised their internal affairs, he became a sharer in the company, entitled thenceforth to ten per cent of the profits. While most professional writers and many of those writers struggling for preferment at court were living in dire penury, Shakespeare had won through financially, not, interestingly enough, in direct payment for his writings but through his share in the player group whose success his fertile genius was helping to assure. From now to the end of his life his standard of living was secure, and details of various property investments both in London and in the Stratford area testify to the income he was deservedly enjoying. His mood, however, seemed to grow more pensive as his social and financial position improved, and the themes which were to absorb his energies in the period of his greatest eminence reflect a mind which, for all its delighted response to the comedy of life, was increasingly disturbed by the darker aspects of the human condition.

10

This side idolatry

THE maturer phase of Shakespeare's art reveals not only an
enrichment of his poetic imagination but also a deepening
complexity in his leading characters. Richard III, Prince Hal,
or Shylock, vividly as they had come to life upon the stage,
were still in many respects two-dimensional figures, the
purpose of their actions being comparatively simple to discern
throughout, whether it be self-serving villainy, the choice of
pleasure before duty, or the desire for vengeance. Now, however, there enters an enigmatic quality, the baffling realisation
that something in the motivation of his tragic heroes will
always elude us. They remain ultimately unfathomable,
beyond the reach of total definition, not through dramatic
failure on Shakespeare's part, but through his enhanced
respect for the profundity of human nature. This is the
mystery which Hamlet treasures within himself, responding
angrily to any attempt by others to affix easy labels to him
in explanation of his melancholy brooding. It is a warning he
addresses obliquely to us, too, as audience or critic. He thrusts
a recorder into the reluctant hands of Guildenstern, sent to
pry out of him the reasons for his gloom:

HAMLET: Will you play upon this pipe?
GUILD: My lord, I cannot.
HAMLET: I pray you.
GUILD: Believe me, I cannot.
HAMLET: I do beseech you.
GUILD: I know no touch of it, my lord . . .
HAMLET: Why, look you now, how unworthy a thing you make
     of me! You would play upon me; you would seem to know my
     stops; you would pluck out the heart of my mystery; you would
     sound me from my lowest note to the top of my compass: and
     there is much music, excellent voice, in this little organ; yet can-
     not you make it speak. 'Sblood, do you think I am easier to be
     played on than a pipe? Call me what instrument you will, though
     you can fret me, you cannot play upon me.   [III,ii]

In this aspect too, Shakespeare was not isolated from the movements on the continent which had slowly been reaching England. That heightened interest in the labyrinthine complexity of man's being, the inner world of contradictory emotions, of love mingled with hate, of longing checked by fear, which make up the riddling self of which each human is composed, had left a similar mark on High Renaissance painting, as Leonardo da Vinci introduced the technique of *sfumato*. By means of a shading at the corners of the eyes and mouth in portraits, a smoky blurring of the lines of a face, he had added a new subtlety to art, a note of enigma, so that his *Mona Lisa* puzzles and intrigues us with her inscrutability. She is, like Shakespeare's Hamlet, Othello, or Cleopatra, immensely fascinating precisely because she remains beyond our final comprehension, teasing us out of thought, and thereby evoking a renewed respect for the infinite intricacies, varieties, and paradoxes of the human character.

This concern with the complexities of man's inner being was to find its most natural setting within the tragedies, but even the comedies of this middle period were to benefit from it. In the earlier comedies, love had been a generally uniform phenomenon, a source of sparkling vitality but producing an essentially similar response from all those fortunate enough to bask in its rays. There is little intrinsic difference between the amorous passion of the King of Navarre for the Princess of France, of Hermia for Demetrius, of Bassanio for Portia, or of Lorenzo for Jessica. Indeed, the lovers could easily be interchanged (as they were in *A Midsummer Night's Dream*) without noticeably affecting the relationships. The same could not now be said of the battle of wits between the reluctant lovers Beatrice and Benedick in *Much Ado About Nothing* (*c.*1599), who delight us by the abnormality of their love, the overt scorn and withering irony which they pour on each other both in public and private, although nursing a secret admiration, an admission that the other is the only opponent worthy of such duelling. That admiration needs only a little prompting by others for it to blossom into mutual love, strong yet still wary, barbed, and highly idiosyncratic:

BENEDICK: Come, I will have thee; but, by this light, I take thee for pity.

> BEATRICE: I would not deny you; but, by this good day, I yield
> upon great persuasion; and partly to save your life, for I was told
> you were in a consumption.

In *Twelfth Night* (1600—1), probably the most satisfying of all these comedies, the idiosyncrasy is not confined to one pair of lovers, but spreads throughout the play, and the eccentricity of each lover becomes the key to the plot as well as a primary source of the pleasure the comedy provides. Returning to a theme he had first used much earlier in his *Comedy of Errors*, the confusion created by the unexpected appearance of twins, Shakespeare no longer remains satisfied with the comic situations of mistaken identity it produced, but instead uses it as a finely honed instrument for discriminating between the various gradations, versions, and distortions of love, each arising out of the individual traits of the lovers themselves.

Everybody in this play, except for the choric figure of the clown, is in love. In the centre is the misdirected circle of the type we have met earlier — Viola loving Orsino, who loves Olivia, who loves Viola/Cesario; beyond the circle are Malvolio and Sir Andrew Aguecheek in foolish pursuit of Olivia's favours; at another level there is the pairing of Sir Toby Belch with the irresistible Maria, and for good measure the Platonic love of Antonio for Sebastian, who will himself come to adore Olivia. Here is love's plenty, but love in carefully discriminated and diversified forms.

Orsino, as his opening speech reveals, is in love less with Olivia than with the romanticised picture of himself in the role of the rejected Petrarchan lover. Wallowing in self-pity, he calls for relief of his pain not through less love but through more:

> ORSINO: If music be the food of love, play on,
> Give me excess of it, that, surfeiting,
> The appetite may sicken, and so die.

The object of his supposed passion, the fair Olivia, suffers from a similar lack of proportion in love, having determined to cherish the memory of her deceased brother by turning her back on the world for a mourning period of seven long years. Amusingly, Shakespeare inserts into her declaration (as reported by a messenger) an unconscious admission of her own exaggerated purpose, to 'pickle' her brother's memory in salt-water as one does in seasoning some delicacy. Withdrawn from the world:

> . . . like a cloistress she will veiled walk,
> And water once a day her chamber round
> With eye-offending brine: all this to season
> A brother's dead love, which she would keep fresh
> And lasting in her sad remembrance.   [I,i,28—32]

Into this atmosphere heavy with misapplied love comes the sensible, attractive Viola like a fresh breeze blown in from the sea. She too must play a role, but in contrast to the native inhabitants she remains fully conscious throughout of her true identity as she finds her place within her host country of Illyria, the lyrical world of illusion as its name suggests. There is no separation here between the 'green world' of the imagination and the harsh reality of parents obstructing the course of true love. The two worlds are represented in the meeting of Viola with the residents of Illyria, and the only obstacle to love in this play is the perversity within the characters themselves. Only the self-knowledge to which Viola and the play at large will lead them can enable them to overcome their own delusions. Olivia must learn the message conveyed by one of the charming songs of the play, not to indulge in an excessive love for the dead nor to postpone true love till it be too late:

> What is love? 'Tis not hereafter,
> Present mirth hath present laughter:
> What's to come is still unsure.
> In delay there lies no plenty,
> Then come kiss me, sweet and twenty:
> Youth's a stuff will not endure.   [II,iii,48—53]

Another song provides Orsino with an instructive parody of his own mournful pose as the rejected lover, to encourage him to shake it off at last:

> Come away, come away, death,
> And in sad cypress let me be laid,
> Fly away, fly away, breath,
> I am slain by a fair cruel maid.   [II,iv,51—5]

And Malvolio must be taught the difference between genuine love and its selfish use for purposes of self-aggrandisement.

There is, however, a further aspect of the play which modern scholarship has helped to identify by its anthropological perception that comedy originates from an ancient fertility rite celebrating the release from winter and the coming of the spring.[36] As its title recalls, this play was originally written for performance at the festivities for the twelfth night after Christmas. 'Winter' in this play, represented by repressive Ill-Will (Mal=volio) wishes to silence the light-hearted festive spirit, the late-night carousals of Sir Toby and his fellow revellers. Such strait-laced pomposity must in such a celebration be vanquished and routed ('Dost thou think because thou art virtuous, there shall be no more cakes and ale?'), and by a brilliant stratagem exploiting his self-love and self-delusion, Maria compels this wintry figure unwittingly to perform with comic incongruity the role of the presiding figure at the revels, donning bright yellow stockings (the colour traditional for the Lord of Misrule), and wearing, even more inappropriately, a perpetual forced smile on his face out of the mistaken assumption that such is his mistress's loving wish. With the festive spirit restored by such hilarity, the true lovers are, in a splendid moment of dramatic dénouement as the twin brother and sister finally appear on the stage together, all happily paired off. In this period, even in such light comedy, a note of melancholy remains, the touch of sadness as Feste the clown reminds us in the concluding song that '. . . the rain it raineth every day.'

Tragic depths

In the earlier tragedy *Romeo and Juliet* (c.1595), fate had been an outside force trapping the innocent, star-crossed lovers. Their only fault was to fall in love within a society riddled by bigotry and vicious family feuding. A message which fails to arrive on time, again through no fault of their own, leads to their death. Ultimately it is the nature of the world about them which dictates their fate. In contrast, the tragedies of Shakespeare's major period are internalised; they evolve from the inner being of the protagonist, and whatever the pressures of the situation in which he finds himself, he alone must bear the final responsibility for his own death and for the suffering of those affected by his fall.

Although the plot of *Hamlet* (*c.*1601) adopts the Senecan theme of vengeance demanded for a father's murder, it is the philosophical brooding of the central figure which absorbs attention, the profundity of his inner quest, rather than the events of the story itself. No play of Shakespeare's attaches such weight to the soliloquies, the series of introspective meditations in which Hamlet searches for answers to the spiritual predicament in which he finds himself. Action there is in abundance – the appearance of a ghost, some spying behind an arras, an unpremeditated murder, a play within a play, the madness of Ophelia, and a duel to the death with poisoned goblet and poisoned sword; yet all these seem subordinate to those quieter moments when the main figure stands alone upon the stage contemplating his own and the human condition.

Any theory that the cause of his brooding is some form of sickness, whether the Elizabethan malady of melancholia or, as Coleridge argued, a morbid oversensitivity to contemplative thought, must be suspect; for Hamlet's procrastination, however it may anger or frustrate him, is presented in the play as in some way ennobling. Those very 'foils' against which his own hesitation is held up for contrast, Laertes ready to slit the throat of his father's murderer even in the church, or the militant Fortinbras ('Strong in arms') unperturbedly sacrificing scores of men to avenge his father's death, appear callous beside the far richer and sensitive personality of Hamlet. There is, moreover, a universality not only in the play at large but in Hamlet's own search for meaning, a recognition that his problem is in the highest degree our problem too, and that universality would vitiate any implication that his is merely an illness of which he needs to be cured. The splendour of the figure he once was, glimpsed in those rare moments of exhilaration when he momentarily forgets his gloom, as he teases Polonius or joyfully welcomes the players, suggests an admirable personality, a learned scholar and poet, a skilled swordsman, a successful lover, a witty satirist, a loyal friend, an eager playgoer, in brief, the ideal Renaissance man:

OPHELIA: The courtier's, soldier's, scholar's eye, tongue, sword;
            The expectancy and rose of the fair state,
            The glass of fashion and the mould of form,
            The observ'd of all observers . . ..   [III,i,159—162]

In some indefinable way, the canker that eats at his heart is made to seem a product of these very virtues, inherent in the sensitivity which raises him so far above the other characters in the play.

If his predicament remains beyond precise formulation, there are hints to point its direction. The pervasive imagery of the play is of putrefaction and decay, and even the humour, which so often in Shakespeare reflects the fundamental themes of a drama, is obsessed with similar thoughts. The slain Polonius, Hamlet announces, is at supper, '. . . not where he eats, but where he is eaten: a certain convocation of politic worms are e'en at him . . . we fat all creatures else to fat us, and we fat ourselves for maggots.' His most famous speech questions what lies beyond that bourn from which no traveller returns, and he enquires anxiously from the gravedigger how long a body must lie in the earth before it rot. His gloomy preoccupation with death, preceding the vision of the ghost as he sits garbed in sombre mourning admidst the celebrations at court, has been prompted, as so often happens, by his father's passing, and it is there that the source of his melancholy must be found. The nagging question to which he can find no answer lies at the very core of the Renaissance worldview. On the one hand the new era had eagerly embraced the validity of this world, the enormous possibilities for human achievement on earth, pushing aside the medieval concern with the world to come. But the decay of the body, the stench even of Alexander the Great's skull within the grave, raises the disturbing problem whether in the final analysis anything of man's glory survives the tomb. In that context, his bitterness towards his mother is not for her re-marriage but its excessive haste. That haste seems an insult to his father's memory, a proof that he has not survived the grave even in the heart of the one who supposedly loved him most dearly. As Hamlet remarks sardonically: 'O heavens! Die two months ago and not forgotten yet? Then there's hope a great man's memory may outlive his life half a year.'

In the midst of this perturbation of spirit, he is called upon to take action to avenge a murder at a time when the settling of scores in this world seems utterly pointless. His repeated dissipation of action into words, words, words is a desperate attempt to stave off decision, to find any means of postponement until he has reached some kind of solution to his deeper quest concerning the significance of life. The tragedy lies in its timing, in fate's selection of him as avenger just when, unlike Laertes or Fortinbras, he is temporarily incapacitated for action. Hence his anguished cry:

> The time is out of joint. O cursed spite,
> That ever I was born to set it right.   [I,v,189—90]

As he moves into a form of madness, which serves both as a disguise and refuge from his own distraught mood, his spiritual search can only evoke our understanding and sympathy. If we cannot plumb the depths of his brooding to their fullest extent, the hints they offer are sufficient to suggest their nature and to prompt our further questioning. As the plot works itself out to culminate in Hamlet's own fall, we can, in the light of his quest, respond more fully to the reverberations of his dying plea to Horatio, that after his death he may, unlike his father, be remembered for a while in his friend's heart with a little grief and pain:

> HAMLET: If thou didst ever hold me in thy heart,
> Absent thee from felicity a while,
> And in this harsh world draw thy breath in pain,
> To tell my story.

Perhaps no play of Shakespeare's suggests with such vividness both the splendour and the ignominy of man's lot. In the midst of the gloom and disillusionment into which Hamlet is plunged, the vivacious jesting with his fellow students, the high-spirited punning and capping of puns, the risqué flirting with Ophelia, the amused chaffing of Osric with its warning against false fashions both in speech and dress, the careful instructions to the players (one of our only sources for Shakespeare's views on acting) and, not least, the genuinely comic exchanges with the gravedigger which can set an audience rocking with laughter even though it knows in whose grave the clown is standing, all these create an exhilarating sense of life's colourful variety, its challenges, its opportunity for artistic inventiveness, and its enormous potential for self-fulfilment. That a person as gifted as Hamlet, blessed with such talents and majesty should have fallen into such despair testifies to the range and complexity of the human spirit; and if Hamlet himself dies at the play's end, there is still a sense that, given time, he might have won his way through to spiritual victory over that temporary despair. On that more satisfying note for mankind at large, the play ends:

> FORTINBRAS: For he was likely, had he been put on,
> To have proved most royal.

The Jacobean phase

In March 1603, Queen Elizabeth died, ending a long reign of nearly fifty years which, with all its disturbances, such as the Earl of Essex's abortive rebellion, the murmuring of the poor against oppressive landlords, the simmering religious controversy, and the failure to provide a natural heir, had nevertheless seen England's advance from military, financial, and cultural mediocrity to a leading position in Europe. Shakespeare's company was in fact to benefit from her death. Only two months later, James I, who might be thought to have had more urgent state matters on his mind, bestowed upon them the signal honour of appointment as the King's Servants and Grooms of the Chamber (to be generally known henceforth as The King's Men), supplying them as members of his staff with red livery for his coronation procession the following year. Their position was now assured. In the winter of 1604 alone, they were summoned to perform at court eleven times, an average of one appearance per week, and such court appearances were particularly remunerative for the actors, as for each performance they received a sum of money equivalent to the profits of a packed house at the Globe. Yet such royal recognition and the widened prestige it brought produced no lightening of mood in Shakespeare's plays, which responded rather to the overall feeling prevailing in the country. The new monarch was an unknown entity. He lacked the grace to win the people's affection and his accession to the throne aroused suspicion and anxiety. Above all, he was not blessed with Elizabeth's discrimination in selecting for advancement men of genuine capability. James's ear was open to flattery and sycophancy, and Shakespeare, who now had more direct contact with the court, must himself have witnessed at first hand the ruthless scheming and calculated self-interest whereby lesser men now wormed their way into positions of power.

Within the Jacobean phase of his drama, probably in response to that change, there emerges an essentially new figure, the Machiavellian schemer, based less on the actual writings of Machiavelli than on the more popular conception of his philosophy. In *Othello* (1603–4) Iago constitutes the anti-pole of Christian love and generosity, scorning traditional morality in his coldly pragmatic view of the universe. Unlike Richard III or Claudius who had been driven to villainy by ambition, Iago is a villain on principle. He scorns the ethically upright as mere credulous fools blinded by superstition and, for their failure to see the simple truths before them, as deserving to be tenderly '. . . led by the nose' into the traps he prepares for them. He possesses an insatiable appetite for intrigue in its own right; not employing cunning to attain an end, but rather inventing an end in order to employ cunning. His reason for destroying the Moor is not the belief that he has been cheated of the lieutenancy (he scarcely notices when it is finally bestowed upon him), nor even the suspicion that Othello has been sleeping with his wife. That is merely an after-thought to rationalise an instinctive antipathy:

> IAGO: I hate the Moor,
> And it is thought abroad, that 'twixt my sheets
> He's done my office; I know not if 't be true;
> Yet I, for mere suspicion in that kind,
> Will do, as if for surety.   [I,iii,384–8]

The power of the play derives largely from the fascination that Iago exerts upon us, however we may consciously abhor him. Shakespeare refuses to oversimplify. In the same way as he had in Falstaff presented the attractions of a life of pleasure before finally reasserting the virtues of duty and honour, so here he is aware of the dangerously alluring philosophy Machiavellianism offered to his age in its freedom from moral restraint and the uninhibited pursuit of self-satisfaction. Iago is the only character in the play with a sense of humour, sardonic yet amusing, as he toys with the stupid Roderigo or is himself entertained by his own duplicity:

> IAGO: And what's he that says I play the villain,
>   When this advice is free I give, and honest . . .
>   [II,iii,327—8]

He is a brilliant tactician, and we are permitted to witness the
absorbing process of a plan first forming in his mind, being
put into execution and, under his stage-management, succeeding superbly as in an instant he resourcefully turns some
unexpected draw-back into a striking advantage. He is the
organiser and controller throughout, the others his mere
pawns. In that Machiavellian context, the term 'honest Iago'
so frequently applied to him by others for his supposed bluff
loyalty and frankness takes on a secondary quality. For in a
subtler sense he is indeed the only 'honest' person in the play,
free from all illusions about himself or others, and seeing everything with the unclouded vision of a cool empiricist. Through
that clarity of vision, he can pinpoint with unnerving accuracy
the weak point of each person about him, and use that knowledge to cause his downfall. By that means, Shakespeare creates
the tragic ambience of the play since those who succumb to
him remain ultimately responsible for their own doom; for
Iago has not so much destroyed them, as helped them to
destroy themselves. In one impressive scene, within the brief
space of some two hundred lines we watch him transform
Othello from a loving and unsuspicious husband into an
anguished cuckold, cursing marriage; and all by no more than
suggestions and half-muttered hints which Othello seizes
upon only too readily:

> IAGO: Ha, I like not that!
> OTH.: What dost thou say?
> IAGO: Nothing, my lord, or if — I know not what.
> OTH.: Was not that Cassio parted from my wife?
> IAGO: Cassio, my lord? . . . no, sure, I cannot think it,
>   That he would sneak away so guilty-like,
>   Seeing you coming . . ..   [III,iii,35—41]

Othello, thus, although a victim of Iago's cunning is still
the cause of his own fall. It is true that, had he never been
subjected to Iago's malice, he might have lived and died untroubled. There lies the pity of it all; but the weakness was
his own, waiting there to be exposed. An incorrigible romantic,
dreaming of his royal forebears, he is, as a blackamoor alien

to Venetian society, acutely sensitive to his social standing in
Venice. He carefully waits for Desdemona to reveal her love
to him before he will risk the humiliating possibility of a
refusal. Having won the love of the fairest lady in Venice, that
love becomes for him the coping-stone of his life's achievement, the affirmation of his intrinsic merit in an alien society,
without which chaos would return. Iago's evil suggestion that,
both during that courtship and after, he had been no more
than a useful camouflage for Desdemona's continuing affair
with Cassio is a blow to his pride far more grievous to him as
a Moor than it would be to any other man; and in the barbaric
fury it releases, his demand for proof becomes an empty
phrase as he moves inexorably towards the obliteration of
that source of humiliation in the terrible scene of the murder.
Hence that strange calm which descends upon him when,
after her death, Iago's machinations are exposed. His own as
well as her life may have been destroyed, but at least he has
been vindicated. The nightmare of cuckoldry has been removed, and he knows at last that Desdemona was steadfast
in her love. Secure in that knowledge, his pride returns once
more, and he can proceed to the atonement of suicide,
restored to honour. Beyond the specific tale of tragedy, this
play constitutes a dramatic meeting between the polarised
world-views of the era, the exquisite poetry of Othello's love:

> O my soul's joy,
> If after every tempest come such calms,
> May the winds blow, till they have waken'd death . . ..

set against the harsh prose of Iago, seeing in that splendid
love no more than the physical animalistic actuality of 'an
old black ram . . . tupping a white ewe'.

   In his next tragedy, *King Lear* (1605), Shakespeare remained
disturbed by the threat of the Machiavels, the vicious Regans,
Gonerils, and Edmunds of this world, challenging the traditional virtues of hierarchical order; and here too the challenge is at times presented with an engaging humour. After
his father's pious fears of ominous eclipses and astrological
warnings, Edmund in soliloquy laughs them to scorn and if
those older values are gradually to be reinstated through the
Christian virtues of Cordelia, the damaging doubts he has cast
on that moral system are never wholly repaired. He asks

disarmingly why a muscular bastard begotten in amorous lust should be thought inferior to a weakling conceived in the 'dull, stale, tired bed' of marriage, and with a perception rare for his time ridicules the current tendency to shrug off personal responsibility by attributing all failures to the movements of the distant planets:

EDMUND: This is the excellent foppery of the world, that, when we are sick in fortune, often the surfeits of our own behaviour, we make guilty of our disasters the sun, the moon, and stars; as if we were villains on necessity, fools by heavenly compulsion, knaves, thieves, and treachers by spherical predominance, drunkards, liars, and adulterers by an enforc'd obedience of planetary influence; and all that we are evil in, by a divine thrusting on. An admirable evasion of whore-master man, to lay his goatish disposition to the charge of a star!   [I,ii,115]

In this play, however, the Machiavel no longer occupies the centre stage, for the focus of the play has moved to the victim. The theme here is the naked vulnerability of man, be he king or pauper, exposed to the predators of this world and ultimately defenceless against their cruelty. Edgar strips to the shivering pathos of a deranged beggar perpetually moaning of the cold, the Fool huddles for protection in the pitiless storm and Lear himself, forcibly divested by others of his retinue of knights, his royal authority, and his paternal dignity, at last himself tears off his robes of office to join symbolically the wretched of this earth, becoming that poor, bare, forked animal, unaccommodated man. The loyal Kent, the gentle Cordelia, and the tender Edgar, for all their respect and love, remain ineffective in protecting him, for there is little man can do against the malicious forces of crude self-interest; and the most comforting advice Edgar can offer is that men must endure their going hence even as their coming hither. In this, the most pessimistic play that Shakespeare wrote, although by the end the villains have been slain, such retribution has come too late to prevent the dreadful suffering at their hand, and we know there will be more Regans and Gonerils to replace them.

If, however, the play has so grim a message, to relieve that gloom it does offer a nobility and splendour in its concept of man's spiritual being. The physical world may lie within the grasp of the ruthless, but man's inner maturity is his own. Ripeness is all. Out of the simple tale of *King Leïr* in the chronicles with its happy ending there, Shakespeare forged an archetypal drama of a man's spiritual odyssey from autocratic pride to humility, a journey through the agony of madness to sanity, paralleled by Gloucester's progression through blindness to true insight. As Lear stands bareheaded in the storm which projects symbolically his own inner turmoil, he experiences the first twinges of guilt at his unjust dismissal of Cordelia, and thereby takes the first hesitant steps on the path to the knowledge he will eventually gain in full, that only through experiencing the suffering of the poorest wretches of this earth can a king be indeed worthy of his crown, a human being be deserving of that name:

> LEAR: Poor naked wretches, wheresoe'er you are,
> That bide the pelting of this pitiless storm,
> How shall your houseless heads and unfed sides,
> Your loop'd and window'd raggedness, defend you
> From seasons such as these? O! I have ta'en
> Too little care of this. Take physic, Pomp;
> Expose thyself to feel what wretches feel,
> That thou mayst shake the superflux to them,
> And show the Heavens more just.
>
> [III,iv,28—35]

Against the callousness of the new philosophy is set the compassion and mercy of the old. Such compassion may avail little in blocking the schemes of the Machiavels, but the wisdom its attainment brings is an ennobling achievement of the human soul, beside which death itself seems less significant.

The conscienceless villains whom Shakespeare had presented until now from Richard III to Goneril, had been devils in human form, moving imperviously towards the attainment of power untouched by pity or remorse. Whether individually or as exponents of the new doctrine of self-interest, they fascinated as embodiments of human evil, but by their ruthless sadism could arouse little responsive sympathy from the audience. In *Macbeth* (1606—7) Shakespeare undertook a task dramatically more challenging, to present as a tragic hero (whose fate must engage us and evoke a measure of identification and understanding) a man guilty of the most abhorrent crime of regicide, not out of zeal for the public good like

Brutus in *Julius Caesar* but through sheer lust for the throne. It was a formidable enterprise. Some hint of this interest had appeared in *Hamlet*, where Claudius was no heartless villain but a man grievously tempted by the dual prizes of the throne and the queen, later falling upon his knees within the chapel in a genuine if vain attempt to win divine forgiveness. But to sympathise with him momentarily as he succumbs to remorse long after the perpetration of his crime is very different from identifying with a tragic hero during the contemplation and planning of the assassination and during its actual execution.

The dramatic technique Shakespeare introduced here was to add a second character. Lady Macbeth, the driving force initiating the plan, unshakeable in her manly determination and scorning his fears as womanish, is never the primary focus of the play, but serves to draw away from him and towards herself our bitterest condemnation, leaving Macbeth by comparison with her as the basically good man diverted from his nobler purposes by the forces working upon him. Moreover, the workings of his soul are projected before us by an enlargement of perspective beyond the natural world to include the world to come; the witches' forewarning of Macbeth, his own foreboding through apparitions that he has forfeited heavenly grace and stands before the threat of eternal damnation. Like the gravedigger scene in *Hamlet*, so here the comic scene of the drunken Porter, reluctantly waking from his stupor to answer the incessant knocking at the door immediately after Duncan's murder, offers a grotesque reflection of the play's real theme. Macbeth has indeed transformed the quiet domesticity of his castle, with the martlets nesting in its eaves, into a Hell of which this Porter guards the gate; and the topical allusions to the recent Gunpowder Plot in which King James so nearly lost his life underscore the enormity of the regicide committed within these walls.

Prompted by his own ambitious longing for the throne, incited by his formidable wife, yet intimidated by his own horror at the act, Macbeth is racked by torment both before and after the murder. And as he is inevitably drawn into further dastardly acts to protect what has been achieved, his inability to answer 'Amen' to the simple prayer 'God bless us', the terrible dreams that shake him nightly, and the apparitions which haunt him, together provide a penetrating psychological study of guilt. Even the unswerving Lady Macbeth succumbs to the anguish of remorse in the famed sleepwalking scene, the suppressed human conscience exacting its dread retribution in the dark recesses of her mind; and as the doctor watches her desperate attempts to wash away the blood of her guilt, he delivers chorically the message of the play:

DOCTOR: Unnatural deeds
Do breed unnatural troubles: infected minds
To their deaf pillows will discharge their secrets.
More needs she the divine than the physician. —
God, God forgive us all!   [V,i,68—72]

In sharp contrast to this drama of guilt and divine retribution, of clear distinction between good and evil, perhaps the most magnificent of all these major tragedies takes us into a realm where such moral sanctions seem suddenly to shrink into insignificance beside the blazing splendour of royal love. In *Antony and Cleopatra* (1606—7) the conventional standards we may bring to the play are discarded as we are swung back and forth from the stern world of Rome demanding duty and obedience to the lush and colourful exoticism of Egypt, amoral, self-indulgent, and at times wonderfully attractive. With a fluidity of movement reflecting the fluidity of ethical precept, the drama presents a Rome at one moment the symbol of honour and order and at the next repelling by its pedantry, coldness, and barrenness. Egypt is warm, rich, fertile, and passionate, but it is also lewd, treacherous, and corrupt. And the unpredictability is superbly embodied in the commanding presence of Cleopatra herself who wins the enslaved devotion of emperors not by the constancy and fidelity of her love but by a provocative coquetry which leaves them permanently intrigued, unsure of their hold upon so elusive a beauty, and enchanted by her infinite changeability. She sends a servant to enquire after Antony:

CLEOPATRA: See where he is, who's with him, what he does:
I did not send you. If you find him sad,
Say I am dancing; if in mirth, report
That I am sudden sick. Quick and return.
                                    [I,iii,3—6]

The swift oscillation between the contrasted worlds of Rome and Egypt is presented strikingly at the opening of the play. Traditionally, the initial speech in the Elizabethan playhouse, whether spoken by a prologue or by a minor figure in the drama, was choric in effect, establishing the controlling viewpoint of the play — the prologue in *Romeo and Juliet*, the loyal soldiers in *Hamlet*, the witches in *Macbeth* — and as such it carried an air of authority. Here a Roman officer informs us unhesitatingly that Antony's sordid affair with Cleopatra is mere dotage, his martial valour wasting away as he becomes the bellows and the fan to cool a gypsy's lust. The triple pillar of the world has, we are informed, become transformed into no more than a 'strumpet's fool'. And at that very moment, the strumpet enters, superb in her majesty, utterly feminine in her wish to hear his love expressed, and conveying in the playful exchange between them a mutual love immeasurable in range, surpassing the petty limits and duties of Roman mentality, beside which the concerns of that trivial empire merely grate on the ear:

CLEOPATRA: If it be love indeed, tell me how much.
ANTONY: There's beggary in the love that can be reckon'd.
CLEOPATRA: I'll set a bourn how far to be belov'd.
ANTONY: Then must thou needs find out new heaven, new earth.
ATTENDANT: News, my good lord, from Rome.
ANTONY: Grates me, the sum.   [I,i,14—19]

Simply to describe in narrative so mesmerising, infuriating, and captivating a woman might be thought difficult enough, but Shakespeare places her on the stage before us, presenting her in all her contrariness and charm in a manner to convince us beyond doubt of the extraordinary ability of the boy actors, without which he would never have dared to create so powerfully feminine a role.

In his later version of this play, *All for Love* (1678), Dryden offered a simpler choice for Antony between noble Roman honour and Egyptian lust. Here, however, in its original Shakespearean form, we are ever more persuaded as the drama progresses that Antony not only cannot but must not leave the superb Cleopatra for the decorous but colder Octavia in Rome. The problem arises, therefore, wherein the tragic blemish of his character lies, that element of his being, whether morally culpable or not, which must lead inevitably to his doom. This play should be seen, I would argue, as intrinsically different from its predecessors, marking an advance beyond the normal framework of tragedy; and a hint of the change can be found in the imagery of the play which is vast in scope, eternal in time, and cosmic in conception. A war between Antony and Octavius would be 'as if the world should cleave and that slain men / Should solder up the rift', eternity was in their lips and in their eyes, Antony's face was as the heavens and therein stuck a sun and moon to 'light this little O the earth'. Within that context can be perceived the transcendental quality of the drama. The love of Antony and Cleopatra is too vast ever to be contained within the narrow world typified by the bounds and limits of Rome. It needs the infinite reaches of the heavens. For Antony embodies within him the divine qualities both of Mars the god of war and of the curled Apollo, the god of male love, and no human frame can contain such immensity. Significantly, when he dies, the image offered is of a heart bursting out of its case. Moreover, again with the imagery to direct us, both lovers are seen as soaring beyond the normal limits set for humanity. He is an autumn that grows the more by reaping, while she defies all natural limits of age or satiety, making defect perfection and, breathless, power breathing forth:

> ENOBARBUS: Age cannot wither her, nor custom stale
> Her infinite variety: other women cloy
> The appetites they feed, but she makes hungry,
> Where most she satisfies.   [II,ii,235—8]

Hence it is that this play alone of all that Shakespeare wrote presents death not as cold, fearsome, and putrefying but as a warm enriching experience through which the lovers will pass to the wide-ranging splendour of eternal and undisturbed love. Death here is as a lover's pinch which hurts but is desired, a baby which sucks its nurse asleep, a marriage bed into which the bridegroom joyfully leaps. And at its conclusion, the play offers not, as in *Romeo and Juliet*, two corpses to be mourned, but creates imaginatively a picture of an Antony 'past the size of dreaming' waiting on the heights of Olympus to be joined by his Cleopatra, there to walk hand in hand for eternity where souls do couch on flowers, the admiration of all the spirits as the lasting epitome of transcendent love. As Cleopatra prepares for her suicide, she is in fact preparing for immortality, dressing in her most royal garments, eager for that kiss from Antony which it is her heaven to have:

CLEOPATRA: Give me my robe, put on my crown, I have
             Immortal longings in me. Now no more
             The juice of Egypt's grape shall moist this lip.
             Yare, yare, good Iras; quick: methinks I hear
             Antony call. I see him rouse himself
             To praise my noble act. I hear him mock
             The luck of Caesar, which the gods give men
             To excuse their after wrath. Husband, I come:
             Now to that name, my courage prove my title!
                                              [V,ii,279—87]

This play marks the last of the great tragedies. Although Shakespeare was only in his mid-forties and to the best of our knowledge in good health, he began shortly afterwards to withdraw from active life in the theatre and, for reasons which have never been firmly established, henceforth to spend most of his time at Stratford, until his death in 1616. He now wrote only rarely for the stage, sometimes, in contrast to his previous practice, in co-operation with other dramatists. His daughter Susanna had married in 1607, and the birth of his only grandchild in the following year may have provided the bait to draw him away from London.

Retirement to Stratford

There were, however, changes within the London theatre which may have influenced his decision, and convinced him that his place was no longer there. The accession of James I had, with the active participation of Queen Anne, witnessed the introduction at court of the Italian masque. It was a form of musical extravaganza, with court ladies appearing in non-speaking roles wearing sumptuous costumes as blackamoors, birds, or whatever other guise took their fancy, with lyrics recited or sung by professionals, and above all with elaborate stage scenery. Clouds opened to reveal wonderful vistas, a group of posed goddesses would be disclosed within a golden sphere above, to descend slowly from the skies, and an illuminated globe gently turning would suddenly be made to disappear from sight. Ben Jonson was commissioned to compose the lyrics and Inigo Jones, later to become England's leading architect of the Palladian style, was made responsible for devising the sophisticated machinery for producing these spectacular effects.

Clearly, the interest here was not in the subtle interplay of human characters nor the maturing of a central figure towards self-knowledge. It was simply a light entertainment for ear and eye. The masque took place within the court, the audience being restricted to the courtiers and staff (of which Shakespeare was now one) but the techniques it adopted began to spread beyond its confines. Private playhouses such as Blackfriars (recently acquired by Shakespeare's company) had, with their indoor location, from the first included musical performances, lighting effects, and some degree of spectacle, and with Jonson active in the playhouse as well as in preparing the masques, some interaction necessarily took place.

Both in the themes of his last plays and at times in the form of presentation, there are signs that Shakespeare was aware that fashions had changed and that audiences expected some of these effects in the playhouse too. The plays he now wrote drift towards the world of fantasy, not as a 'green world' operating as an imaginative entity interlocking with the real, but simply fantastic in itself. In *Pericles* (c.1608), *Cymbeline* (c.1609), and *The Winter's Tale* (c.1610), there is a recurrent theme of dead people magically reappearing into life and being restored to a husband or lover in a manner more than straining belief, and Shakespeare seemed uncomfortable and less effective in that new fashion. His charming play *The Tempest* (1611) is certainly the best of them, but it marks a falling-off in dramatic quality after the great series we have been examining. It is set on an island where the all-seeing and all-powerful magician Prospero directs his spirit Ariel to arrange a shipwreck, to lead Prince Ferdinand to his fair daughter Miranda, to cause the usurping duke to repent, and to punish some foolish courtiers led into feeble attempts at rebellion by Caliban. At a wave of the hand, a banquet appears miraculously upon the stage, and when all is neatly ended, Ariel obtains his freedom and Prospero discards his magical powers.

That renunciation speech of Prospero's has often been interpreted as Shakespeare's farewell to the stage, his casting away of the creative rod whereby he has conjured up characters and scenes to entertain his audiences. But it is specifically the world of magic that Prospero rejects, and if it does have any autobiographical allusion, it may rather mark Shakespeare's rejection of the world of mere fantasy into which he had found himself edged by the new fashion, a fantasy divorced from reality, no longer exploring the human condition, and with the dead miraculously returning from the tomb to suit the new need for spectacle:

PROSPERO: graves at my command
Have wak'd their sleepers, op'd, and let 'em forth
By my so potent art. But this rough magic
I here abjure, and, when I have requir'd
Some heavenly music, which even now I do,
To work mine end upon their senses that
This airy charm is for, I'll break my staff,
Bury it certain fathoms in the earth,
And deeper than did ever plummet sound
I'll drown my book.

[V,i,48—57]

What he casts away is the staff of the enchanter and the book of magic spells, not the pen of the creative artist.

For the very last play he wrote, he turned back, indeed, from fantasy to the world of reality, to the tradition of the history plays dealing with affairs of state and the fate of individuals functioning within it. *The Famous History of the Life of King Henry VIII* (1613) had it been written by a minor dramatist would, like any of Shakepeare's lesser-known plays, have been sufficient to win him an honoured place in the annals of the drama. But it could not compete with those master works whereby he had at last raised the English stage not only to the level of the continental drama but well beyond. For both in comedy and tragedy, he had created for England the crystallisation of the Renaissance ideal, dramatically integrating in superb poetry the sharply perceived actuality of human experience with the infinite range and splendour of the human imagination.

Notes

The place of publication is London unless otherwise stated.

1. T. Nashe, *Works*, ed. R. B. McKerrow and F. P. Wilson (1904–10), II, 159.

2. C. S. Lewis, *English Literature in the Sixteenth Century, Excluding Drama* (Oxford: OUP, 1954).

3. M. Levey, *Early Renaissance* (Harmondsworth: Penguin, 1977), p. 181.

4. E. M. W. Tillyard, *The Elizabethan World Picture* (Chatto, 1943) and Hiram Haydn, *The Counter-Renaissance* (New York: Atheneum, 1960).

5. A. L. Rowse, *The England of Elizabeth* (Macmillan, 1964), p. 24.

6. G. Saintsbury, *A History of English Prose Rhythm* (Macmillan, 1912).

7. Thomas Elyot, *The Book Named Governor* (1531), I.i.

8. H. C. Gardiner argues for that view in his *Mysteries' End: an Investigation of the Last Days of the Medieval Religious Stage* (New Haven: Yale University Press, 1946).

9. Jean Luis Vives, *St. Augustine 'Of the City of God'*, tr. J. H. Healey (1610), p. 337.

10. Glynne Wickham, *Early English Stages, 1300–1600*, 3 vols (London/New York: Routledge, 1959–1972).

11. Nikolaus Pevsner, *The Englishness of English Art* (Penguin, 1956), p. 26.

12. *Epistle Exhortatory of an English Christian* (1544), published under the pseudonym of Henry Stalbridge.

13. F. S. Boas, *University Drama in the Tudor Age* (Oxford: OUP, 1914), pp. 4–11.

14. F. P. Wilson, *The English Drama 1485–1585* (Oxford: OUP, 1969), p. 112.

15. G. G. Coulton, *Medieval Panorama* (New York: Longman, 1955), p. 311.

16. H. B. Charlton, *The Senecan Tradition in Renaissance Tragedy* (Manchester: Manchester University Press, 1946).

17. Una Ellis-Fermor, *The Frontiers of Drama* (Methuen, 1948), p. 130.

18. *See* J. C. Adams, *The Globe Playhouse* (Cambridge, Mass.: Harvard University Press, 1943), C. W. Hodges, *The Globe Restored*

(Ernest Benn, 1953) and J. L. Hotson, *Shakespeare's Wooden O* (Rupert Hart Davis, 1959).

19.   E. H. Miller, *The Professional Writer in Elizabethan England* (Cambridge, Mass.: Harvard University Press, 1959).

20.   T. Nashe, *Preface to Greene's 'Menaphon'* (1589).

21.   Edward Blount, in the preface to his edition of *Six Court Comedies* (1632).

22.   G. K. Hunter, *John Lyly: the humanist as a Courtier* (Cambridge, Mass.: Harvard University Press; London: Routledge, 1962) p. 260.

23.   Thomas Morley, *A Plain and Easy Introduction to Practical Music* (1597).

24.   *Hamlet* II, ii.

25.   T. Warton, *A History of English Poetry*, orig. 1778–81 (1840), p. 622.

26.   Hallett Smith, *Elizabethan Poetry* (Cambridge, Mass.: Harvard University Press 1966), p. 2.

27.   Cf. J. S. Lawry, *Sidney's Two Arcadias* (Ithaca: Cornell U.P., 1972).

28.   W. Webbe, *A Discourse of English Poetry* (1586) and George Puttenham, *The Arte of English Poesie* (1589).

29.   J. L. Hotson, *The Death of Christopher Marlowe* (Cambridge, Mass.: Harvard University Press, 1925), F. S. Boas, *Christopher Marlowe: a biographical and critical study* (Oxford: O.U.P., 1940), and J. B. Steane, *Marlowe: a critical study* (Cambridge: C.U.P., 1965).

30.   Leo Kirschbaum, 'Marlowe's *Faustus*: A Reconsideration' *Review of English Studies* XIX (1943), 229.

31.   John Melton, *Astrologaster* (London, 1620), p. 31.

32.   E. K. Chambers, *The Elizabethan Stage* (Oxford: O.U.P., 1923), iii, 424.

33.   Muriel C. Bradbrook, *Shakespeare: the Poet in his World* (Weidenfeld and Nicolson, 1978) p. 74.

34.   See C. F. E. Spurgeon, *Shakespeare's Imagery and What It Tells Us* (Cambridge: C.U.P., 1936), W. Clemen, *The Development of Shakespeare's Imagery* (Methuen, 1951), and the series of books on Shakespeare by G. Wilson Knight (Methuen and Routledge).

35.   Here too E. M. W. Tillyard in his well-known *Shakespeare's History Plays* (Chatto, 1944) oversimplifies the background in terms only of divine right within the Elizabethan hierarchy.

36.   Northrop Frye, *The Anatomy of Criticism* (Princeton: Princeton U.P. and Oxford: O.U.P., 1957) and C. L. Barber, *Shakespeare's Festive Comedy* (Princeton: Princeton U.P.; and Oxford: O.U.P., 1959).

Further reading

J. C. ADAMS, *The Globe Playhouse* (Constable, 1961).

P. J. ALPERS, (ed.) *Elizabethan Poetry: Modern Essays in Criticism* (Oxford: O.U.P., 1967).

J. W. ATKINS, *English Literary Criticism: The Renascence* (Methuen, 1947).

C. L. BARBER, *Shakespeare's Festive Comedy* (Princeton: Princeton U.P.; Oxford: O.U.P., 1959).

D. BEVINGTON, *From Mankind to Marlowe: Growth of Structure in the Popular Drama of Tudor England* (Cambridge, Mass., Harvard U.P.; Oxford, O.U.P., 1962).

S. T. BINDOFF, *England Under the Tudors* (Penguin, 1950).

J. W. BLENCH, *Preaching in England in the Late Fifteenth and Sixteenth Centuries* (Oxford: O.U.P., 1964).

F. S. BOAS, *University Drama in the Tudor Age* (Oxford: O.U.P., 1914).

M. C. BRADBROOK, *Themes and Conventions of Elizabethan Tragedy* (Cambridge: C.U.P., 1935). *The Rise of the Common Player* (London, Chatto, 1962).

T. BROOKE, 'The Renaissance 1500—1660' in A. C. Baugh *A Literary History of England* (Routledge, 1950; 1967).

F. F. BRUCE, *The English Bible: a History of Translations* (Oxford: O.U.P., 1961).

D. BUSH, *Classical Influences in Renaissance Literature* (Cambridge, Mass., Harvard U.P., 1952).

M. C. BYRNE, *Elizabethan Life in Town and Country* (Methuen, 1961).

L. B. CAMPBELL, *Divine Poetry and Drama in Sixteenth Century England* (Berkeley: C.U.P., 1959).

M. CAMPBELL, *The English Yeoman* (New York: Merlin Press, 1942).

E. CASSIRER, *et al* (eds) *The Renaissance Philosophy of Man* (Chicago: University of Chicago Press, 1948).

E. K. CHAMBERS, *The Elizabethan Stage*, 4 vols (Oxford: O.U.P., 1923).

H. B. C. CHARLTON, *The Senecan Tradition in Renaissance Tragedy* (Manchester: Manchester U.P., 1946).

K. CHARLTON, *Education in Renaissance England* (Routledge, 1965).

G. N. CLARK, *The Wealth of England, 1496—1760* (Routledge, 1946).

T. W. CRAIK, *The Tudor Interlude: Stage, Costume, and Acting* (Leicester: Leicester U.P., 1958).

M. DORAN, *Endeavors of Art: a Study of Form in Elizabethan Drama* (Madison: University of Wisconsin Press, 1954).

L. FORSTER, *The Icy Fire: Five Studies in European Petrarchism* (C.U.P., 1969).

S. J. FREEDBERG, *Painting of the High Renaissance,* 2 vols (Cambridge, Mass.: Harvard U.P., 1961).

H. C. GARDINER, *Mysteries' End: an Investigation of the Last Days of the Medieval Religious Stage* (New Haven: Yale U.P., 1946).

H. HAYDN, *The Counter-Renaissance* (New York: Atheneum, 1960).

C. W. HODGES, *The Globe Restored* (Ernest Benn, 1953).

J. HOLLANDER, *The Untuning of the Sky: Ideas of Music in English Poetry 1500—1700* (Princeton: Princeton U.P., 1961).

L. HOTSON, *Shakespeare's Wooden O* (Rupert Hart Davis, 1959).

P. HUGHES, *The Reformation in England,* 3 vols (New York: Macmillan, 1950—54).

F. R. JOHNSON, *Astronomical Thought in Renaissance England* (Baltimore: John Hopkins U.P., 1937).

F. KERMODE, *English Pastoral Poetry from the Beginnings to Marvell* (Harrap, 1952).

A. KERNAN, *The Cankered Muse: Satire of the English Renaissance* (New Haven: Yale U.P., 1959).

P. H. KOCHER, *Science and Religion in Elizabethan England* (San Marino: Huntington Library Publications, 1953).

P. O. KRISTELLER, *Renaissance Thought: the Classic, Scholastic, and Humanistic Strains* (New York: Harper and Row, 1961).

L. LERNER (ed.), *Shakespeare's Comedies: an Anthology of Modern Criticism* (Penguin, 1967) *Shakespeare's Tragedies: an Anthology of Modern Criticism* (Penguin, 1963).

J. W. LEVER, *The Elizabethan Love Sonnet* (Methuen, 1956).

H. LEVIN, *The Myth of the Golden Age in the Renaissance* (Bloomington: Indiana U.P., 1969).

C. S. LEWIS, *English Literature in the Sixteenth Century, Excluding Drama* (Oxford: O.U.P., 1954).

H. A. MASON, *Humanism and Poetry in the Early Tudor Period* (Routledge, 1959).

J. MAZZARO, *Transformations in the Renaissance English Lyric* (Ithaca: Cornell U.P., 1970).

E. H. MILLER, *The Professional Writer in Elizabethan England* (Cambridge, Mass.: Harvard U.P., 1959).

K. MUIR and S. SCHOENBAUM, *A New Companion to Shakespeare Studies* (Cambridge: C.U.P., 1971).

D. J. PALMER, *Shakespeare's Later Comedies* (Penguin, 1971).

B. PATTISON, *Music and Poetry of the English Renaissance* (London, 1948).

B. PENROSE, *Travel and Discovery in the Renaissance* (Cambridge, Mass.: Harvard U.P., 1955).

D. L. PETERSON, *The English Lyric from Wyatt to Donne* (Princeton: Princeton U.P., 1967).

A. L. ROWSE, *The England of Elizabeth: the Structure of Society* (Macmillan, 1964).

J. SEZNEC, *The Survival of the Pagan Gods: the Mythological Tradition*

and its Place in Renaissance Humanism and Art, trans. B. Sessions
(New York: Pantheon, 1953).
J. SIMON, *Education and Society in Tudor England* (Cambridge: C.U.P.,
1966).
H. SMITH, *Elizabethan Poetry: a Study in Conventions, Meaning, and
Expression* (Cambridge, Mass.: Harvard U.P., 1966).
J. E. SPINGARN, *A History of Literary Criticism in the Renaissance*
(New York: Greenwood Press, 1925).
J. STEVENS, *Music and Poetry in the Early Tudor Court* (Methuen,
1961).
C. R. THOMPSON, *Schools in Tudor England* (Washington, D.C., 1958).
G. M. TREVELYAN, *English Social History* (Longman, 1940).
R. TUVE, *Elizabethan and Metaphysical Imagery* (Chicago: University
of Chicago Press/Phoenix Books, 1947).
E. K. WATERHOUSE, *Painting in Britain, 1530—1790* (Penguin, 1953).
G. WICKHAM, *Early English Stages, 1300—1660*, 3 vols (London/New
York: Routledge, 1959—72).
F. P. WILSON, *The English Drama, 1485—1585* (Oxford: O.U.P., 1969).
C. WINTER, *Elizabethan Miniatures* (1943).
R. WITTKOWER, *Architectural Principles in the Age of Humanism* (War-
burg Institute, 1952).
L. B. WRIGHT, *Middle-Class Culture in Elizabethan England* (Chapel
Hill: University of North Carolina Press, 1935).
F. YATES, *The Art of Memory* (Routledge; Chicago: Chicago U.P.,
1966).

BIBLIOGRAPHICAL GUIDES
F. W. BATESON (ed.), *The Cambridge Bibliography of English Literature*,
vol. I (Cambridge: C.U.P., 1940).
A. E. CASE, *A Bibliography of English Poetic Miscellanies, 1521—1750*
(Oxford: O.U.P., 1935).
V. de SOLA PINTO, *The English Renaissance, 1510—1688* (Routledge,
1962).
A. HARBAGE, *Annals of English Drama, 975—1700*, rev. S. Schoenbaum
(Methuen, 1964).
J. HAYWARD, *English Poetry: a Catalogue of First and Early Editions*
(Cambridge: C.U.P., 1950).
T. H. HOWARD-HILL, *Shakespearean Bibliographical and Textual Criticism*
(Oxford: O.U.P., 1971).
S. JAYNE, *Library Catalogues of the English Renaissance* (Berkeley:
University of California Press, 1956).
W. M. JONES (ed.) *The Present State of Scholarship in Sixteenth Century
Literature* (Columbia, Missouri and London, 1978).
C. S. LEWIS, *English Literature in the Sixteenth Century, Excluding
Drama* (Oxford: O.U.P., 1954).
J. L. LIEVSAY, *The Sixteenth Century: Skelton through Hooker* (New
York: Appleton, 1968).
T. P. LOGAN and D. S. SMITH (eds.), *The Predecessors of Shakespeare:
a Survey and Bibliography of Recent Studies in English Renaissance*

Drama (Lincoln, Nebraska: University of Nebraska Press, 1973).

J. G. McMANAWAY and J. A. ROBERTS, *Selective Bibliography of Shakespeare* (Charlottesville, Va.: University Press of Virginia, 1975).

G. WATSON (ed.), *Supplement to the Cambridge Bibliography of English Literature* (Cambridge: C.U.P., 1957).

S. WELLS (ed.), *English Drama Excluding Shakespeare: Select Bibliographical Guide* (Oxford: O.U.P., 1975), *Shakespeare: Select Bibliographical Guide* (Oxford: O.U.P., 1973).

Chronological table

Literary and dramatic works are listed according to their approximate date of composition or first stage performance.

DATE	ENGLISH WORKS	EVENTS
1485		Richard III dies at Bosworth. Henry VII founds Tudor dynasty
1497	H. Medwall. *Fulgens and Lucrece*	
1498	J. Skelton 'Bowge of Court'	
		Leonardo Da Vinci: 'Mona Lisa'
1508	J. Skelton 'Philip Sparrow'	
1509		Henry VIII succeeds to throne. Marries Catherine of Aragon. Michelangelo works on Sistine Chapel ceiling, Raphael on Stanza. Colet founds St Paul's school
1513	T. More *History of Richard III*	Machiavelli's *The Prince*
1515	J. Skelton *Magnificence*	Wolsey made cardinal
1516	T. More *Utopia*	Ariosto *Orlando Furioso*
1517	J. Skelton 'Elinor Rumming'	Luther's 95 theses nailed to Wittenberg church begins Protestant Reformation. Machiavelli's *La Mandragola*
1519	J. Heywood *Four P's, John John*	Magellan begins voyage around the world. Cortez invades Mexico
1526	W. Tyndale *New Testament* in English	
	J. Skelton 'Speak Parrot' etc.	
1528		Castiglione: *The Courtier*
1529	T. More 'Dialogue Concerning Heresies' and 'Supplication of Souls'	Wolsey falls from power

DATE	ENGLISH WORKS	EVENTS
1531	T. Elyot *Governor*	
1532	J. Redford *Wit and Science*	Henry VIII divorces Catherine. More resigns
1533	J. Heywood *Play of Weather*	Cranmer appointed. Henry VIII excommunicated and marries Anne Boleyn
1534	T. Elyot *Castle of Health*. T. More 'Dial of Comfort'	Act of Supremacy. More and Fisher executed
1535	Coverdale Bible	
1536	T. Wyatt active as poet	Anne executed. Henry marries Jane Seymour. Tyndale strangled to death
1538	J. Bale *King John*	English Bible required in every church
1539	'Great' Bible	Dissolution of the monasteries
1543	Surrey active as poet	Copernicus 'theory of heliocentricity'
1545	R. Ascham, *Toxophilus*	Council of Trent opens
1547		Henry VIII *d.* Edward VI succeeds. Surrey executed
1548	E. Hall, *York and Lancaster*	
1549	Cranmer's *Book of Common Prayer,* Sternhold and Hopkins, *Psalms*	
1550	R. Sherry, *Treatise of Schemes.* Latimer active as preacher	Vasari, *Lives*
1553	T. Wilson, *Art of Rhetoric,* N. Udall, *Ralph Roister Doister*	Edward VI *d.* Mary succeeds and re-introduces Catholicism. *Lazarillo de Tormes*
1554		Mary m. Philip of Spain. Wyatt rebellion
1555	*Mirror for Magistrates*	Protestants persecuted. Latimer and Ridley burnt at stake, Cranmer soon after
1557	Tottel's *Miscellany*	War with France
1558	R. Ascham, *Schoolmaster*	Mary dies. Elizabeth I succeeds. Calais lost

DATE	ENGLISH WORKS	EVENTS
1559	J. Heywood, tr. Seneca's *Troas* Enlarged *Mirror for Magistrates*	Church attendance made compulsory. Peace with France. Revolution in Scotland
1560	*Gammer Gurton's Needle,* Norton & Saville *Gorboduc,* Geneva Bible	Peace with Scotland
1561	T. Hoby, tr. Castiglione *Courtier*	
1563	J. Foxe, *Book of Martyrs*	Plague in London. First Poor Law
1565	J. Hall, *Court of Virtue*	
1567	A. Golding, tr. Ovid's *Metamorphoses,* G. Gascoigne, *Supposes*	
1568	T. Garter's *Susannah*	Mary Queen of Scots flees to England
1569	T. Preston, *Cambises*	
1570		Elizabeth excommunicated
1572		Unpatronised actors declared vagabonds
1575	G. Gascoigne, *Posies, Notes of Instruction, Glass of Government*	New Poor Law
1576	*Paradise of Dainty Devices*	James Burbage builds Theatre
1577	Holinshed, *Chronicle*	Drake sets out round world
1578	J. Lyly, *Euphues*	
1579	S. Gosson, *School of Abuse,* Lyly, *Euphues & his England,* E. Spenser, *Shepheardes' Calender,* T. North, tr. Plutarch's *Lives,* P. Sidney, *Arcadia, Astrophel, Defence of Poesy*	
1581	T. Newton, *Seneca His Ten Tragedies*	Tasso, *Gerusalemme Liberata*
1582	Hakluyt, *Voyages*	
1583	J. Lyly, *Campaspe*	Irish rebellion crushed

DATE	ENGLISH WORKS	EVENTS
1584	T. Lodge, *Alarum*, Ralegh active as poet	William of Orange assassinated. Ralegh unsuccessful in Virginia. G. Bruno, *On the Infinity of the Universe*
1586	T. Kyd, *Spanish Tragedy*	Sidney dies near Zutphen
1587	C. Marlowe, *Tamburlaine I*	Mary Queen of Scots beheaded
1588	*Tamburlaine II*, J. Lyly, *Endimion*, Marprelate controversy	Defeat of Spanish Armada. Montaigne, *Essays*
1589	R. Greene, *Menaphon, Friar Bacon, Tully's Love,* Lodge and Greene, *Looking Glass,* C. Marlowe, *Jew of Malta, Dr Faustus.* G. Puttenham, *Art of English Poesy*	
1590	T. Lodge, *Rosalind,* E. Spenser, *Faerie Queene, i—iii*	
1591	R. Greene, *Cony-catching,* Shakespeare, *Henry VI*	
1592	R. Greene, *Groatsworth, Repentance,* T. Nashe, *Pierce Penniless,* Marlowe, *Edward II,* Shakespeare, *Richard III*	
1593	Shakespeare, *Venus and Adonis,* R. Hooker, *Laws of Ecclesiastical Polity i—iv,* T. Nashe, *Christ's Tears, Strange News.*	Plague closes theatres. Marlowe dies
1594	T. Nashe, *Unfortunate Traveller,* G. Peele, *David and Bethsabe,* Shakespeare, *Rape of Lucrece*	
1595	Spenser, 'Colin Clout', *Amoretti,* 'Epithalamium'. Shakespeare, *Midsummer Night's Dream, Romeo and Juliet*	Drake and Hawkins die on expedition
1596	*Richard II, Merchant of Venice,* Spenser, *Faerie Queene, iv—vi,* 'Prothalamium', *Four Hymns*	Calais captured by Spanish. Cadiz expedition
1597	F. Bacon, *Essays,* Hooker, *Laws v,* Nashe, *Isle of Dogs,* Shakespeare, *Henry IV*	T. Morley, *Plain Introduction to Practical Music,* J. Dowland, *Songs of Four Parts*

DATE	ENGLISH WORKS	EVENTS
1598	B. Jonson, *Everyman in his Humour*	Burghley dies. Further Poor Law
1599	Shakespeare, *Much Ado, As You Like It, Henry V, Julius Caesar,* T. Dekker, *Shoemaker's Holiday*, B. Jonson, *Everyman Out of his Humour*	Essex imprisoned. Globe Playhouse opened
1600	Shakespeare, *Merry Wives, Troilus*	G. Bruno executed. East India Company founded. W. Gilbert *De Magnete*
1601	*Twelfth Night, Hamlet*	Essex rebellion and execution
1603	*Othello, All's Well, Measure for Measure*	Elizabeth dies, James I succeeds. King's Men appointed. Court masque introduced

Index